SUNDAY HOMILIES

To my sister, Terry

Liam Swords

Sunday Homilies for the three-year cycle

the columba press

First published in 1995 by
the columba press
93 The Rise, Mount Merrion, Blackrock, Co Dublin
Reprinted 1996

Cover by Bill Bolger
Origination by The Columba Press
Printed in Ireland by Colour Books Ltd, Dublin.

ISBN 1 85607 131 6

Contents

YEAR C

Preface

A national survey of popular attitudes to preaching in Ireland was carried out in 1986-87. From the responses received from priests, adults and young laity, it concluded:

> Good homilies are brief (five to seven minutes), have one clear message, interpret the word of God while applying it to daily life. Such homilies make use of concrete language, as well as illustrations, stories and images drawn from the experience of the preacher himself and of the congregation.

The homilies presented here attempt to follow this blueprint.

They were, for the most part, preached and recorded live. Later they were worked over and edited for the print medium. The first drafts were circulated to a select few who offered comments and criticism, which were incorporated into the final texts.

Like Christ's words recorded in the gospel, the preacher's homily has its own *sitz im leben*, the listeners for whom the message is intended. These homilies were preached to the congregation at the Irish Sunday Mass in Paris. Most of them were young adults between 18 and 25, male and female, all of them with second or third level education. They belong to the category which the survey found showed the highest level of dissatisfaction (79%) with preaching.

Each homily has a single theme, most often selected from the gospel reading, occasionally from the first or second reading, and once (*Exile*) inspired by the responsorial psalm. A wide range of Christian topics are treated over the three-year cycle. An attempt has been made to marry the pre-Vatican II idea of *Catechetical Instruction* with the gospel of the day. Some repetition of topics is inevitable (where it occurs a cross-reference is given) as the choice of liturgical readings seems more concerned with providing continuous extracts from the four gospels over

11

the three-year cycle than with the problems of the preacher. For this reason, appropriate quotations from the *Catechism of the Catholic Church* are added at the end of each homily. These are commentaries on the scripture readings and are intended, not as back-up for the homily, though they often are, but as a supplementary source for the preacher. On those rare occasions where the texts or themes are not indexed in the *Catechism*, no reference is given.

All preachers need help, as the survey underlined. If the author presumes to offer these to others, it is only because he knows from experience that anything that makes this difficult task a little easier is appreciated.

Liam Swords
Via degli Ibernesi 20
Roma
June 1995

Year A

First Sunday of Advent A

Readings: Is 2:1-5. Rom 13:11-14. Mt 24:37-44.

Introduction.

Today, the First Sunday of Advent, we look forward to Christmas and the birth of Christ. But beyond that we look forward to the Second Coming when Christ will come in glory at the end of time. We should keep ourselves ready as 'we know not the day nor the hour.'

Following the signs (Second Coming)

The famous Czechoslovakian film-maker Milos Forman, was interviewed a few years ago on television. It was the period when all the political changes were taking place in eastern Europe after the collapse of communism. He was asked about the prospects for the future. The Czechs, he said, were exchanging the zoo for the jungle. For three generations they had lived in a zoo under communist dictatorship. Now that the zoo-keepers were disposed of and their cages unlocked, they had all the freedom of the jungle. His comment has since proved prophetic. In the zoo they were fed and looked after by their keepers, sufficiently though frugally. They had their cages which protected them from the elements and other predators. Their days were passed with regular supervised exercises. All they lacked was the freedom to roam at will. Such was the socialist society under communism. It provided its citizens with housing, education and health services, however basic. Unemployment did not exist officially. They were now released into the wild, to survive in the jungle of capitalist society. Here, the norm is the survival of the fittest. Jobs are scarce, housing is in short supply and expensive, health services and education are two-tiered. Society is divided into the 'haves' and the 'have-nots'. It is 'a dog eat dog' world. In any case, most zoo-raised animals would not survive in the wild. They have lost the knack of surviving. Forman's prediction came true. A few short years later, they welcomed back their former zoo-keepers. Poland, Lithuania, Romania, Hungary, Czech Republic etc., re-elected communist governments.

The poet, William Butler Yeats, in his poem, *The Second Coming*, comes close to describing what they experienced:

Things fall apart, the centre cannot hold,
mere anarchy is loosed upon the world,

the blood dimmed tide is loosed
and everywhere the ceremony of innocence is drowned.
The best lack all conviction
while the worst are full of passionate intensity,
Surely some revelation is at hand,
surely the Second Coming is at hand.

Today, the First Sunday of Advent, we prepare for Christmas and the coming of Christ. But beyond that we look forward to the Second Coming which Christ speaks about in the gospel. Recent political events, spectacular though they were, do not herald the imminence of the Second Coming, when Christ will return at the end of the world. But they are straws in the wind that bring it to mind. The present Russian programme to convert their tank factories into tractor-production seems almost the fullfilment of Isaiah's prophecy:

These will hammer their swords into ploughshares,
their spears into sickles.
Nation will not lift sword against nation,
there will be no more training for war.

But as the gospel says we 'know not the day or the hour'. We must go on living from day to day, yet always remain ready for the Second Coming.

To travel anywhere by Métro in Paris, you must look up the name of the end-line terminus in the direction you wish to go. Once in the underground, you follow the signs with that name. It leads you to a platform, over which hangs a sign with the word 'Direction' and the name of that terminus. The next train will take you there. Life is full of cross-roads, spaghetti junctions, criss-crossing routes going in all directions. It is easy to lose the way, to get lost. We can spend all our lives going everywhere and getting nowhere. Advent is a sign-post on our way, giving us direction. The end of the line for us is Christ's glorious advent and eternal life.

Suggested additional Bidding Prayers
We pray
– that we will welcome Christ into our lives this Christmas.
– that he will give direction to our lives.
– that we will ready ourselves for the coming of 'the day of the Lord'.

Catechism of the Catholic Church

524 When the church celebrates the *liturgy of Advent* each year, she makes present this ancient expectancy of the Messiah, for by sharing in the long preparation for the Saviour's first coming, the faithful renew their ardent desire for his second coming. By celebrating the precursor's birth and martyrdom, the church unites herself to his desire: 'He must increase, but I must decrease.'

673 Since the Ascension Christ's coming in glory has been imminent, even though 'it is not for you to know times or seasons which the Father has fixed by his own authority.' This eschatological coming could be accomplished at any moment, even if both it and the final trial that will precede it are 'delayed'.

Second Sunday of Advent A

Readings: Is 11:1-10. Rom 15:4-9. Mt 3:1-12.

Introduction

John the Baptist's role was to prepare the way for the coming of Christ. He is a role model for all of us. Once Christ had arrived, there only remained for John to disappear gracefully. Like John, we should make way for Christ in the lives of others.

Man for all seasons (John the Baptist)

The first two years of my education took place in a mixed school. At four years of age, it was not considered a threat to my morals. Besides it was a convent school. There was a large picture in the infant classroom which I can still recall vividly. It showed a teenage boy with long hair, bare arms and legs, draped in a knee-length tunic, with a belt round his waist. He held a staff in his hand. It was John the Baptist. He became my hero immediately. He was the stuff a young boy's fantasies are made of. As I grew older, I should have grown out of John the Baptist – as I did out of Santa Claus – but I didn't. The older I became, the more I learned about him, and the more I liked him. He was my man 'for all seasons'.

To start with, he was a 'voice crying in the wilderness'. The type of person every age needs and none more than our own. Somebody prepared to speak out. Willing to take on the system, the powers-that-be. People who have the courage of their convictions, who dare to confront low standards in high places. Who do 'not judge by appearances' but give 'their verdict for the poor of the land'. Isaiah knew the type; he was one himself:

His word is a rod that strikes the ruthless,
his sentences bring death to the wicked.

They are few and far between. But mercifully every age produces all too rare examples. Somebody who can articulate for the silent majority, for the rest of us, who lack the courage to speak out. And we turn out in our thousands to applaud them from the safety of our anonymity. 'Then all Jerusalem and all Judea and the whole Jordan district made their way to him.' We can always melt away when the tear-gas and the baton-charges start. All of them pay a price for their outspokenness, and some of them, the ultimate price. It was long years imprisonment for Aleksandr Solzhenitsyn and Nelson Mandela. It was the assassin's bullet for Martin Luther King. It was both for John the Baptist. And it was not surprising. Anyone foolhardy enough to describe the religious establishment of his time as a 'brood of vipers' was certain to become a marked man. He didn't mince his words. And when he pointed a finger at the sexual scandals of the government in the person of Herod, he was a condemned man.

What makes John the Baptist unique, is that all the fame or notoriety he achieved was not for himself but for another. 'The one who follows me is more powerful than I am and I am not fit to carry his sandals.' His was no ego-trip, which is a charge that could be laid at the feet of all those others who challenged the system, no matter how admirable their causes were. History has no other example of people who achieve that sort of adulation, yielding centre-stage to another as yet unknown. That extraordinary moment has been immortalised in the Mass, fittingly just before Communion, when the priest lifts up the Host and says 'Behold the Lamb of God.' These were the words the Baptist first pronounced when he spotted the unknown Jesus standing at the fringe of a crowd who had come to hear John preach. His job was to prepare the way for Christ and then make way for him.

He is a model for any Christian and for all Christians. For parents for their children, husbands for their wives, and wives for their husbands. Teachers for their pupils, priests for their people, neighbours for their neighbours. Christians should lead others to Christ. And sometimes this may entail taking themselves out of the way. Interference in others' lives, even with the best of intentions, rarely if ever discovers Christ for them. The

reverse is more often the case. How many young people have
drifted away from the Mass because of the constant harassment
of their parents. Such parents could take a leaf out of the
Baptist's book. Preachers like them and like me rarely influence
people. We can't see past our egos to Christ. Those like John the
Baptist never fail.

Suggested additional Bidding Prayers
We pray
– that we will prepare the way for Christ in the lives of others.
– that we will not frustrate the young in our efforts to evangelise
them.
– that we will know when it is time to take ourselves out of
Christ's way.

Catechism of the Catholic Church
    523 St John the Baptist is the Lord's immediate precursor or
forerunner, sent to prepare his way. 'Prophet of the Most High',
John surpasses all the prophets, of whom he is the last. He inaugurates the gospel, already from his mother's womb welcomes
the coming of Christ, and rejoices in being 'the friend of the
bridegroom', whom he points out as 'the Lamb of God who
takes away the sin of the world'. Going before Jesus 'in the spirit
and power of Elijah', John bears witness to Christ in his preaching, by his baptism of conversion, and through his martyrdom.

Third Sunday of Advent A

Readings: Is 35: 1-6, 10. Jas 5:7-10. Mt 11:2-11.

Introduction
    Society finds it very difficult to tolerate dissent. Those who
step out of line are often very harshly treated. We should remind
ourselves that John the Baptist castigated the religious and civil
authorities of his day. Only by doing so could he prepare his
contemporaries for the coming of Christ.

Tomorrow's heroes (Dissent)
    When the history of the Soviet Union is re-written, as it cer-
tainly will be soon, one man will loom large in its recent past.

His name is Andrei Sakharov. He died this week just five years ago. He was a most unlikely prophet, a small, quiet-spoken, scholarly man, with none of the attributes usually associated with great public figures. For years, he confronted what must have been the greatest totalitarian regime the world has ever seen. He was a very distinguished scientist; in fact, he was one of Russia's greatest scientists of this century. He could have had anything the Soviet system had to offer its favourite sons. Instead he chose to fight it, for the freedom and the civil rights of its citizens. For this he paid dearly, spending years in prison and labour camps in Siberia. But he never wavered.

Sakharov was a Russian Jew and in some striking ways bears comparison to that other Jew in Palestine two thousand years ago – John the Baptist. His too was a lone 'voice crying in the wilderness'. He spoke out courageously against the corruption of a powerful regime. He resisted all the blandishments his talents would have earned him. He could have 'worn fine clothes and lived in palaces' by the standards of ordinary Russians in that harsh regime. And when they could not buy his silence, they locked him away. He was in prison when the world first heard of him. From there, his message of dissent escaped to make disciples in Russia and abroad. He was no 'reed swaying in the breeze'. His heroic dissent was a contagion which his captors were powerless to contain. Eventually, yielding to world opinion – he had been awarded the Nobel Prize while in prison – they were forced to release him. His health was irretrievably broken. Nevertheless, he continued his crusade. The seed he had sown in the wilderness so many years before was coming to harvest. Then almost within sight of the promised land, he died. Had he lived another few months he might have been, like a Lech Walesa or a Vaclav Havel , elected President of Russia. But he didn't. Perhaps history will be all the kinder to him because of that.

As Christians, we should cherish our dissidents. So often today's dissidents are tomorrow's heroes. Recognition, if it comes at all, comes posthumously. They belong in the tradition of John the Baptist, whom Christ praised so warmly in today's gospel. Melito of Sardis wrote in the second century:

If you wish to see the mystery of the Lord,
it is he who endures many things:
it is he who was in Abel murdered,
and in Isaac bound,

and in Jacob exiled,
and in Joseph sold,
and in Moses exposed,
and in the lamb slain,
and in David persecuted,
and in the prophets dishonoured.
Their role is best described by Isaiah in today's reading:
Strengthen all weary hands, steady all trembling knees
and say to all faint hearts,
'Courage! Do not be afraid.
Look, your God is coming …
he is coming to save you.'

Suggested additional Bidding Prayers
We pray
– that we will always show special concern for those who dissent from us.
– that we will always be tolerant of the opinions of others.
– that we will cherish those who have the courage of their convictions.

Catechism of the Catholic Church
719 John the Baptist is 'more than a prophet'. In him, the Holy Spirit concludes his speaking through the prophets. John completes the cycle of prophets begun by Elijah. He proclaims the imminence of the consolation of Israel; he is the 'voice' of the Consoler who is coming. As the Spirit of truth will also do, John 'came to bear witness to the light.' In John's sight, the Spirit thus brings to completion the careful search of the prophets and fulfils the longing of the angels. 'He on whom you see the Spirit descend and remain, this is he who baptises with the Holy Spirit. And I have seen and have borne witness that this is the Son of God … Behold, the Lamb of God.'

Fourth Sunday of Advent A

Readings: Is 7:10-14. Rom 1:1-7. Mt 1-18:25.

Introduction
Our Lady played a unique role in our salvation. We honour

her especially at Christmas when she gave birth to our Saviour. Our world mocks the virgin birth. We accept it on faith and 'in the totality of Christ's mysteries'.

'A female figure with a child' (Virgin Birth)
'When that the Eternal deigned to look
on us poor men to set us free,
He chose a maiden whom he took
from Nazareth in Galilee.'

The English writer, Hilaire Belloc, came across an item in a newspaper in the early part of this century. It concerned a dispute between an Anglican vicar and his bishop. It appears that the vicar had decided to erect a statue of Mary, the Mother of God, in one of the niches of his church.

These mysteries profoundly shook
The Reverend Doctor Lee, D.D.,
Who forthwith stuck into a nook,
or niche of his encumbancy,
high on the wall for all to see,
a statue of the undefiled
the universal mother, she,
a Female figure with a Child.

Some of the parishioners complained to the bishop about it. Whereupon, the bishop:

wrote off at once to Doctor Lee,
in manner, very far from mild,
and said: 'Remove them instantly,
this Female figure with a Child!'

The bishop, it seems, was 'not satisfied with trying the patience of men, (or at least that of Dr Lee) without trying the patience of God too.' He does not appear to have been familiar with today's reading from Isaiah:

The Lord himself, therefore
will give you a sign.
It is this: the maiden is with child
and will soon give birth to a son
whom she will call Immanuel,
a name which means 'God-is-with-us'.

From the beginning, faith in the virginal conception of Jesus has always met with 'the lively opposition, mockery or incomprehension of non-believers, Jews and pagans alike'. It continues to be the one teaching of the church which attracts most contempt from unbelievers and most doubt from believers. It is pointless trying to placate the one or convince the other. It can be accepted only on faith and 'in the totality of Christ's mysteries'. What separated the vicar from his bishop was faith.

The next time we meet will be at Midnight Mass on Christmas Eve, to celebrate the Virgin Birth. It is too late now to send you a Christmas card. But I can suggest one to you. It is a simple line drawing of a 'female figure with a child'. Underneath, is the little prayer Belloc concluded his poem with:

Prince Jesus, in mine agony,
permit me, broken and defiled,
through blurred and glazing eyes, to see
a Female figure with a Child.

Suggested additional Bidding Prayers
We pray
– that Mary will always intercede for us with her Son.
– that because of Mary we will always cherish single mothers.
– that society will accord mothers the rights that are their due.

Catechism of the Catholic Church
497 The gospel accounts understand the virginal conception of Jesus as a divine work that surpasses all human understanding and possibility: 'That which is conceived in her is of the Holy Spirit', said the angel to Joseph about Mary his fiancée. The church sees here the fulfilment of the divine promise given through the prophet Isaiah: 'Behold, a virgin shall conceive and bear a son.'

Christmas Day, Years A, B and C

Readings: Is 9:2-7. Tit 2:11-14. Lk 2:1-14.

Introduction

Today we celebrate the birth of Jesus Christ. He was born in a stable because 'there was no room at the inn'. We best celebrate his birthday by opening our hearts and our homes to the less fortunate in our communities.

No room (Nativity)

I have never quite been able to make up my mind about Christmas cards. From year to year, I blow hot and cold about it. There is a commercialism about them which I find mildly offensive. The real problem is deciding who to send them to. My friends are easily counted. If I settled for that as the criterion, I would add little to the postman's load. But the lines get blurred and the list expands. In the end, I include everybody who might be vaguely suspected of choosing me as a recipient of their seasonal greetings. The lists never match and invariably there is a last minute rush to fill the gaps. Whatever the defects of the custom are, the thought behind it is undeniably good.

It is a pity Christmas cards so rarely reflect an authentic gospel message about the birth of Christ. My ideal one can only be transmitted verbally. It is a simple black and white line drawing, depicting a street with a row of houses. A few subtle touches – a milk bottle outside the door, a cat curled up on a windowsill, an open window with a fluttering curtain – indicating that all the houses are lived in. In the centre of the picture, a man stands knocking at a door. His head is turned towards the street, where a woman stands waiting. Below, there is a caption, only visible to the inner eye. What is remarkable about this card is that the street depicted is instantly recognisable to each recipient. It is, in fact, the street where each lives. The stranger is standing at the door of *your* home. To read the caption, you must look deeply into your own heart. There, unless you are a Mother Teresa or an Abbé Pierre, you will find in bold capitals: NO ROOM.

The litmus-test is easy and foolproof When last did you stretch out a helping hand to someone in need? Or open your heart and your home to somebody in want? How often have you shut your eyes and your door on the needs of others? Every knock on our door left unanswered is a rejection of Christ. If

Christ is not born in our hearts and in our homes this Christmas, then what happened in Bethlehem some two thousand years ago is no cause for celebration.

Suggested additional Bidding Prayers
We pray
– that Jesus Christ will be born in our lives today.
– that we will open our hearts and our homes to the needy.
– that Christians will show a special concern for the homeless.

Catechism of the Catholic Church
525 Jesus was born in a humble stable, into a poor family. Simple shepherds were the first witnesses to this event. In this poverty heaven's glory was made manifest. The Church never tires of singing the glory of this night.

The Holy Family, Years A, B and C

Readings: Sir 3:2-6, 12-14. Col 3:12-21. Lk 2:22-40.

Introduction
The family today is experiencing a crisis. Economic hardship alone cannot account for it. The Holy Family thrived in adversity. Their example is more relevant than ever.

Family album (The Holy Family)
The family photo-album is not produced very often, and even then only on very special occasions and only for very special people. Our past is a very intimate part of us. We would not like strangers to 'burgle our bank of youth'. When the daughter of the house becomes engaged, it is customary to invite her fiancé to peruse the family album. Here, he will meet his future partner at all the important moments of her past. There will be snap-shots of her as a baby in her mother's arms, sleeping in her cot, playing on the nursery floor. Baptism, birthdays, First Communion, Confirmation, holidays, school outings, graduation, etc. The record seems virtually complete. And yet, in most cases, what is missing from the album is far more important than what it contains. For one thing, the camera catches only the smiles and they were both fleeting and false. There is not a single shot of baby's tantrums and they were far more frequent and

furious. The events recorded are all special. Our past has no rov-
ing camera to catch us unawares, doing what we did everyday.
There is no film of our sickness and setbacks. There are no tears
framed here, no pain, no sorrow.

Strangely, in the infancy narrative, Luke has albumed a different set of pictures of the Holy Family. He does not shy away
from the sordid or the sad. The animal eating-trough where
Mary cradled her baby is included. There is a dark side to each
of the events pictured here. The innkeeper's refusal, Herod's
death-threat, exile in Egypt, Simeon's warning, lost in
Jerusalem. The annals that trace the early years of that family between Bethlehem and Nazareth, with its stint as emigrants in a
foreign country, fairly reek of poverty and deprivation.

Few would dispute that the family today is a threatened institution. In most developed countries it is ravaged by divorce.
The break-down rate hovers around the fifty per cent mark.
Parental authority is seriously undermined. Television has replaced the hearth as the focal point in the living-room.
Commercials, beamed into the sanctuary of the home, raise expectations which many budgets can never hope to satisfy. Even
the very young are targeted as potential consumers. While
poverty can sometimes be benign, debt often proves malignant.
For marriage it can prove terminal. Adversity, on the other
hand, only serves to strengthen family ties. Such was the experience of the Holy Family.

If marriage today is in crisis it may be because we are following the wrong models. Perhaps we have traded the Holy Family
for our favourite soap-opera. We should peruse again that family
album. Family solidarity comes through in each incident recorded,
in bold relief. Mary's concern and care for her child is transparent. Joseph hovers in the background protectively. The danger,
the poverty that overshadowed their early marriage, bonded
them more closely together.

Suggested additional Bidding Prayers
We pray
– for our families, that they may model themselves on the Holy
Family.
– for deprived families, that they may be given a share of the
good things in life.
– for broken families, that they may be re-united in love.

Catechism of the Catholic Church
2204 'The Christian family constitutes a specific revelation and realisation of ecclesial communion, and for this reason it can and should be called a *domestic church.*' It is a community of faith, hope and charity; it assumes singular importance in the Church, as is evident in the New Testament.

Mary, Mother of God, Years A, B, and C

Readings: Num 6:22-27. Gal 4:4-7. Lk 2:16-21.

Introduction

We become attached to our religion by its stories and images. One of the first and most powerful is that of the Christmas crib. Here we meet Mary, the Mother of God. She is our mother too and we should always turn to her for help.

The Mary-image (Mother of God)

The American sociologist Andrew Greeley, addressing the question 'Why do Catholics stay in the Church?' – particularly nowadays when so many of them seem to disagree with much of its official teaching – suggests that it is because of its images, metaphors and stories. And the most powerful image of all is Mary, the Mother of God.

It all begins when a mother brings her little child to see the Christmas crib. The child gazes in wonder at this exotic scene of angels, animals, shepherds, kings, mother and father, all gathered around a little baby in its cot.

'Who is the baby?' the little child asks.

'That is Jesus'.

'And who is Jesus?'

'Jesus is God.'

'Oh!' the little child says.

'And who is the lady?'

'That is Mary, God's mammy.'

It is a hard story to beat. It is many children's first introduction to theology and a most effective one at that. Nothing in later life shakes their attachment. They may disagree and sometimes violently with the Church's pronouncements on certain issues. They may fall foul of its discipline in areas as intimate as marriage and family life. They may be disillusioned by the lifestyle of their clergy but they remain Catholics or at least the great majority of them do. An American survey has shown that the Catholic defection rate has remained constant over the last thirty years. It was 15% in 1960 and it is 15% today. Some have dismissed them as *à la carte* Catholics, preferring to choose their own menus than swallow the official line. But *Pobal Dé* (People of God) remains unimpressed and Catholic to boot. They have their stories, images and rituals and nobody will detach them from them. And the most powerful object of attachment is the metaphor of Mary, the Mother of God. Research on Catholic young people in America shows that the Mary image continues to be their most powerful religious image. I knew myself some older people, very often men, whose attachment to religion was tenuous, to say the least. Yet they carried in their pockets a rosary beads and stopped occasionally in places like Knock to pray before a statue of Our Lady. And the people I knew, were far to intelligent to be duped by superstitious charms or miraculous madonnas. I remember reading somewhere that Brendan Behan wrote a letter to the newspaper protesting vehemently against some journalist who described him as a 'non-Catholic'. He was not a non-Catholic, he insisted, but a bad Catholic and there was a world of a difference between the two.

Greeley tells a story heard from nuns who taught him as a young boy in Chicago. One day God made a tour of heaven to check out the recent arrivals. He was taken aback at the quality of many of those allowed in and he went out to confront Peter about it.

'You've let me down again' he told Peter.

'What's wrong now?' Peter asked.

'You let a lot of people in that shouldn't be there.'

'I didn't let them in.'

'Well, who did?'

'When I turned them away at the front gate, they went round the back and your mother let them in.'

It is the sort of story that may make intellectuals squirm or non-Catholics sneer. But it strikes deep cords in our Catholic sensibility. It tallies well with our own conception of mother and the gospel image of Mary. She is the Mother of God and our mother too and like any mother, she will not be baulked by bureaucratic red-tape or hair-splitting moralists, when it comes to the happiness of her children.

Some Additional Bidding Prayers
We pray
– that Mary, the Mother of God will lead us to her Son.
– that Mary, the Mother of God will be the model of our concern
for others.
– that Mary, the Mother of God will protect us 'now and at the
hour of death'.

Catechism of the Catholic Church
963 ... 'The Virgin Mary ... is acknowledged and honoured
as being truly the Mother of God and of the redeemer ... She is
"clearly the mother of the members of Christ"... since she has by
her charity joined in bringing about the birth of believers in the
Church, who are the members of its head.' 'Mary, Mother of
Christ, Mother of the Church.'

Second Sunday after Christmas Years A, B and C

Readings: Sir 24:1-2, 8-12. Eph 1:3-6, 15-18. Jn 1:1-18.

Introduction
The more our standard of living improves, the less, it seems,
we practice the virtue of hospitality. It is not an optional extra
for a Christian. We, like the Chosen People, reject Christ, when
we fail to share our bread with the hungry.

'Come in to the parlour' (Hospitality)
'If you're Irish, come into the parlour,
There's a welcome here for you.
If your name is Timothy or Pat,
As long as you come from Ireland
There's a welcome on the mat.'
This Irish-American come-all-ye underlines the tradition of
welcome associated with the Irish. It has deep roots in our
Gaelic past. *Céad Míle Fáilte* (a hundred thousand welcomes)
was our traditional greeting. Hospitality was the queen of the
virtues in Gaelic society. The Annals of the Four Masters record
the obituaries of Gaelic chieftains and ecclesiastics. By our stan-
dards now, many of them were corrupt and unsavoury. Yet, the
Annals describe them in glowing terms as men renowned for

their hospitality. The lives of the early Irish saints highlight those incidents which show their hospitableness, especially for the poor and needy. We know little more about St Brigid other than her extraordinary concern to provide food and shelter for the deprived. One charming legend links her to the Holy family in Bethlehem. It recounts how the dour innkeeper turned away Joseph and his pregnant wife Mary, who then took shelter in his outhouse. Mary's time had come and Joseph ran back to the inn, pleading for someone to help deliver the baby. No one would come except the innkeeper's daughter who was severely handicapped. She was blind and had no hands. But she came gladly. When the child was born, she was the first to hold him in her arms, miraculously restored: the first one these once sightless eyes were to see was the Saviour of the world. Legends such as these earned for her the title, Mary of the Gael.

Such stories are no longer handed down from generation to generation, but some customs evoking our ancestors' high regard for hospitality still survive in some rural parts. There are places where a lighted candle is placed in the window at Christmas time, offering hospitality to the Holy Family.

With the urbanisation of modern society, that custom and the virtue of hospitality it symbolises, are well on the way to extinction. High-rise flats with their burglar-proof locks, alarm systems, Judas-windows and door codes, are hardly intended to encourage the casual visitor. We do throw the occasional party or give the odd dinner for a few intimate friends, but it is a far cry from setting an extra place at our table for the hungry stranger. Our standard of living may have risen considerably but the same cannot be said for the quality of our lives.

Hospitality is not an optional extra for the Christian. It is the very language in which the story of our salvation is couched. It is in these terms that the gospel describes the rejection of Christ. 'He came to his own domain and his own people did not accept him.' Whatever else the Christmas crib illustrates – most of them are so pretty, only the eyes of faith could unlock their secret – it is that there was 'no room in the inn' for the Son of God. Our faith is an invitation to an eternal banquet in our Father's house. Our hospitality here will determine our fate later. 'For I was hungry and you gave me to eat.'

Suggested additional Bidding Prayers
We pray
– that our hospitality may not be limited to social acquaintances only.
– that we will always welcome the stranger in our homes.
– that we will always share our bread with the world's hungry.

Catechism of the Catholic Church
291 'In the beginning was the Word ... and the Word was God ... all things were made through him, and without him was not anything made that was made.' 'The New Testament reveals that God created everything by the eternal Word, his beloved Son. In him 'all things were created, in heaven and on earth ... all things were created through him and for him. He is before all things, and in him all things hold together.'

Epiphany Years A, B and C

Readings: Is 60:1-6. Eph 3:2-3, 5-6. Mt 2:1-12.

Introduction
The Wise Men had to follow a star to discover the birth of God's Son in Bethlehem. If ever there is to be a real epiphany in our lives, we too, like them, must use our heads as well as our hearts in our search for Christ.

Star of Bethlehem (Orientation)
Nobody disputes the fact that Jesus Christ was born on Christmas day. But dating it is quite another matter. Historians have never been able to agree on the year Jesus was born. There is even less certainty about the day or the month. Oddly enough, almost the only scientific data they have to help them in their search is today's star. Astronomers can, with reasonable accuracy, date the appearance of this star. Inter-stellar activity follows its own fixed rhythms and thus the appearance of new stars in different regions can be determined by computation. Fact is stranger than fiction. That part of the Infancy Narrative one would be most tempted to discard as fairy-tale, turns out to be the only thing that is scientifically verifiable. Whatever else has changed since Christ was born, the sky at night remains the

same. Star-gazers today can follow the same star the Wise Men followed.

Western tradition chose three as the number of the Wise Men and even found exotic names for them, Caspar, Melchior and Balthasar. Some suggest that they travelled from Persia or South Arabia, though Matthew simply indicates that they came from the East. The gospel leaves no doubt that they were individuals of strong conviction, enquiring minds and adventuresome spirit. In a word, intellectuals.

The point should not be overlooked. The church has not often shown such welcome to that beleaguered community as its infant-founder. In those rare periods when it did, religion truly blossomed. Oddly enough, the recent epiphany in the communist east traces its origin to an alliance between the churches and the dissidents. They make natural bed-fellows though it often takes persecution to convince them. It was intellectuals who first discovered the star of Bethlehem. No church, no religion can be authentic, that does not cherish specially its poets, its writers and its thinkers. The true church in the world is an island of saints and scholars. Stars reveal their secrets only to dreamers.

Their astronomical enquiries brought the Wise Men as far as Jerusalem. Astronomy could take them no further. There, they had to consult other experts. The Jews were the people of the Book. Only biblical scholars could shed further light on where the Messiah was to be born. Thus the chief priests and the scribes were called in, through the intervention of Herod. They had not long to wait for an answer. The bible quickly yielded up its awesome secret. 'And you Bethlehem, in the land of Judah, you are by no means least among the Leaders of Judah, for out of you will come a leader who will shepherd my people Israel.' Their search had narrowed down to Bethlehem. Enquiries at the inn might well have led them to the manger. The star, the symbol of their inquiring minds, went forward and halted over the place where the child was. Or did they hear a baby crying?

The investigation of the Wise Men is a fine illustration of the Latin adage *intelligentia quaerens fidem* (intelligence seeking faith). The message for us is simple. If ever there is to be an epiphany in our lives we will need our heads as well as our hearts. We can ill-afford to ignore the insights of intellectuals.

Suggested additional Bidding Prayers

We pray
– that our minds may always enlighten our faith.
– that the church may always cherish its writers and intellectuals.
– that a spirit of probing scholarship be nurtured and respected.

Catechism of the Catholic Church

528 The *Epiphany* is the manifestation of Jesus as Messiah of Israel, Son of God and Saviour of the world … In the magi, representatives of the neighbouring pagan religions, the gospel sees the first-fruits of the nations, who welcome the good news of salvation through the incarnation. The magi's coming to Jerusalem in order to pay homage to the king of the Jews shows that they seek in Israel, in the messianic light of the star of David, the one who will be king of the nations …

Baptism of the Lord Years A, B and C

Readings: Is 42:1-4, 6-7. Acts 10:34-38. Mk 1:7-11.

Introduction

Terrorism is the scourge of our age. Isaiah depicts the Messiah as the apostle of non-violence. We seek the kingdom of God through our commitment to non-violence.

'The lash goes one' (Non-violence)

Helen is twenty two but could pass for somebody in her mid to-late teens. She is pretty, healthy and fairly bristling with cheerfulness. She says she doesn't know how the time flies. Which is somewhat surprising because Helen is a prisoner in a foreign jail, awaiting her trial on terrorist-related charges. Most of her fellow-prisoners are serving sentences for drug related crimes. Many of them are diagnosed as carriers of the deadly AIDS virus. Why Helen decided to embark on a career of terrorism, virtually certain to land her in prison, is almost beyond comprehension. She shows no sign of remorse for the killings and the injuries. She has no regrets. Even in her prison cell, her commitment to the cause is unwavering. Yet in every other way, she is like any other girl of her age. She is religious too, more than many of her contemporaries. She laughs easily and she cries easily too, especially when she sees others treated cruelly and unjustly. Her terrorist activities seem completely out of keeping with her nature.

There seems to be a tremendous proliferation of terrorist groups in the last two decades. Almost no part of the world is free of them. Almost no news-bulletin is without its gruesome coverage in word and pictures of the latest bomb attack. Politicians and churchmen quickly exhaust their vocabularies in expressing vehement condemnations. All so futile and frustrating. Many a peace-proclaiming modern state was born out of terrorism. Today's statesmen were often yesterday's terrorists. 'Glorious' revolutions were often little more than tyrannies exchanged.

Hurrah for revolution and more cannon-shot!
A beggar upon horseback lashes a beggar on foot.
Hurrah for revolution and cannon come again!
The beggars have changed places, but the lash goes on.

Violence breeds violence. Helen is the product of a culture that for far too long preached the sword If the words of anthems such as the Marseillaise or Amhrán na bhFiann are anything to go by, our commitment to non-violence is steeped in ambiguity. Abbé Pierre recently requested the French government to change the words of the Marseillaise. The reply was a model of sweet reasonableness It would be happy to do so when the church changed the words of the Psalms! Touché!

Too much of our religion is laced with the blood and guts language of war. 'Onward Christian Soldiers!' we sing, with a gusto more congenial to the battlefield than to the altar. God's blessing is invoked for our conquering armies and their dead are martyrised. The jingoism in Britain arising out of the Falklands war, should serve us all as a warning. The spirit of the crusades still lingers in our churches. Holy War is not just the preserve of Muslims.

Much as we would like to disclaim it, religion bears a large responsibility for the violence of our time, whether it be in Belfast, Beirut or Baghdad. While Christians retain a certain ambiguity on the subject of violence, they betray their Master, and will continue to fill their jails with people like Helen and her comrades-in-arms.

Suggested additional Bidding Prayers

We pray
– for the victims of violence, that you may heal their wounds.
– for the perpetrators of violence, that you may extinguish the hatred in their hearts.
– for ourselves, that we may love our country without hating its enemies.

Catechism of the Catholic Church

535 Jesus' public life begins with his baptism by John in the Jordan. John preaches 'a baptism of repentance for the forgiveness of sins'. A crowd of sinners – tax collectors and soldiers, Pharisees and Sadducees, and prostitutes – come to be baptised by him. 'Then Jesus appears.' The Baptist hesitates, but Jesus insists and receives baptism. Then the Holy Spirit, in the form of a dove, come upon Jesus and a voice from heaven proclaims, 'This is my beloved Son.' This is the manifestation ('Epiphany') of Jesus as Messiah of Israel and Son of God.

First Sunday of Lent

Readings: Gen 2:7-9, 3:1-7. Rom 5:12-19. Mt 4:1-11.

Introduction

Today we remember Christ's victory over temptation in the desert. The beginning of Lent is a good time for us to confront the temptations in our lives. We should pray for the gift of discernment between good and evil.

Noonday devils (Temptation)

One day, an elderly devil was taking a stroll in the desert. He was a senior member of Hell's politburo. It was his custom to take a stroll each afternoon to clear his head after spending a long hard morning discussing various high-level strategies with his colleagues regarding media take-overs. The desert was his favourite place as it was much frequented by hermits and anchorites and other holy eccentrics. Though he was no longer a field-operator he liked to keep his hand in. So he was quite pleased when he spotted a cluster of noonday devils surrounding a kneeling hermit, deep in contemplation. He observed them for a while. Some transformed themselves into lewd women offering their favours to the holy man. Others carried trays filled with delicious foods to eat and the choicest wines to drink. But the hermit was impervious to their blandishments. Without ceasing his contemplation he brushed them aside as nonchalantly as a cow swishing his tail to rid himself of flies. The old devil shook his head sadly. 'What is hell coming to at all?' he said to himself, 'Standards are not what they used to be. I don't know where they recruit these young devils from.' 'Desist!' he cried, clapping his hands imperiously and he waved the young devils aside. 'Let the master show you.' Thereupon, he tiptoed gently up to the holy man and stooping down he whispered softly in his ear, 'Your brother, the priest, has just been elected Patriarch of Antioch.' Whereupon the holy man leaped to his feet, his eyes blazing with fury and his face suffused with anger. He shook his fist at the heavens and began to curse and swear and blaspheme God. Smiling contentedly, the old devil resumed his walk while the noonday devils looked after him in admiration.

Temptations are rarely spectacular. You are unlikely to run away with your colleague's wife, much as you admire her, but stealing his character is quite another matter, particularly, as rumour has it that he is in line for promotion. Embezzling the company's funds has never even occurred to you, but you have no scruples about padding out your expenses. The old devil assigned to cover you is not even stretched most of the time. He knows your soft spot. A mere tickle and he chalks up another score. The tabloids you read every Sunday with their lurid tales of the scandalous goings-on of the high-fliers lull you into a false sense of your own righteousness. Just the way the old devil likes to have you.

We live in an age where sin has virtually disappeared. And if sin has disappeared, temptation has gone with it. We have become very naïve, like Eve in the garden of Eden. One has only to read the daily newspaper to see that sin is thriving as never before. Look into your own heart and you will see that temptation is not gone nor likely to go. We are full of petty spites and jealousies and murderous thoughts. Unfortunately, they are often our blind spots. Everybody else is more aware of them than we are. When God said to Solomon, 'Ask what you would like me to give you,' Solomon replied, 'Give your servant a heart to understand how to discern between good and evil.' On this first Sunday of Lent we should pray for a little bit of the wisdom of Solomon.

Suggested additional Bidding Prayers
We pray
– that Christ will give us the wisdom to recognise temptation.
– that Christ will give us the discernment to distinguish between good and evil.
– that Christ will give us the strength to resist temptation.

Catechism of the Catholic Church
2847 The Holy Spirit makes us discern between trials, which are necessary for the growth of the inner man, and temptation which leads to sin and death. We must also discern between being tempted and consenting to temptation. Finally, discernment unmasks the lie of temptation, whose object appears to be good, a 'delight to the eyes' and desirable, when in reality its fruit is death.

Second Sunday of Lent

Readings: Gen 12:1-4a. 2 Tim 1:8-10. Mt 17:1-9.

Introduction

Peter, James and John saw Christ transfigured on the mountain. They themselves were transfigured by the sight. By prayerful meditation on Christ our lives too will be transfigured.

The Transfiguration (Meditation)

If there is one thing most TV cameramen have a penchant for it is 'the face in the crowd'. It has become a cliché of the trade. Whatever the event being filmed, the camera loves to steal away and zone in on some anonymous person to capture their reaction. The best faces are those of the very young and the very old. The young are incapable of counterfeiting their emotions while the old are past caring about the world and its opinions. But there are moments when everybody is capable of registering pure emotion without a hint of affectation. These are those all too rare occasions when the 'camera never lies'. What makes a televised football match truly exciting is not the expert camera work following the intricate moves of the ball through the field to the back of the net but the absolute joy on the face of a fan in the crowd. The viewer at home feels that he is there too in the middle of that roaring crowd. In every live broadcast, there is a camera incessantly panning the audience, searching for a face that best expresses the emotion of the moment, with the producer, hovering like a bird of prey in his crow's nest, ready to zone in and pounce on that face. The enraptured face of the young girl listening to a Mozart aria momentarily captures the sublimity of the soprano's voice. It is a moment of transfiguration.

Had it been possible then, when Christ was transfigured on the mountain, some two thousand years ago, no doubt the camera would have lingered on the faces of Peter and James and John to capture the exultation of that sublime moment. At least that is what their ancestral cousins, the artists, have done in depicting that scene. In any case, it is most unlikely that such a vision would be accessible to electronic eyes. It would be reserved only to the eyes of faith. Beauty, they say, is in the eye of the beholder. Often, it is best expressed in the faces of those who witness it. Peter and his companions were transfigured by the transfiguration.

Since then, only the great mystics have had similar experiences. And they have reached such heights through meditative prayer. In fact, today's gospel charts the way. Prayer begins with an invitation from Christ to find a place to be alone. It may well be that the dearth of such places in our modern world is why we find it so hard to pray. 'Climbing a mountain' signifies raising our vision above the humdrum daily chores that press us down. Remember Martin Luther King and his moving 'I have a dream' speech to civil rights activists in the Sixties. 'I have climbed the mountain and I've seen the promised land.' Only up there alone will we shed all our everyday burdens and concerns and encounter Jesus. And when we do we will feel like Peter. 'Lord, it is good for us to be here!' Only by prayer, will our lives be transfigured.

Suggested additional Bidding Prayers
We pray
– that Christ may invite us to come to him alone.
– that we will always remain faithful to prayer.
– that our lives may be transfigured by prayer.

Catechism of the Catholic Church
556 ... the Transfiguration 'is the sacrament of the second regeneration': our own resurrection. From now on we share in the Lord's resurrection through the Spirit who acts in the sacraments of the Body of Christ. The transfiguration gives us a foretaste of Christ's glorious coming, when he 'will change our lowly body to be like his glorious body.' But it also recalls that 'it is through many persecutions that we must enter the kingdom of God'.

Third Sunday of Lent

Readings:Ex 17:3-7. Rom 5:1-2, 5-8. Jn 4:5-48.

Introduction
Christ quenches our spiritual thirst with the living water of grace: the love of God which is poured into our hearts by the Holy Spirit. We should remain true to our baptism and hope that this living water will turn into a spring inside us, welling up to eternal life.

Going to the well (Grace)

Few of the many visitors to Rome who stand and admire its many splendid fountains realise that they are not only artistic gems but that the water gushing from all those sculptured heads is perfect drinking water. I have seen tourists throw their coins into the Trevi fountain and make a wish on a sweltering summer's day, when their most immediate wish could be realised by simply scooping up the water to slake their thirst. These fountains are the result of various public works undertaken by popes to provide the citizens of Rome with an abundance of good safe drinking water. It was a major engineering feat, tapping wells miles away in the hills outside Rome and piping it into the heart of the city. And doubtlessly, it saved numerous lives. They lived then, as many still do today in the Third World, under the constant threat of deadly plagues such as typhoid resulting from contaminated drinking water.

It is hard to believe now that for most of history the mass of humanity could be aptly described as 'hewers of wood and drawers of water'. The well was the great centre of community life. Everybody met there daily. Local politics revolved round the 'parish pump'. Even after the introduction of running water into most homes, the local well continued for years to be the only source of drinking water. We simply called it 'spring water'. I remember well as a child, that my first chore when I came home from school, was to go to the well for a bucket of water. And in that pre-pocket-money era, I earned a few pennies by doing the same for an elderly spinster who lived in our street.

It is not surprising that the ancients included water, with air, fire and earth as the four elements of life. A person can survive a relatively long time without food, but will die fairly quickly without water. The term the French use for a well is *la source*. Particularly, in that parched and semi-desert land where Christ first preached the gospel, the well was the source of life. To poison a well was a crime against humanity. Even in pre-Christian Ireland wells were sacred places and when the Irish became Christians they kept their holy wells, attaching the names of their saints, like Patrick and Bridget, to them. They remained places of pilgrimage up to recent times. Their demise came, like those of their secular sisters, with the introduction of running water. Since then, the very notion of 'well' has largely lost its fascination for us. And we are the poorer for it.

In today's gospel, Christ offers the Samaritan woman living

water. For us, as for her, he is the source of life, the only well where we can quench our thirst for happiness. 'Anyone who drinks the water that I shall give,' Christ said, 'will never be thirsty again: the water that I shall give will turn into a spring inside him, welling up to eternal life.'

Suggested additional Bidding Prayers
We pray
– that Christ will be our source of life.
– that we will receive from him the living water of grace.
– that it 'will turn into a spring, welling up to eternal life'.

Catechism of the Catholic Church
694 The symbolism of water signifies the Holy Spirit's action in baptism, since after the invocation of the Holy Spirit it becomes the efficacious sacramental sign of new birth: just as the gestation of our first birth took place in water, so the water of baptism truly signifies that our birth into the divine life is given to us in the Holy Spirit ... Thus the Spirit is also personally the living water welling up from Christ crucified as its source and welling up in us to eternal life.

Fourth Sunday of Lent

Readings: 1 Sam 16:1, 6-7, 10-13. Eph 5:8-14. Jn 9:1-41.

Introduction
We walk in darkness, blind to our own shortcomings and the needs of others; but Christ lights up our way, curing our blindness and leading us to his kingdom.

Finding the way (Blindness)
One Sunday morning, I had to cross Paris to celebrate Mass. By a strange coincidence, it happened to be, like today, the fourth Sunday of Lent. As I was approaching the Métro, I was stopped by a young girl. She was blind. She asked me to help her cross the street to the entry to the Métro. When we got there, I offered to help her find her train. She thanked me but declined my offer, assuring me that she would have no difficulty finding her way. I watched in fascination as she made her way confidently,

tapping her little white cane, through the maze of corridors leading to her platform, where she duly boarded the train. The system is so user-friendly that it is almost impossible to go astray. This presumes, of course, that you have eyes and can read. Everything depends on following the directions. This shows the *direction* and leads you to your train. How that blind girl navigated her way with only a white cane and her other senses to guide her almost defies explanation. But she did, and without scarcely hesitating. I nearly got lost myself trying to keep her in view.

The beggar in today's gospel was blind from birth. He had never seen another human being. And yet, like the blind girl in the Métro, he must have had an awareness of his environment that would make sighted people seem almost handicapped. Nature has a marvellous knack of exploiting the potential of the other senses to compensate for the one that is lost. What this blind beggar lacked by sight, he made good by insight. As a beggarman, he encountered huge numbers of people everyday. Many of them would turn their heads, lest they prick their consciences and hurt their pockets. He did not see that but he saw their indifference, their meanness. He sensed their disapproval, their anger. He could see what the teachers of religion were blind to – that his blindness was not the result of sin. They, like their counterparts today who see in the AIDS epidemic the punishing hand of an angry God, suffer from spiritual blindness.

It is an ailment that seems to thrive particularly in a religious environment and its symptoms are easily recognised. The closed mind that refuses to be enlightened. The narrow prejudice that distorts the truth. The overbearing intolerance that brooks no dissent. The blind fanaticism that masquerades as religious zeal. None of them strangers in our modern world.

The message of today's gospel is that the blind see, while those with sight are blind. The real miracle was that the blind man recognised Christ as the Messiah, which the religious experts failed to see. As the poet expressed it: 'There are none so blind as those who do not wish to see.' St Paul draws the conclusion for us:

> You were darkness once, but now you are light in the Lord:
> be like children of light, for the effects of the light are seen in
> complete goodness and right living and truth.

Suggested additional Bidding Prayers

We pray

– that Christ will open our eyes to our own sinfulness.

– that Christ will take away our prejudice against others.

– that Christ will open our eyes and our hearts to the most deprived in our communities.

Catechism of the Catholic Church

588 Jesus scandalised the Pharisees by eating with tax collectors and sinners as familiarly as with themselves. Against those among them 'who trusted in themselves that they were righteous and despised others', Jesus affirmed: 'I have not come to call the righteous, but sinners to repentance.' He went further by proclaiming before the Pharisees that, since sin is universal, those who pretend not to need salvation are blind to themselves.

Fifth Sunday of Lent

Readings: Ez 37:12-14. Rom 8:8-11. Jn 11:1-45.

Introduction

We learn in today's gospel how much Christ valued the friendship of two sisters and their brother. Raising Lazarus was the proximate cause of his own death. We all need the support of friends.

Greater love than this (Friendship)

Some years ago, I took up a temporary assignment in a parish in Los Angeles. It is customary for priests there to take their day-off on Mondays. Usually, they get together in a foursome to play golf during the day and eat out in a restaurant in the evening. The time-honoured custom among the clergy in the US is to wear civilian clothes when off-duty. In the climate of Southern California, this usually consists of open-neck shirt and pants. While there, I followed the local custom. One such evening, with three of my clerical friends, all in our early thirties, I ended up in a restaurant. We exchanged a few pleasantries with the pretty young waitress who came to serve us, taking a little advantage of our anonymity. Then we settled down to the serious business of eating. Half-way through the meal, the waitress returned. 'Everything O.K., Fathers?' she enquired. I was dumbfounded. How did she know we were priests? It was a new twist on the old dictum: 'Once a priest, always a priest.' One of my American colleagues enlightened me. 'In this country,' he said, 'four males sitting together are either four homosexuals or four priests.' Recent disclosures suggest that these categories are not always mutually exclusive.

I was saddened then and I am more saddened now. In all other ages we would have been automatically assumed to have been friends. In a world obsessed by sex, the only real casualty is friendship. Every relationship is now deemed to have a hidden agenda, invariably sexual. There is no place for a platonic friendship free from suspicion. It was not always so. In the ancient world friendship was among the cardinal virtues. Cicero wrote one of his finest treatises on the subject. Any historical researcher could reproduce correspondence among friends whose language would be regarded today as ambiguous, to say the least. An Irish Jacobite writing to his friend on the eve of a battle where he was to lose his life, forgave him a debt, 'since no man breathing loves you more than I do'.

Strange that the Christian churches neglect friendship so much in its preaching. It has become the Cinderella of the virtues. And yet, Jesus Christ valued it so much, as today's gospel records, that he was willing to give his life for it. Jesus had many disciples and numerous followers but he had only three friends, two girls and their brother, in the village of Bethany. 'Jesus loved Martha and her sister and Lazarus.'

When he wept at the tomb of Lazarus, the Jews remarked, 'See how much he loved him.' His friendship for Lazarus was to cost Jesus his life. Even his disciples had warned him against returning to Bethany, a mere stone's throw from Jerusalem. There, the established religion, threatened by the growing Jesus-movement among their adherents, were seeking a pretext to do away with him. The raising of Lazarus, right there in Bethany under their noses, was the final provocation. 'Greater love than this no man has, that a man lays down his life for his friend.' The story of our salvation is also the story of a great friendship.

Adolescence is the great period of friendship in our lives. Every teenager finds a best friend before he ever finds his first love. And friendships made then endure a life time. Neither time nor space seems to diminish the relationship. It is strange how even after long separation, we can pick up again years later where we left off in our schooldays. As we grow older, the number of our acquaintances multiply but real friendship remains elusive. We become more economic with our affections and less inclined to invest them even in those we like. But friendship is not one of life's peripheral options. If Jesus Christ, the Son of God, treasured the friendship of Mary, Martha and their brother Lazarus, it would be foolish of us to think we can manage without them.

Suggested additional Bidding Prayers
We pray
– that God will give us the grace of friendship in our lives.
– that we will always remain faithful to our friends.
– for our friends that they will always remain true to God and to us.

Catechism of the Catholic Church
2347 The virtue of chastity blossoms in friendship ... Chastity is expressed notably in friendship with one's neighbour. Whether it develops between persons of the same or opposite sex, friendship represents a great good for all. It leads to spiritual communion.

Passion Sunday Years A, B, and C

Readings: Is 50:4-7. Phil 2:6-11. Mt 26:14-27, 66. (A). Mk 14:1-15:47. (B).

Introduction
The passion is the historical record of Christ's death, but its message is outside time. The world continues to crucify Christ. There is no role in that drama, be it Judas or Peter or Pilate, that we are incapable of playing.

Complete let-down (The Passion)
Jesus Christ was not the first man to die for a cause, nor the last. He was not the first or the last innocent man to be put to death. He was not the only one ever crucified. There were on that very same day two others. Even as regards physical pain it is at least possible that others have suffered as much. What then makes the passion so different? And it is undeniably different.

The gospel account is roughly about two newspaper columns long, and even though I've read it, or heard it read

hundreds of times, it still affects me. I wonder why? I think the
answer lies in the details – the completely human and utterly
shabby circumstances in which Christ died.

Take for example the behaviour of his friends. Was there ever
such a complete let-down? Judas, one of the twelve, especially
chosen. One can feel the hurt, almost the unbelief in Christ's
gentle words, 'Friend, why are you here? Judas would you betray the Son of Man with a kiss?'

One could almost stomach the betrayal of Judas had the
other eleven remained faithful. No way. One short line tells their
story: 'And they all forsook him and fled.' And Peter – surely
not Peter. Think of all those miracles Christ worked, specially
for him. He raised the dead child to life, set him walking on
water, was transfigured before him. Only a few short hours before, Peter had boasted, 'Even though all abandon you, I will follow you to prison and to death.' He followed alright – in the
words of the gospel – at a distance, a safe distance. And when he
was cornered – it wasn't even that – a jibe or two from a servant
girl looking for notice, Peter the Rock disintegrated. 'He began
to curse and to swear that he knew not the man.' That must really
have hurt Jesus. 'And Jesus turning looked at Peter and Peter
went out and wept bitterly.' And these were his friends, his only
friends. The people he lived with and loved. The people he
showered his miracles on and shared his secrets with. And not
one of them lifted a finger for him.

What has this story to do with us? It is the story of our salvation. But it is more, much more. It is the story of our lives. There
isn't a part in the whole sordid script that we, you and I,
wouldn't play to perfection. Peter in his pride and Peter in his
fall and, hopefully, Peter in his repentance too. We'd fit in perfectly with the disciples who fled at the first sign of danger, or
with Caiaphas and the high priests, with their self-righteousness
and eagerness to reform others while ignoring themselves, or
with Pilate in his abuse of authority, or with the mob with its
thirst for excitement and blood. And Judas? Let's face it – there's
a Judas in all of us. There are times and situations in all our lives
when Jesus could easily say to us as he said to Judas, 'Friend,
why are you here?' The truth is, it was only his friends who
could really have crucified him so.

Suggested additional Bidding Prayers

We pray

– for the victims of tyranny and injustice everywhere.

– for those who suffer mental, physical or spiritual anguish.

– for the courage to defend those who are oppressed.

Catechism of the Catholic Church

613 Christ's death is both the Paschal sacrifice that accomplishes the definitive redemption of men, through 'the Lamb of God, who takes away the sin of the world', and the sacrifice of the new Covenant, which restores man to communion with God by reconciling him to God through the 'blood of the covenant, which was poured out for many for the forgiveness of sins'.

Easter Sunday, Years A, B and C

Readings: Acts 10:34, 37-43. Col 3:1-4. Jn 20:1-9.

Introduction

The Easter Alleluia is a great cry of joy. When Christ broke the death-barrier on the first Easter morning, he did so for all of us. Hence our joy. 'By dying he destroyed our death; by rising he restored our life.'

A life before death (Resurrection) see also Year B

One of the features that characterises the last decades of this century is the extraordinary proliferation of grafitti, particularly in urban areas. If you travel by train through the suburbia of any modern city, you cannot fail to notice how the railway sidings on both sides of the tracks are crammed with grafitti. What motivates those anonymous artists to ply their lonely trade, often in almost inaccessible places and always in unsociable hours? Is it the cry of the dispossesssed, one of the faceless masses in densely populated cities seeking recognition? More recently, these grafitti and their artists have taken some tentative steps towards entering the mainstream of modern art. They are emerging from the underground to mount photographic exhibitions of their work. Like modern art they too seem to have gone from the representational to the abstract.

In the Shankill area of Belfast there is a grafitto which makes no pretense to art. It reads: 'Is there a life **before** death?' It is a bleak reminder of the brutal precariousness of life of those who live in war-torn communities. Their existence is a daily passion, struggling to survive under the constant shadow of death. They huddle in fear in bomb-scarred tenements in Sarajevo, like the frightened disciples in the upper room, keeping what seems to them an endless vigil. And on this Easter morning, the Christians among them venture out, braving snipers' bullets and exploding shells, to celebrate the risen Lord, in bombed-out churches. Those like them who have experienced the crucifixion, have a heightened hope in the resurrection. 'Dying, he destroyed our death, rising he restored our life' is more than a pious Easter jingle for them. Those who live so close to death have greater cause to hope for life.

Women bear the brunt of war, nursing the wounded, sheltering the very old and the very young, foraging for food and fuel and water to stave off death and starvation. And when their best efforts fail, it falls to them to bury and mourn the dead. It is no surprise that it was women who kept vigil with the dying Christ. Nor that it was a woman, Mary of Magdala, who first experienced the risen Lord. Those who bear the first stirrings of human life were destined to bear the first tidings of eternal life. The empty tomb was where Christ became 'the first-born from the dead.' He broke the death-barrier not only for himself but for us. Following fast on Mary's discovery, Peter and John rushed back to the tomb where they 'saw and believed'. 'Till this moment,' the gospel tells us, 'they had failed to understand the teaching of scripture, that he must rise from the dead'. From that moment, a community of belief began, of which we are its latest members. We are the heirs to eternal life.

'Is there a life before death?' the despairing may well ask. St Paul gave the answer to the Colossians, which he gives us today:

> Since you have been brought back to true life with Christ, you must look for the things that are in heaven, where Christ is, sitting at God's right hand. Let your thoughts be on heavenly things, not on the things that are on the earth, because you have died, and now the life you have is hidden with Christ in God. But when Christ is revealed – and he is your life – you too will be revealed in all your glory with him.

Suggested additional Bidding Prayers
We pray
– that we will experience the joy of the resurrection this Easter.
– that we will live the new life of the risen Christ.
– that the dead, who have died in Christ, will rise to glory with him.

Catechism of the Catholic Church
641 Mary Magdalene and the holy women who came to finish anointing the body of Jesus, which had been buried in haste because the Sabbath began on the evening of Good Friday, were the first to encounter the Risen One. Thus the women were the first messengers of Christ's resurrection for the apostles themselves. They were the next to whom Jesus appears: first Peter, then the twelve. Peter had been called to strengthen the faith of his brothers, and so sees the Risen One before them; it is on the basis of his testimony that the community exclaims: 'The Lord has risen indeed, and has appeared to Simon!'

Second Sunday of Easter

Readings: Acts 2:42-47. 1 Pet 1:3-9. Jn 20:19-31.

Introduction

Belief and doubt are natural bed-fellows. Belief thrives in a climate of doubt. Certainty is anathema to faith. By submitting to the test, Christ endorsed Thomas' approach. We should never be afraid to question our faith.

Seeing is believing (Doubt) see also Year B

When something strange or unusual happens in the modern world, for example, the shooting of the president of the United States, John F. Kennedy, people demand an explanation. There is a call for a public enquiry. Usually a supreme court judge is asked to preside over this judicial enquiry. If what happened on Easter Sunday two thousand years ago were to happen today, there would be an immediate call for such an enquiry. Should it be reported that a human being had come back from the dead, it would be headlined around the world and demands would be made for all the facts to be brought out into the open.

With the facts as reported in the gospels we could easily visualise such an enquiry. The witnesses who claimed to have seen and met the risen Jesus would be called and thoroughly cross-examined. First of all his death would have to be established. This should not create any problem. It was a public event and there were numerous witnesses. His death was so brutal, it was surprising that he did not die even before he did. This could be testified to by impartial witnesses like the soldiers, the man who helped to carry his cross etc. Then there was the soldier who just to make sure he died, stuck a spear into his side. There was Joseph of Arimathea who put him in the tomb and the women who wrapped his body. About his death there could be no great argument.

His coming back from the dead is a different story altogether. Here the witnesses would be called one by one, in the order they made their extraordinary discovery. Mary of Magdala would be the first to take the witness stand. She discovered an empty tomb. The other women would corroborate this. There could be thousands of rational explanations of that. The only implausible one is that the occupant rose from the dead. Under cross-examination they would admit they saw angels. Imagine the laughter

that would cause in a modern courtroom. Mary Magdalen
would be forced to admit that when she met Jesus, she didn't
recognise him. It would be easy to demolish her as a credible
witness, not to mention her dubious past which would be bound
to be brought up.

Peter would be sworn in next, followed by John. Peter could
be easily discredited. Any expert psychiatrist could demonstrate
that both he and John had been deeply traumatised the previous
two days. Their lives had been shattered. They had gone into
hiding, fearing they might be next. The servant-girl would be
found to testify that Peter swore three times that he didn't know
Jesus while the trial was in progress. The two disciples on the
road to Emmaus spent a few hours in the company of the risen
Jesus, without recognising him. So much for the main witnesses.

Finally, Thomas takes the witness-stand. He was the one
who refused to believe all the rumours that Jesus had risen from
the dead. He demanded positive proof. Nothing less than to put
his hands into the wounds. Either he is committing perjury or he
is telling the truth. He is the only credible witness that would
stand up in a modern court. And because of this, he has got a
bad press for almost two-thousand years. He has given the expression 'doubting Thomas' to the English language and that is
not a compliment. And he has earned this reputation unfairly
for two reasons. Firstly, Christ submitted himself to Thomas'
test. The second reason is given in the last lines of today's
gospel:

There were many other signs that Jesus worked and the disciples saw, but they are not recorded in this book. These are
recorded so that you may believe that Jesus is the Christ, the
Son of God, and that believing this you may have life
through his name.

Suggested additional Bidding Prayers
We pray
– that we may believe in the risen Christ, in spite of our doubts.
– that we may continue to probe the mysteries of religion in
search of new insights.
– that we will never fear to submit our religion to intellectual in-
quiry.

Catechism of the Catholic Church
644 Even when faced with the reality of the risen Jesus the

disciples are still doubtful, so impossible did the thing seem: they thought they were seeing a ghost. 'In their joy they were still disbelieving and still wondering.' Thomas will also experience the test of doubt and St Matthew relates that during the risen Lord's last appearance in Galilee 'some doubted.' Therefore the hypothesis that the resurrection was produced by the apostles' faith (or credulity) will not hold up. On the contrary their faith in the resurrection was born, under the action of divine grace, from their direct experience of the reality of the risen Jesus.

Third Sunday of Easter

Readings: Acts 2:14, 22-28. 1 Pet 1:17-21. Lk 24:13-35.

Introduction

At the present time there is a consistent downward trend in the numbers of those attending Sunday Mass. We should remember that the Eucharist is the only place that we are guaranteed to recognise the risen Christ 'in the breaking of bread.'

The breaking of bread (Mass)

A few years ago a survey was carried out on the religious attitudes of Irish university students. It covered all Irish universities for the period 1987-88. The survey was confined to Christians. Its findings are important because this group will emerge as the future leaders of Ireland and it may safely be assumed that where this group leads, many others will follow. Christian missionaries, notably the Jesuits, tended to target the elite for conversion, believing rightly that the masses would follow. It was true even of St Patrick in his conversion of Ireland. Now, that the process has begun to be reversed, it will more than likely follow the same pattern. While the survey confirms the downward trend in religious belief and practice in recent times, it does highlight some peculiar anomalies. The number of those who believe in sin, 68%, was marginally higher than the number of those who believe in a personal God, 65%. Those two three-letter words are reverse sides of the same coin. 64% believe in the Easter message, Christ's resurrection. 59% believe in the soul and afterlife, though there is a sharp division between those who believe in heaven, 56%, and hell, 28%, (though the devil does slightly better at 30%), confirming the modern *à la carte* tendency to choose the more savoury dishes on the menu. These figures confirm a downward trend from a similar survey carried out twelve years previously, e.g. belief in God, down from 81% to 65%. One figure, however, remains more or less static, i.e. the number of those who attend church once or more than once a week, which for Catholics is presumably Sunday Mass. Strangely, at 72%, it is slightly more than those who believe in God. Here, Irish students show a marked difference from Catholic adults recently surveyed in England. There, 81% believe in God, while less than 20% attend Sunday Mass. More Catholics in England believe and far less practise, slightly more Irish practise than believe. The Irish, it seems, continue to defy modern trends by clinging doggedly to Mass-going, so typical of their ancestors. But an heroic past is no guarantee of constancy in the future.

This survey has a relevance to today's gospel which recounts the encounter between the risen Christ and two of his disciples on the road to Emmaus. They had heard the rumours in Jerusalem of his resurrection but remained unconvinced. They were deep in conversation about the traumatic events of the last few days when a stranger joined them. He began to explain the scriptures to the them. When they reached Emmaus, they pressed him to stay with them. Only when he blessed and broke the bread at table with them did they recognise Jesus. It was the earliest recorded Mass after the resurrection.

Many say today – and it is borne out by the figures, particularly in the English survey – 'You don't have to go to Mass to encounter God.' True. St Paul, bent on an altogether different mission, encountered him on the road to Damascus. 'The Spirit breathes where he wills.' But the only place we are assured of meeting him is at the Eucharist. There, where every Sunday the scriptures are opened up to us, are we given the opportunity of 'recognising him at the breaking of bread.'

Suggested additional Bidding Prayers
We pray
– that we will always remain faithful to the Sunday Mass.
– that we will recognise the risen Lord in the 'breaking of bread.'
– that priests in their homilies will 'open up the Scriptures' for us.

The Catechism of the Catholic Church
1346-1347 The liturgy of the Word and the liturgy of the
Eucharistic together form 'one single act of worship'; the
Eucharistic table set for us is the table both of the Word of God
and the Body of the Lord.

Is this not the same movement as the Paschal meal of the
risen Jesus with his disciples? Walking with them he explained
the scriptures to them; sitting with them at table 'he took bread,
blessed and broke it, and gave it to them.'

Fourth Sunday of Easter

Readings: Acts 2:14, 36-41. 1 Pet 2:20-25. Jn 10:1-10.

Introduction
Today is Vocations Sunday. We live in a world where our
young are subjected to many competing voices and where there
is a crisis in vocations to the priestly ministry. We should pray
that God will continue to provide wise and caring pastors for his
church.

Hearing voices (Vocations) see also Second Sunday Year B
Some years ago, I worked with *Radharc*, an Irish television
team specialising in religious documentaries. Once, I went to
film with them in Spain. One day we stopped for a picnic lunch
somewhere in the sierras. It was a bleak and mountainous countryside and the midday sun beat down mercilessly. There we
witnessed what was for me a strange encounter. A shepherd approached, leading his flock of some few hundred sheep.
Another shepherd approached from the opposite direction with
a similar flock. Their paths crossed about a hundred yards in
front of us, where the shepherds stopped for a chat. We watched
in fascination, as the two flocks mingled. There must have been
close to a thousand sheep in all. 'Boy! Are they going to have a
problem separating that lot!' my colleague remarked. Ten minutes later, the two shepherds shook hands and parted, each
moving off in the opposite direction. The sheep too separated,
each following his own shepherd, who after making a few calls,
scarcely looked over their shoulders to check on their flocks,
leaving a modern television crew gazing after them in amaze-
ment. Our only regret was that we hadn't filmed the scene.

My only experience in Ireland of sheep was seeing them driven to fairs and markets by an angry stick-wielding farmer with his equally irritable dog snapping at their heels. It may explain why our pastors of the recent past had a reputation for browbeating their flocks into conformity. The big stick was more in evidence than the shepherd's staff. A 'belt of an episcopal crozier' was every reforming politician's greatest fear. Courting couples, lurking behind bushes after a dance, went in fear of their parish priest and his probing stick.

Sheep, like other domestic animals, come to know their master and especially his voice. They depend on him to find 'fresh and green' pastures. Far from threatening them, his 'crook and his staff' are there to pull them out when occasionally they fall into creeks and gullies. The worst fate that can befall them is to stray from the right path. Even then, the shepherd will go in search of him, clambering over rocks and crags, calling out and listening to the answering bleat that will lead him to the stray.

We live in a media age, very far removed from that idyllic pastoral scene in the Spanish sierras. The only bleating we hear is far more likely to be pop-music from the earplugs of a Walkman or the bleeping of the cellular phone in our pockets. All sorts of voices are competing for our attention. They scream at us from transistor on the beaches and TV commercials in our sitting-rooms. 'Please, turn down the volume!' is the almost constant plea of a deafened parent to its wired-up offspring. Sound-free zones are as important for our health as 'no smoking' zones and there is a case to be made for putting a health-warning sign on all that sound-producing gadgetry. And things are getting worse rather than better. We are now going to be deluged with information from personal computers. The cyberspace age has arrived with the Internet and e-mail. Information is not synonymous with knowledge; technique is no substitute for wisdom. Wherever else it may lead us, it will not lead us to the promised land.

Today, the feast of the Good Shepherd, is Vocations Sunday. The church is experiencing a crisis in vocations which is likely to deepen following recent disclosures of clerical scandals. Like their mountainy brothers, they are becoming a threatened species. More than ever the church needs wise and good pastors to guide what must be by now a very bewildered flock.

Father, eternal shepherd,
watch over the flock, redeemed by the blood of Christ
and lead us to the promised land.

Suggested additional Bidding Prayers
We pray
– that God will provide wise and caring pastors for his church.
– that those he calls to the priestly ministry will answer his call.
– that the church will use imaginatively all those whom God
calls to the service of the gospel.

Catechism of the Catholic Church
754 The church is, accordingly, a sheepfold, the sole and necessary gateway to which is Christ. It is also the flock of which
God himself foretold that he would be the shepherd, and whose
sheep, even though governed by human shepherds, are unfailingly nourished by Christ himself, the Good Shepherd and
Prince of Shepherds, who gave his life for his sheep.

Fifth Sunday of Easter

Readings: Acts 6:1-7. 1 Pet 2:4-9. Jn 14: 1-12.

Introduction
    Life is a pilgrimage. Like all journeys, it is important that we
keep our eyes fixed on our destination which is eternal life.
Christ assured us: 'I am the Way, the Truth and the Life.' With
him as our guide we will not go astray.

Beginning at the end (The Way)
    About twenty years ago, Archbishop Donal Lamont stayed
with me on a brief visit to Paris. A short time before, he had first
been imprisoned and later expelled from Rhodesia, since re-
named Zimbabwe, for his outspoken criticism of the white racist
regime there. It took the form of a letter smuggled out of prison
and published in the international press. He was now invited to
Paris to give a lecture in OECD on his experiences. The night before, he consulted me on how best to get to the OECD headquarters. His talk was scheduled for early the following morning,
during rush hour traffic, when delays would be unavoidable. As
there was a direct line on the underground, I suggested he take
the Métro. It was his first visit to Paris and he baulked at the
prospect. It was strange to see this man who had braved persecution and imprisonment for his convictions, terrified of taking
the underground. He only agreed finally, when I offered to go

with him. When he returned that evening, I asked him how he got on, meaning how was his lecture received. 'Fine,' he said, 'and I came back on the Métro all on my own.'

Paris must be the easiest city in the world for tourists to get around. This is very much due to its underground system. There are other undergrounds, like the London tube or the New York subway, but at least in my opinion, the Paris Métro surpasses them all. Nowhere in Paris is further than 500 yards from the nearest underground station and all addresses in Paris list their nearest underground. Tickets are all the same price, regardless of the length of the journey and regular users are supplied with monthly tickets. Queues are rare, or non-existent. But it is the underground system itself that gives Paris the edge over all others. I cannot speak for Tokyo, among many others, and Rome is fine as far as it goes, though it doesn't go very far. There are only two lines and their magnificent archeological heritage precludes further development. The Métro is an example of French logic at its very best. You begin at the end, where all good journeys should begin. It's the destination that counts. Where you want to go is what decides the direction you take. Each line is named by its terminus. Your direction is determined by whichever of the two termini serves your purpose. Having made your choice, you can't go wrong. No wonder Parisians have a saying: 'If you get lost in the Métro, don't tell anyone!'

The 'Christian Way' is not dissimilar. Life is a journey. Older generations preferred to call it the 'pilgrim way'. It begins at birth and ends at death. In between, at every juncture, we are confronted with a multiplicity of choices. Life is a network of criss-crossing routes and spaghetti junctions. Getting lost is a constant possibility. We can easily end up in all sorts of blind alleys or get trapped in narrow cul-de-sacs from which we can barely extricate ourselves. We are often tempted to stray from the 'straight and narrow path' that leads to salvation, preferring the easier paths to perdition. Like the Paris Métro, finding their way is only a problem for those who don't know their destination.

To Thomas' question, 'How can we know the way?', Jesus replied:

I am the Way, the Truth and the Life.

No one can come to the Father except through me.

James Thurber, the American fable writer put a similar message in verse:

All men should learn before they die,
where they are going to, from where and why.

Suggested additional Bidding Prayers
We pray
– for the courage to make the right moral decisions in our lives.
– for the grace to resist temptations that lead us astray.
– for perseverance in following the Christian way.

Catechism of the Catholic Church
1696 The way of Christ 'leads to life'; a contrary way 'leads to destruction'. The gospel parable of the two ways remains ever present in the catechism of the church; it shows the importance of moral decisions for our salvation: 'There are two ways, the one of life, the other of death; but between the two, there is a great difference.'

Sixth Sunday of Easter

Readings: Acts 8:5-8, 14-17. 1 Pet 3:15-18. Jn 14:15-21.

Introduction
We live in a world which has largely lost its sense of the sacred. If God is no longer sacred for us, all our other relationships suffer as a result. We should reverence God, respect others and show courtesy to all.

A sense of the sacred (Reverence)
As a young boy, I was encouraged to show respect for adults. Our teachers as well as our priests were always acknowledged with a military-style salute when we passed them in the street. Other adults we greeted with 'Good morning, Sir' or 'Good evening, Ma'am' depending on their sex and the time of day. In spite of my good intentions, I didn't always get it right. One old lady who lived in my street took me aside one day to explain to me that I should call her 'Miss' not 'Ma'am'. 'I am a spinster,' she rather haughtily informed this ten-year old who should have known better. These courtesies were invariably observed among adults themselves. My father always raised his hat or doffed his cap to the opposite sex. Strangely enough, the only occasion where that gesture still survives, at least in rural Ireland, is as a

mark of respect for the dead. Men there still uncover their heads when a funeral hearse passes. Now all those little formalities have disappeared like the world of my childhood which valued them so highly.

I suspect their end was hastened by the cinema and its strong diet of American egalitarianism. The cowboys and crooks, the cops and hoodlums, who filled the big screen and dominated my teenage imagination, were not idolised for the nicety of their manners. These 'guys and dolls' shot from the hip, with their mouths as well as with their six-shooters. And we were eager students. We parroted their every phrase and every gesture. We shed our earlier cissiness like an embarrassing relative. Incidentally, the old-world formalities seem to have survived better in places like France. 'Monsieur', 'Madam' and 'Mademoiselle' are still *de rigueur* among colleagues and neighbours there. I recently watched an old John Wayne Western which was dubbed in French. Wayne sauntered into the saloon in search of the bad guy. He found him sitting at the bar. Wayne approached, tapped him on the shoulder and drawled in impeccable French. 'Excusez-moi, Monsieur!' When the crook turned round, Wayne slugged him. With dubbing like that, one wonders why the French continue to fight so hard to keep out American films.

Nowhere seems to have escaped this new wave of informality. What Hollywood did for secular society, ironically, the new liturgy introduced into the church. When I was an altar-boy, my awkward gait and sleepy Latin responses might have caused offence to purists. At least, they occasionally irritated priests, though irritability seems to have been a feature of priests then. But, like all my contemporaries, I had a deep sense of the sacred. For us, the Real Presence was very real indeed. Whatever contribution the new liturgy has made, and its contribution has been enormous, this sense of the sacred has been an unintended casualty. It demystified the Mass and like the earlier Reformation, 'stripped the altars'. Gone are the 'Thee's' and 'Thou's' of God language, like the altar-rails that enclosed the sanctuary. God has joined our egalitarian ranks.

'Reverence the Lord Christ in your hearts,' Peter tells us in today's reading. If God is not sacred, there is nothing sacred anymore. Neither husband for wife, nor wife for husband, neither parents for children, nor children for parents. Maybe that accounts for the growing break-down in families. And in a timely warning to those in Ireland and elsewhere engaged in religious debate, he urges them to make their arguments 'with courtesy and respect'. These two qualities are notably absent in most religious disputes. Reverence for God, respect for persons and courtesy are all facets of the same virtue. Those who are courteous may not always be believers, but the discourteous can never be true followers of Jesus Christ.

Suggested additional Bidding Prayers
We pray
– that we may always treat others with respect especially those who differ from us.
– that we will always 'reverence the Lord Christ in our hearts.'
– that we will always treat others with courtesy especially the weaker members of society.

Catechism of the Catholic Church
2120 Sacrilege consists in profaning or treating unworthily the sacraments and other liturgical actions, as well as persons, things or places consecrated to God. Sacrilege is a grave sin especially when committed against the Eucharist, for in this sacrament the true Body of Christ is made substantially present for us.

Ascension Years A, B, and C

Readings: Acts 1:1-11. Eph 1:17-23. Mt 28:16-20 (A).
Mk 16:15-20 (B). Lk 24:46-53 (C)

Introduction
We celebrate today Christ's ascension to his eternal glory in heaven and express our hope that where he has gone before us, we will one day follow to live forever in the kingdom of our Father.

Saying goodbye. (Ascension) see also Sixth Sunday of Easter C
To speak a foreign language well, one needs to think in that language. Most beginners tend to translate from their mother-tongue. I remember when I first started speaking French and I squirm now at the thought of what the unfortunate natives were subjected to. I was spending the summer working in a parish in

the suburbs of Bordeaux. On one occasion I was invited out to
dinner by a family in the parish. At one point during the meal,
Madame offered me a second helping, which I declined. I
should have said, *Merci, non. J'ai bien mangé.* (No thank you. I
have eaten well.) Instead, I used an expression which was commonly used in Ireland on such occasions and translated it literally
into French. 'No thanks. I'm full.' I said. There was a sudden
burst of laughter from the younger members of the family which
earned them a stern rebuke from *Maman.* Later I discovered the
reason for their amusement. Their priest-guest had just informed them that he was pregnant. 'To be full' was a local expression to describe the state of pregnancy.

French is a more precise language than English. It often has
two words, where English has only one. 'Goodbye' is a case in
point. The French use *Au revoir* for those everyday temporary
separations, while *Adieu* is reserved strictly for final definitive
departures. There is no English translation but it means roughly
'until we meet in heaven'. Life is a succession of Adieus. The
number grows with the passing years. Our past is peopled with
faces that once were dear to us. Some, like our parents, died.
Others moved away out of our lives never to reappear again.
Sometimes their names crop up in conversation and we say, 'I
wonder what became of so-and-so.' They probably make the
same remark about us occasionally. Life is a series of little deaths
until our own death which for us will be the last great *Adieu.*
Paris must be the capital of 'goodbyes'. People live there for a
while and then move on and settle down elsewhere. With all its
charm, it doesn't seem the kind of city where people strike roots.
More a temporary haven for nomads. The modern world is becoming more and more like Paris. It is said that Americans
change home on average every four years. More often than you
and I change our cars. And in this, as in so many other facets of
life, we are all becoming more and more Americanised. Our
'goodbyes' are growing at an ever accelerating rate.

We are, as never before, a pilgrim people. We need faithful
friends who travel with us. In today's gospel, Jesus is alerting his
disciples to his immanent departure, his ascension into heaven.
He doesn't say *Adieu* but *Au revoir.* 'I am going away and shall
return'. We never say goodbye to God: He always goes with us.
'Know that I am with you always; yes, to the end of time.' It is
striking to note how emigrants who leave their families, friends,
language and cultures, and settle, often penniless and in a hos-

tile environment, on the other side of the globe, begin by building houses of worship. Such was the case with the Irish in the
second half of the nineteenth century in America or Australia.
Such is the case today with Muslims from North Africa and elsewhere building mosques in France. God is all they have left to
cling on to. It is a striking proof that God has kept his promise to
be with us always. He will always keep his side of the bargain. It
is up to us to keep ours. And when we come to the end of our
pilgrimage here and have to make our final farewell, it will be
literally *Adieu* – 'until we meet in heaven' with the ascended
Christ.

Suggested additional Bidding Prayers
We pray
– that one day we too may follow Christ into the kingdom of our
Father.
– that we will be reunited with our departed friends in heaven.
– that the faithful departed may be reunited with the ascended
Christ.

Catechism of the Catholic Church
659 'So then the Lord Jesus, after he had spoken to them, was
taken up into heaven, and sat down at the right hand of God.' …
Jesus' final apparition ends with the irreversible entry of his
humanity into divine glory, symbolised by the cloud and by
heaven, where he is seated from that time forward at God's right
hand.

Seventh Sunday of Easter

Readings: Acts 1:12-14. 1 Pet 4:13-16. Jn 17: 1-11.

Introduction
   Today's gospel recounts Christ's final prayer before his ascension into heaven. It should be a reminder to us of the importance
of prayer in our lives.

Lost treasure (Prayer)
   Nostalgia is a dangerous illusion. Taking refuge in the past is
a form of escapism. In any case, memory is highly selective.
Strange, isn't it, that the summers of our childhood were always
sunny. Like the schoolmaster's cane, we easily forget the chill-

blains and fleabites of our early schooldays. The shivering cold
of the mornings' ablutions and the refined torture of mother's
finecomb too often escape our hazy recollection. If I seem, rather frequently, to recall the past, it is not to indulge in nostalgia. My generation, unlike most others, have straddled two worlds, an experience
I consider an enrichment. Rummaging in the attic of memory, occasionally one recovers a lost treasure, whose value is no way diminished by the passage of time. In any case, we are endowed with
memory as well as imagination and those who have passed their
middle years have more to look back on than forward to.

A smell can conjure up memories of the past like nothing
else. Recently, an all too rare smell of incense brought me back to
my teen years and what we used to call the 'May devotions'.
During that month, we went every evening to the church for the
Rosary and Benediction in honour of Our Lady. It was also an
occasion for meeting our girlfriends and going for long strolls
together in those lengthening evenings. And all that with our
parents' blessing, unaware of our other hidden agenda. Our
lives then seemed to revolve around a cycle of devotions.
Besides the great religious festivals of Christmas and Easter,
there were Sunday devotions, First Fridays, Lenten masses,
school retreats, parish missions and October devotions. It's
amazing we had time for anything else in our lives but prayer.

But there was no television then. No *Coronation Street* to
watch. And the cinema did not open until 9 pm, (probably in
deference to the parish priest). Religion then consumed a frac-
tion of the staggering 202 minutes a day every Irish person over
the age of four now spends in front of the TV screen. In the
'couch potato' order of merit, we come fourth in Europe, according to a recent survey. Little wonder that prayer has become virtually non-existent. It's our lost treasure. Prayer is what makes
sense of our lives and puts our problems in perspective. It is
what the disciples did in the upper room, immediately after the
trauma of the crucifixion, 'together with several women, including Mary the mother of Jesus'. It was with a prayer that Jesus finally parted with his disciples before his ascension into heaven.

With all the blessings that modern science has showered us
with, including television, without prayer our lives are impover-
ished. A poet once wrote:
    A poor world this, if full of care,
      we have no time to stand and stare.'
I think he might forgive my slight alteration:
    'we have no time for private prayer.'

Suggested additional Bidding Prayers
We pray
– for the gift of prayer.
– that we will live as we pray.
– that our lives may be transformed by our fidelity to prayer.

Catechism of the Catholic Church
2746 When 'his hour' came, Jesus prayed to the Father. His prayer, the longest transmitted by the gospel, embraces the whole economy of creation and salvation, as well as his death and resurrection. The prayer of the Hour of Jesus always remains his own, just as his Passover 'once for all' remains ever present in the liturgy of his church.

Pentecost Sunday Years A, B and C

Readings: Acts 2:1-11. 1 Cor 12:3-7, 12-13. Jn 20:19-23.

Introduction
For much of history, the Holy Spirit was the neglected Cinderella of the three divine persons. Rediscovered in our own age, the Spirit is now monopolised by charismatic groups. But 'the Spirit breathes where we will,' and works best with individuals who place themselves under his guidance.

Generous impulses (The Holy Spirit)
Some years ago, at the very beginning of the seventies, I spent a summer working in a parish in San José, about fifty miles south of San Francisco. During my stay, some parishioners invited me to what appeared to be a prayer-meeting. There were thirty or forty people present, men and women, young and old. We sang hymns, we held hands, we prayed and we meditated. While we were meditating in silence, suddenly one of the group began to speak or, rather, language began to pour out of him. The problem was, it was completely incomprehensible gibberish. It was an eerie experience and I felt a shiver run down my spine. When the outburst came to an end, another member of the group prayed for the gift of understanding and after a decent interval a third member translated or interpreted the gibberish. There was nothing extraordinary about the content of the message. What was extraordinary was the event itself. I did not

realise then but I learned shortly afterwards that this was an early meeting of what was called a charismatic group. It was in fact the second such group ever founded in the world. During the rest of that decade, the Charismatic Movement spread rapidly all over the world. What I had experienced that night in San José was an expression of the gift of tongues, first practiced by the apostles on the day of Pentecost.

Despite the obvious good the Charismatic movement achieved and achieves, I have always had two reservations about it. I felt that it had privileged access to the Holy Spirit and that the latter had a marked preference for communicating with organised groups. There was also a tendency, as on that night in San José, to highlight the extraordinary manifestations of the Holy Spirit, as the gift of tongues and the gift of healing, very much to the detriment of the far more numerous routine out-pourings of the Spirit. Everybody has access to the Holy Spirit and he has access to everybody, and that includes those who are not religious as well as those who are, those who are affiliated to a religion as well as those who are not. 'The Spirit breathes where he will.' It is through the individual, with his unique gifts, that the Holy Spirit operates *par excellence*. Everybody has experienced his gentle urgings. Those moments in our lives when we are tempted to surpass ourselves, to do something almost bordering on the heroic, to reach out and help someone in trouble, to sacrifice our time and our well-being for totally unselfish reasons. In reality, these moments are rare and the number of times we yield to these temptations rarer still. Probably the real failures in our lives are not the bad temptations we succumb to but the good ones we resist. We should give way to our generous impulses instead of pulling back at the last moment as we do, thus thwarting the promptings of the Holy Spirit.

He works best with individuals with their unique talents and special opportunities. Look at the history of the world, even in our own century. Every earth-shaking movement every happening that renewed the face of the earth was invariably the brainchild of a single individual. Martin Luther King's crusade for the civil rights of American blacks; Mahatma Ghandi almost single-handedly emancipating an entire subcontinent. What else is the history of the church but the lives of the saints, a succession of individuals of the calibre of Francis of Assisi, Ignatius Loyola, Vincent de Paul, stretching down to a John XXIII and a Mother

Teresa of Calcutta in our own time? More recently, how else to explain the sudden dissolution of the Eastern Bloc except by reference to a Lech Walesa, a Vaclav Havel, a Sakharov or a Gorbachev? History is nothing else but his story and her story. These individuals, together with the Holy Spirit, renewed the face of the earth. You too, together with the Holy Spirit, can do likewise. This is the message of Pentecost.

Suggested additional Bidding Prayers
We pray
– that the Holy Spirit will help us to renew the face of the earth.
– that we will place our own unique talents under the guidance of the Holy Spirit, at the service of the church.
– that we may always follow our generous impulses.

Catechism of the Catholic Church
1076 The church was made manifest to the world on the day of Pentecost by the outpouring of the Holy Spirit. The gift of the Spirit ushers in a new era in the 'dispensation of the mystery' – the age of the church, during which Christ manifests, makes present and communicates his work of salvation through the liturgy of his church, 'until he comes'.

Trinity Sunday Years A, B and C

Readings: Ex 34:4-6, 8-9. 2 Cor 13:11- 13. Jn 3:16-18.

Introduction
We were created in the image of a triune God, the Father, the Son and the Holy Spirit. We best reflect that image when we are creative, compassionate and charismatic.

Fullness of love (Trinity)
Our age has been largely dominated by three outstanding figures, Charles Darwin, Sigmund Freud and Karl Marx. Some have described them irreverently as 'the unholy trinity'. They pushed us into the modern world, very often in spite of our protests. Charles Darwin's theory of evolution was greeted, particularly by the established churches, with howls of derision and had to battle long and hard for recognition. Sigmund Freud

opened up the universe of the unconscious and profoundly affected conventional attitudes. The socialist theories of Karl Marx came to dominate one half of the planet and considerably influenced the other. Of the three, only Darwin and his theory of evolution remain intact. Recent events in the Eastern Bloc have largely discredited Marx. The theories of Freud are more and more contested in recent times. Time has taken its toll of 'the unholy trinity'.

The Holy Trinity, whose feast is celebrated today, is beyond the reach of time and the grasp of human reasoning. It is a mystery of our faith. We can only fumble in the dark in search of glimmers of light. 'Two is company, three is a crowd' is a popular expression. The gospel would have it otherwise. There, the figure three symbolises completeness and perfect symmetry, and re-appears at all the key moments of the Christ story. His life itself constantly reflected the Trinity. Three figures make up the nativity scene in Bethlehem – the Holy Family of Jesus, Mary and Joseph. Their first visitors were the three wise men. Later, in the desert preparing to begin his public life, Jesus was tempted three times by the devil. A good story, we are told should have a beginning, a middle and an end. Christ was a story-teller *par excellence* and three figures prominently in his parables. The Prodigal Son is about a father and his two sons; the Good Samaritan tells of the behaviour of three passers-by, the priest, the levite and the Samaritan; the sower sowed his seed in three different types of terrain, yielding three different levels of harvest. The end of his life, as the beginning, has again the three motif. During his Passion, Peter denied him thrice. On the road to Calvary, he fell three times. The crucifixion scene has three figures, Christ between two thieves. Before his resurrection, he spent three days in the tomb.

God is love. There are Three Persons in the Trinity, the Father the Son and the Holy Spirit. Together they represent the fullness of love. The Father loves the Son, the Son loves the Father. The Holy Spirit is their love for each other. We are made in the image of a triune God. God the Father, who created us, his Son who saved us, and the Holy Spirit who continues to guide us. Our lives should reflect the Trinity. We should be always creative like the Father, compassionate like his Son, and dispose our talents in the service of others like the Holy Spirit.

Suggested additional Bidding Prayers

We pray

– that we may reflect in our lives the image of the Father by our creativity.

– that we may reflect the image of his Son by our compassion for others.

– that we may place our talents at the disposal of the Holy Spirit.

Catechism of the Catholic Church

234 The mystery of the Most Holy Trinity is the central mystery of Christian faith and life. It is the mystery of God in himself. It is therefore the source of all the other mysteries of faith, the light that enlightens them. It is the most fundamental and essential teaching in the 'hierarchy of the truths of faith'. The whole history of salvation is identical with the history of the way and the means by which the one true God, Father, Son and Holy Spirit, reveals himself to men 'and reconciles and unites with himself those who turn away from sin'.

Corpus Christi Years A, B, and C

Readings: Deut 8:2-3, 14-16. 1 Cor 10:16-17. Jn 6: 51-58. (A)
Ex 24:3-8. Heb 9:11-15. Mk 14:12-16, 22-26. (B)
Gen 14:18-20. 1 Cor 11:23-26. Lk 9:11-17. (C)

Introduction

God fed his people in the desert by providing them with food and drink. He continues to feed us with food and drink in the body and blood of his Son, which we celebrate in the feast of Corpus Christi.

Body of Christ (Eucharist)

A modern tourist in cities like Paris and Rome, and particularly the latter, cannot but be struck by the extraordinary number of churches and their close proximity to each other. In Rome, each street has several and occasionally, next door to each other. Most people assume that the explanation for such a density of churches in Rome is that it is the headquarters of the Catholic Church and that many religious orders established houses there. While that may be true, it is not the historical explanation and that certainly is not the case with Paris. There, within the walls of the old city, churches proliferate, often a mere fifty yards from each other, such as the cathedral of Notre Dame and the church of St Julian-le-Pauvre. Like Notre Dame, most of these churches date from the Middle Ages. They all derive from the devotion to Corpus Christi which originated in the twelfth century and whose feast we celebrate today.

It began in the city of Liège in northern France and when a priest of that diocese became Pope Urban IV, he made it a feast of the universal church in 1624. Gradually, the devotion spread throughout Christendom. By the fifteenth century Corpus Christi had become the principal feast of the church almost everywhere. Every city, town and village held its Corpus Christi procession. In some places it became the social event on the calendar. Months were spent preparing for it. Guilds competed with each other to provide the most colourful contribution. Cities like Paris, consisted of clusters of timber-built houses arranged in narrow streets, where humans and animals lived closely together in squalor. Streets were running sewers and rat-infested. Plagues were endemic and fire a constant hazard. Medicine was primitive or non-existent. In such a world, it was little wonder that the Corpus Christi devotion had such enormous appeal. What greater protection could they ask for than the Body of Christ, carried in procession through their streets to inoculate them against all such infections?

After well over a thousand years of Christianity, the Real Presence, God's continuing presence in the consecrated bread, came to dominate the devotional life of the people. New devotions were developed such as visits to and exposition and benediction of the Blessed Sacrament. The notion that no place was too good to house the body of Christ, led to the building of larger and more ornate churches. It became the age of the great Cathedrals, like Notre Dame and Chartres. Changes were introduced into the Mass itself to reflect this new devotion, in particular the elevation was introduced after the consecration. For a medieval, there were very real and down-to-earth reasons why the Body and Blood of Christ should be raised. Blindness was a common affliction then and people believed that looking at the Body of Christ was the best protection against it. Bowing to popular pressure, the church permitted it. The elevation of the chalice was an after-thought because the church feared that the people might believe in only one species. All of which helps to explain the close proximity of churches in cities like Paris and

Rome. Elevations were much in demand and people rushed from one church to another just to watch the elevation.

All this eucharistic devotion dominated religious practice right down to the Second Vatican Council. There the church decided wisely that the Mass needed to be restored to the centre of eucharistic devotion and wittingly or unwittingly the others were down-graded. Within a generation, visits, benedictions, expositions and Corpus Christi processions had virtually disappeared. The bread remained, the circuses had gone. And we are the poorer for it. One cannot pray with others unless one has learned to pray alone. And visits, exposition and benediction were *par excellence* occasions for private prayer. Our Sunday liturgies, no matter how well prepared or executed, are lacking. For virtually the first time in the history of the Mass, the complaint is heard: 'I don't get anything out of it.' A new generation has been deprived of a thousand year heritage of prayer and contemplation.

We don't suffer from blindness, or cholera or plague, at least in the western world, as our medieval ancestors did. Modern medicine has taken care of that. But we suffer from other things, loneliness, alienation, depersonalisation, despair, for which medicine has no cure. As much as ever, we need the comfort of the Real Presence and the protection of Corpus Christi.

Suggested additional Bidding prayers
We pray
– that we may always be nourished by the Body of Christ.
– that its promise of eternal life will be fulfilled for us.
– for eucharistic ministers who bring Christ's Body to the sick.

Catechism of the Catholic Church
1324 The Eucharist is 'the source and summit of the Christian life'. 'The other sacraments, and indeed all ecclesiastical ministries and works of the apostolate, are bound up with the Eucharist and oriented towards it. For in the blessed Eucharist is contained the whole spiritual good of the Church, namely Christ himself, our Pasch.'

Second Sunday

Readings: Is 49:3, 5-6. 1 Cor 1:1-3. Jn 1:29-34.

Introduction
   Today's gospel reminds us of the crucial role we play in leading others to Christ. Each generation is called to hand on the faith to the next. If there is a fall away from the practice of the faith today we must all accept a portion of the blame and examine our lives to see where we are failing.

'Look, there is the lamb of God' (Handing on the faith)
   There are somethings that can only be explained by their history. Take two Catholic countries like Ireland and France. The rate of church-attendance in France is about 16% nationwide, while the figure for Ireland hovers round 80%. The decline in France dates from the period of the French Revolution. In 1789, when the French rose up against the *ancien régime* their decadent church was identified with the oppressive system and was thus targetted by the revolutionaries. Ireland and its church had a completely different history. Because we were an occupied country and that occupier was Protestant, the Catholic church there was on the side of the people against the oppressor. The church emerged from our history in a favourable light when we gained our independence at the beginning of this century.
   When one considers what is happening in eastern Europe today a similar pattern emerges. The remarkable series of revolutions which toppled the communist governments in countries from Poland to Rumania and even within the Soviet Republics themselves, all have one thing in common. Religion played a significant if not dominant role in their liberation. Unlike the French Revolution, the churches there were on the side of the victors. What kept the spirit of liberty alive all during that period of communist totalitarianism was religion. It was the Catholic Church in Poland. In East Germany it was the Protestant Churches. The protests first began around the church in Leipzig. The Russian Orthodox also played its part. And it must have been similar in those other Russian Republics about which so little is known except that some sixty million Muslims live there. In all these places an alliance was formed between the political dissidents and the churches which finally brought about the collapse of communism.

These churches played a truly prophetic role. The purpose of the Christian Church is to reveal Christ to the people. The eastern churches seem to have fulfilled their purpose well in spite of persecution. I lived for a year in Rome with a Ukrainian who worked as an engineer under the communist regime, while he carried out his ministry as a priest in secret after a long hard day at his job. In fact, he was consecrated as a bishop underground. He came to Rome now to learn theology.

The role of John the Baptist was to reveal Christ. As he said, 'it was to reveal him to Israel that I came'. Today's gospel describes him bowing out when Jesus arrived. 'Look,' he said, 'there is the lamb of God that takes away the sin of the world.' Ever since, these words have been enshrined in the Mass when the priest holds up the consecrated host just before communion.

All Christians are called to perform this prophetic role and nobody more than those who have others in their care. Above all parents whose duty is to introduce their children to Christ, to hand on the faith to them. Unfortunately, it doesn't always happen. Sometimes, young people who give up the practice of their religion were put off it by their parents. What they saw they didn't like. It is no wonder we speak nowadays about a credibility gap.

The response to the psalm is a little prayer that sums up our roles as Christians:

Here I am Lord! I come to do your will.

Suggested additional Bidding Prayers
We pray
– for pastors and priests that they may live up to their callings
– for parents and teachers that they may hand on the faith to their children.
– for our departed parents and friends who handed on the faith to us.

Catechism of the Catholic Church
523 St John the Baptist is the Lord's immediate precursor or forerunner, sent to prepare his way. 'Prophet of the Most High', John surpasses all the prophets, of whom he is the last. He inaugurates the gospel, already from his mother's womb welcomes the coming of Christ, and rejoices in being 'the friend of the bridegroom', whom he points out as 'the Lamb of God who takes away the sin of the world'. Going before Jesus 'in the spirit and power of Elijah', John bears witness to Christ in his preaching, by his baptism of conversion, and through his martyrdom.

Third Sunday

Readings: Is 8:23-9:13. 1 Cor 1:10-13,17. Mt 4:12-23

Introduction

We live in a world where recently many ideological barriers have come tumbling down. Those which still remain – between the different branches of the Christian faith – should have been the first to fall. Maybe they have become monuments to our indifference.

Breaking down the barriers (Christian Unity) see Seventh Sunday of Easter Year C

The strange thing about the Berlin Wall was that it was built with bricks and mortar. It physically divided Berlin city into east and west. It served also as a symbol for the division of Germany and indeed of Europe into two ideological camps. It was a concrete symbol of the Iron Curtain. It was probably a tactical mistake on the part of the East Germans to erect the Berlin Wall. While it was there and while people could see and touch it, people thought it should come down. And down it came to everybody's surprise at the time. But while thousands were chipping away at it, taking it apart brick by brick, they were dismantling the ideological Iron Curtain, which collapsed soon afterwards.

If only all the other walls which divide humans were built of bricks! Unfortunately, they are built with myths and ideologies, prejudices and fears. Because we don't see them, we are not always conscious of their existence. They are not easily attacked. It is a slow tortuous process even to make people aware of them. Such is the case with the walls which were erected throughout history to divide religions. When you consider that the Berlin Wall came down after a mere fifty years of existence, it is disturbing to reflect that there is another wall dividing Germany and Europe and the West, which has remained intact for more than five-hundred years. It is the wall that divides the Christian world into Protestants and Catholics. There is little indication that that wall is coming down. It is strange that the barrier which divided the atheistic communist world from the God-believing West could disappear so quickly while the one that separates two sets of Christians who believe that Jesus Christ is Lord should remain as solid as ever.

Of course, we observe Church Unity Week. The priest and

the parson share a cup of tea on the lawn and even exchange pulpits occasionally. The hierarchies get together to issue joint statements on public issues that concern them. The Pope and the Archbishop of Canterbury exchange visits and presents. Theologians work away at finding points of agreement and removing misunderstandings. One might be forgiven for believing that at least some bricks were being dislodged. But other bricks are being added all the time. The decision of the Anglican Church to ordain women is considered by the Catholic Church to be a further obstacle to unity.

Lest we become too depressed about the prospects of Christian unity, it is worth looking again at what led to the collapse of the Berlin Wall and the dismantling of the Iron Curtain. There was a marvellous surge of human spirit, shown by the people of Leipzig and elsewhere who crowded into the streets in sub-zero temperatures night after night and refused to disperse even when threatened with tanks. This massive expression of the peoples' will changed everything. Something similar will be needed to break down our religious barrier. The problem is not with hierarchies; it is with ordinary people. Apparently, they don't feel strongly enough or express their will forcefully. Or even that they don't wish for Christian unity. The Archbishop of Canterbury visited Rome and had a long discussion with the Pope. It was agreed that in a united Christendom Anglicans would accept the Pope as president. When the Archbishop returned to England, a poll was taken among practising Anglicans. The great majority rejected the notion of the Pope as president.

It is easy for us to sit in the pew and think it is time for popes and bishops to get their act together and solve this terrible scandal. The problem may not be there. It may be our indifference or downright hostility. We like to say that our best friend is a Protestant. We may have even stood for his children. We may even have vague aspirations that it would be nice some day if we could all get together again. Five-hundred years of separation will not disappear just like that. Our disunity has a long history. It goes back to the earliest days of Christianity when St Paul pleaded with the Corinthians:

> I do appeal to you, brothers, for the sake of our Lord Jesus Christ, to make up the differences between you, and instead of disagreeing among yourselves, to be united again in your belief and practice.

What St Paul wrote two thousand years ago to the Corinthians, he is writing to us today.

Suggested additional Bidding Prayers

We pray
– that conflicts within our families may be reconciled.
– that conflicts between communities and nations may be settled peacefully.
– that the divided Churches lead the way in reconciliation.

Catechism of the Catholic Church

822 Concern for achieving unity 'involves the whole church, faithful and clergy alike.' But we must realise 'that this holy objective – the reconciliation of all Christians in the unity of the one and only church of Christ – transcends human powers and gifts'. That is why we place all our hope 'in the prayer of Christ for the Church, in the love of the Father for us, and in the Holy Spirit'.

Fourth Sunday

Readings: Zeph 2:3, 3:12-13. 1 Cor 1:26-31. Mt 5:1-12

Introduction

The beatitudes are a charter of the Christian life. They are not a moral code or a set of minimal precepts to avoid God's punishment. They are ideals to raise our perspective above the constraints of worldly interest.

Happy attitudes (Beatitudes) See also Sixth Sunday A

About twenty years ago I made my one and only visit to Palestine. I had always thought it was a barren and desert land. I probably went at the best time of the year, towards late April. I was quite surprised at how beautiful it was and particularly the places Jesus chose for the various happenings recorded in the gospel. One sunny morning I climbed the hill of the beatitudes overlooking the lake and sat down there reflecting on today's reading. The hill was ablaze with flowers. It suddenly dawned on me that Jesus Christ was not only the Son of God but he also had a marvellous eye for the beauties of nature. The beauty of his words on than occasion were fittingly matched by the beauty of his surroundings.

Yet, what he said there was extraordinarily radical. How his listeners reacted to it then, I have no idea. I have some idea what the reaction would be today. Imagine a father or mother giving this list as advice to their eighteen year old son or daughter as they set out to make their way in the modern world. Were they to suggest that the attitudes to get on were the following, to be attached to poverty, to be gentle, to be activists for human rights and peace etc, their offspring might be forgiven for thinking their parents had gone crazy.

If they were 'poor in spirit', that is not dependent on others, especially the influential, to get on, they wouldn't go very far. How often parents have said to me because they think the priest has influence: 'You wouldn't put in a word with so-and-so for my boy?' How often we imply if we do not say to our children: 'It's not *what* you know but *who* you know that counts.' Whatever else gentleness or meekness may achieve, it won't help you climb the ladder of success in the company. To do that you need to be pushy and aggressive and you may well need to be ruthless as well. We know well what happens to those 'who hunger and thirst after right'. Their cases are well documented in history books. They end up, like St Paul or Andrei Sakharov, in a prison cell. Not many like Nelson Mandela become president after twenty-eight years in prison. Most finish up in an unmarked prison grave unknown and forgotten. The attitudes listed by Christ in his sermon are exactly the opposite of what the world demands of the successful. As St Paul says: 'It was to shame the wise that God chose what is foolish by human reckoning ... those whom the world thinks common and contemptible are the ones God has chosen.'

We speak a lot nowadays about 'practising Catholics'. We have reduced practice, very conveniently for ourselves, to one single solitary item. And one that is not too demanding at that, attendance at Sunday Mass. There is no mention of that in the sermon on the mount. Christ did not set up a moral code with the 'i's' dotted and the 't's' crossed. He probably knew we were very good at that ourselves, if the Pharisees were anything to go by. He simply pointed out the attitudes needed to enter the kingdom of heaven.

These 'happy attitudes' are the charter of the kingdom. They are ideals and like all ideals well-nigh unattainable. What is the point of them then? They are the heights we aim at and measure our standards against. Fortunately for us, history throws up rare examples of individuals who incarnate one or other of these beatitudes, like a Francis of Assisi or a Mother Teresa of Calcutta. There are many others whom we know nothing about 'whose godly deeds have not failed.' As St Paul says in today's reading: 'You, God has made members of Christ Jesus and by God's doing he has become our wisdom, and our virtue, and our holiness, and our freedom.'

Suggested additional Bidding Prayers
We pray
– that we may be idealists and always follow the Christian way.
– that God will always bless his church with saints to inspire us.
– for those who are persecuted in the cause of right.

Catechism of the Catholic Church
1719 The beatitudes reveal the goal of human existence, the ultimate end of human acts: God calls us to his own beatitude. This vocation is addressed to each individual personally, but also to the church as a whole, the new people made up of those who have accepted the promise and live from it in faith.

Fifth Sunday

Readings: Is 58:7-10. 1 Cor 2:1-5. Mt 5:13-16.

Introduction
In spite of recent spectacular events, tyranny still flourishes in many parts of the world. It is maintained by terror and propaganda. Other forms of tyranny thrive nearer home: poverty, unemployment and homelessness. Christians best fight these tyrannies by showing their solidarity with the oppressed victims.

The clinched fist (Tyranny)
Revolutions tend to be highly contagious. Such was the case with the French Revolution. The fall of the Bastille resounded even in Ireland where it gave birth to the United Irishmen and the rebellion of 1798. No wonder the Archbishop of Dublin at the time reported despondently to Rome that the 'French disease' was spreading. That was two hundred years ago. Now, because television relays the pictures instantly worldwide, the effects are more immediate. No sooner had the Berlin Wall collapsed than that other wall of shame, apartheid, at the other end

of the world and the other extreme of the ideological spectrum, began to crumble.

Some four thousand years ago, the prophet Isaiah gave what seems a remarkably modern analysis of revolutions and their causes. The tyrannies which they attack, he described as the 'yoke, the clinched fist and the wicked word'. The 'yoke' was the system of apartheid by the white racist regime in South Africa or the totalitarian dictatorship in Soviet Russia. The 'clinched fist' was the system of terror used to maintain the regime. The world knows now how clinched that fist was in Stalinist Russia, with its gulags and Siberian prison-camps. Only now mass graves are being discovered which reveal the enormity of the massacres carried out by Stalin and his cronies, of those who dared to raise their voice in protest. A more modern term for 'the wicked word' is propaganda. Many ordinary white South Africans were indoctrinated so thoroughly that they came to believe in the rightness of apartheid, that, indeed, blacks were sub-human. For tyrannies to thrive, they need at least the acquiescence of the majority population. The people are propagandised virtually from the cradle to the grave. The 'wicked word' becomes the revealed truth. Brain-washing, in what were euphemistically referred to as psychiatric correctional centres, was ruthlessly applied to those few who dared even to think differently. We are only learning now how many of the ordinary citizens collaborated with the system. In Rumania, it is suggested that they were as many as one in four.

Revolutions come and go. Tragically, too often they just exchange one tyranny for another. Lenin was the great liberator of Russia and the tyranny that followed was worse than ever was perpetuated by the Csars. The same might be said of Fidel Castro in Cuba. So often, 'glorious' revolutions are little more than tyrannies exchanged. As the poet, Yeats, described it:

Hurrah for revolution and more cannon-shot!
A beggar on horseback lashes a beggar on foot.
Hurrah for revolution and cannon come again!
The beggars have changed places, but the lash goes on.

Isaiah proposes radical remedies for the underlying causes of revolutions or as he puts it 'to do away with the yoke, the clinched fist and the wicked word.' Firstly, 'share your bread with the hungry'. It is not surprising that the French Revolution began with a march of the women of Paris to the royal palace at Versailles in search of bread or that the downfall of communism

in Russia began with long queues outside Moscow's stores with
their empty food-shelves. Judging by the numbers of starving in
our world, there are a lot of revolutions brewing out there, and
the worst is yet to come. We should hear Isaiah's warning to
'share our bread with the hungry' before it is too late. I'm sure he
wasn't thinking in terms of our paltry foreign aid.

His second remedy is to 'shelter the homeless poor'. For
these we don't have to look very far. You will find them in plenty
in Paris, Rome or Dublin, sleeping rough on the streets or in
doorways with cardboard boxes for covering. Land speculation
by the greedy has led to rocketting house-prices. Even the mod-
erately well-off young couple are obliged to mortgage their lives
to provide a roof over their heads. The huge new office-block
complexes, often largely untenanted, while a growing number
of poor remain unhoused is a terrible indictment of our system.

Nakedness comes in many forms. The long dole-queue is a
line of naked people. People without jobs are just as naked as
people without clothes. Children without education face a lifetime of nakedness. The almost regular summer riots in the deprived urban areas where unemployment is rampant, suggest
they are nurseries of revolutions. To clothe the naked is to solve
unemployment. We ignore it at our peril.

Isaiah, four-thousand years ago, provided the answer we are
still searching for:

Share your bread with the hungry,
and shelter the homeless poor,
clothe the man you see to be naked
and turn not from your own kin.
Then will your light shine like the dawn
and your wound be quickly healed over.

Suggested additional Bidding Prayers
We pray
– for the generosity to share our bread with the hungry.
– for the kindness to shelter the homeless poor.
– for the charity to clothe the naked.

Catechism of the Catholic Church
1930 Respect for the human person entails respect for the
rights that flow from his dignity as a creature. These rights are
prior to society and must be recognised by it. They are the basis
of the moral legitimacy of every authority: by flouting them, or

refusing to recognise them in its positive legislation, a society undermines its own moral legitimacy. If it does not respect them, authority can rely only on force or violence to obtain obedience from its subjects.

Sixth Sunday

Readings: Eccles 15:15-20. 1 Cor 2:6-10. Mt 5:17-37.

Introduction

Every Sunday at Mass we make the sign of peace to each other. The gesture comes immediately before Communion. We should remember that if we cannot reach our hand out in reconciliation to someone in our community, we cannot reach it out to receive Christ.

Sign of peace (Reconciliation)

'In just over two hours from now, Nelson Mandela will be released from prison.' That is how I began this homily, when I first preached it in Paris on this Sunday the year Mandela was released. He had then been in prison for longer than most of my young congregation had been born, and longer than I had been a priest. His prison silence resounded all over the world. For twenty-seven long years he was not allowed to communicate with the outside world. And yet, his message reached everywhere. Largely due to this one silent victim the system of apartheid was brought to an end. There is a moral here for all of us. Nowadays people labour under the impression that the individual is powerless to change the system. Yet Mandela and history teaches us that this is not so. Even this century has produced individuals like Mahatma Ghandi in India, Martin Luther King in the United States and Andrei Sakharov in Russia, who have done just that.

It is a strange thing about prophets that they never seemed fated to see the promised land. It was the case with Moses who led his people out of slavery in Egypt but died within sight of the promised land. Most have followed a similar pattern. Both Ghandi and Martin Luther King were assassinated before their missions were completed. Sakharov came close but he too died before many of the great changes took place in his country. Mandela was seventy when he was released from prison where he had spent a little less than half his life. He too seemed destined to follow the same course. But he has survived.

It seems almost as if God had another mission for him to accomplish, perhaps even more difficult than the destruction of apartheid, the reconciliation of South Africans. It is an awesome task. He has to reconcile himself with his former gaolers who took away more than twenty-seven of the best years of his life. He has to reconcile his black compatriots with their former white masters. So far, he has made a good beginning. Just five years later, as President of South Africa he attended the opening match of the Rugby World Cup being held there for the first time. He rejoiced in the victory of South Africa over the defending champions, Australia. There was only one black player on the field and he was in the Australian squad. It was a reminder to Mandela, though he hardly needed a reminder, of how thoroughly the system of apartheid had done its job and how hard reconciliation was going to be.

There are areas in all our lives which cry out for reconciliation. There are neighbours who are not on speaking terms and sometimes for years. Even within families, brothers and sisters have fallen out and refuse to make up. Some disputes go so far back, that nobody remembers now what exactly caused them. Yet many carry these ancient grudges with them to the church on Sundays and all the way up to the altar. Which is why the Vatican Council re-introduced the sign of peace into the Mass and placed it just before Communion. It is a symbol of reconciliation. When you shake hands with the person beside you in the pew, you are making up with your alienated neighbour. If you can't stretch out your hand in reconciliation to him, you can't stretch it out to receive Christ in Communion.

So then, if you are bringing your offering to the altar and there remember that your brother has something against you, leave your offering there before the altar, go and be reconciled with your brother first, and then come back and present your offering.

Suggested additional Bidding Prayers
We pray
– that we may become reconciled with estranged members of our families.

– that we will make peace with our neighbours with whom we have quarrelled.

– that we will act as go-betweens to reconcile conflicts between others.

Catechism of the Catholic Church

2302 By recalling the commandment, 'You shall not kill', our Lord asked for peace of heart, and denounced murderous anger and hatred as immoral.

Anger is a desire for revenge. 'To desire vengeance in order to do evil to someone who should be punished is illicit', but it is praiseworthy to impose restitution 'to correct vices and maintain justice'. If anger reaches the point of a deliberate desire to kill or seriously wound a neighbour it is gravely against charity; it is a mortal sin. The Lord says, 'Everyone who is angry with his brother shall be liable to judgement.'

Seventh Sunday

Readings: Lev 19:1-2, 17-18. 1 Cor 3:16-23. Mt 5:38-48.

Introduction

Our minds are full of murderous thoughts against those we believe have done us wrong. They come between us and our loving God. We cannot celebrate the Lord of love in today's Eucharist without resolving to be more forgiving like him.

Eye for an eye (Vengeance) see also Seventh Sunday Year C

The old cowboy films of my boyhood Sundays had a scene that always intrigued me. In the bar-room shoot-out, the crook, beaten to the draw, tottered to the floor, riddled with bullets. As the gunman turned away, the dying crook weakly raised his gun and fired a last shot into the gunman's back. Then he slumped back and died, almost contentedly, a wisp of smoke spiralling from his gun and a flicker of a smile on his face. Sweet revenge!

I accepted all this then as part of the Western fantasy-world. I know better now. Life is full of people with chips on their shoulders, real or imaginary, all waiting for a chance to get their own back. They carry their scars through life, refusing to let them heal until they have settled accounts. Feuds, vendettas and grudges are nurtured in parishes, in streets and even in families. Some are even passed down from one generation to the next. A colossal amount of human energy and ingenuity is expended on settling old scores and exacting vengeance. The *lex talionis* – 'an eye for eye and tooth for tooth' – is alive and well and thriving in every human environment, but nowhere more so than in the industrial world. Management singles out troublemakers for redundancy. Blacklists are kept. Workers know where and when to call a lightening strike and who in management is to be sacrificed. Even in the corridors of power, in the velvet setting of plush boardrooms, the knives are long and sharp and are slipped between pin-striped shoulder-blades almost with a smile.

Honour is always at stake when the God of vengeance is invoked. 'Getting one's own back' is raised to the level of a virtue in our world. The injured party could never hold its head up again if the injury is not repaid. Loved ones too are invoked. We owe it to our wives and children. 'Getting even' becomes an obsession. 'I'll fix him if it is the last thing I do.' Shades of the prostrate crook and his smoking six-shooter! The world has nothing but contempt for the one who 'turns the other cheek'. He is a weakling. 'He took it lying down.' It goads us on to vengeance. 'Don't let them get away with it.'

The bible tells us otherwise. The Lord said to Moses: 'You must not exact vengeance, nor must you bear a grudge against the children of your people.' What is refreshing about today's gospel is that it recognises us as we are, full of pettiness, exacting hurt for hurt, trading blow for blow. We all have enemies who persecute us. Letting them get away with it is not easy. Loving them is a call to perfection.

'You must therefore be perfect just as your heavenly Father is perfect.'

Suggested additional Bidding Prayers
We pray
– for the grace to overcome our resentments.
– never to seek revenge on those who have hurt us.
– for the grace to love our enemies.

Catechism oft the Catholic Church
2262 In the Sermon on the Mount, the Lord recalls the commandment, 'You shall not kill', and adds to it the proscription of anger, hatred and vengeance. Going further, Christ asks his disciples to turn the other cheek, to love their enemies ...

Eighth Sunday

Readings: Is 49:14-15. 1 Cor 4:1-5. Mt 6:24-34.

Introduction
Our lives are blighted by worry. Today's gospel reminds us
not to worry about tomorrow but to trust in God's providence.

'Tomorrow will take care of itself' (Anxiety)
I was taking a stroll one summer's evening in Paris. I am a
creature of habit and I usually follow the same route. I go down
Mont Ste Genevieve as far as the Seine, cross over the bridge to
Isle St Louis and return home to the Latin Quarter via Boulevard
St Michel. An old man once advised me always to take a circular
route as every step outwards is a step homewards. That evening
I made a slight diversion to pass by an Irish pub where I had to
leave a message. Just as I was heading up the narrow rue des
Boulangers, where the Irish pub was situated, I was faintly
aware of a young man walking almost parallel to me in the middle of the street. Suddenly, he swung round and began to attack
me. He held me by my jacket and struck me with his fist several
times. I cannot remember the details very clearly as I was deep
in thought when it happened and deeply shocked when it was
over. I thought his fist landed three times but when I counted
the bruises the following morning, they were five. I never struck
back. I must be a pacifist deep down or too long a priest. He
knocked me to the ground. I began to shout 'Help!' and then, realising I was in Paris, I changed to *'au sécours!'* I was only ten
yards from the pub where I could see a face peering out at me.
Frightened by my screams, my assailant took off. I picked myself up, dusted myself down – the two buttons had been
wrenched off my jacket – and with all the dignity I could muster,
I walked into the pub. When I recounted my story there, the
owner of the face at the window told me he heard the shouting
and when he looked out he saw what he took to be a drunk lying
on the street. What a shoddy end it might have been for the Irish
chaplain in Paris! It was the only time I was ever mugged. Ever
since I have been looking over my shoulder.
    One thing is sure, somebody up there was looking after me.
As Isaiah puts it:
    Does a woman forget a baby at the breast,
    or fail to cherish the son of her womb?

Yet even if these forget,
I will never forget you.

We are afraid of something all of the time and of everything
some of the time. We are afraid of failure. We are afraid of letting
others down and of being let down ourselves by others. We are
afraid to love somebody because we are afraid they will not love
us. We are afraid of losing our jobs, our health, our security, our
grip. We are afraid of growing old and of dying. Most of all we
are afraid of being afraid.

It is like a plague that nobody can escape. Everybody suffers
from it. It mars the development of children. It torments adoles-
cents. It affects newly-weds. It ravages those in their forties and
it haunts the old. Adolescence and the forties are regarded as the
crisis years. It comes in a wide variety of forms. Nervousness,
stress, tension, pressure, anxiety. It manifests itself in countless
ways from a nervous tic to a nervous breakdown. Or as in my
case now, a tendency to look over my shoulder at every shadow
in the street.

In today's gospel Christ wants to reassure us:

So do not worry; do not say, 'What are we to eat? What are
we to drink? How are we to be clothed?' It is the pagans who
set their hearts on all these things. Your heavenly Father
knows you need them all. Set your hearts on his kingdom
first, and on his righteousness, and all these other things will
be given you as well. So do not worry about tomorrow: tomorrow will take care of itself. Each day has enough trouble
of its own.

Suggested additional Bidding Prayers

We pray
– that our trust in God will rid us of our anxieties.
– that we will not be over-anxious about the things of this life.
– for all those who suffer nervous breakdowns that they will
find peace of mind in God's love.

Catechism of the Catholic Church

2547 ... Abandonment to the providence of the Father in
heaven frees us from anxiety about tomorrow. Trust in God is a
preparation for the blessedness of the poor. They shall see God.

Ninth Sunday

Readings: Deut 11:18, 26-28. Rom 3: 21-25, 28. Mt 7:21-27.

Introduction

It is not sufficient to worship God by going to Mass on Sunday. We must do the will of the Father. God will only recognise us by our care and concern for others.

The will of the Father (Practice)

Priests have a varied experience of human society. Their pastoral work is a passport that allows entry to all sorts of places, from a prison-cell to a penthouse flat. Apart from doctors, they are the only ones that can at once be confidants to millionaires and paupers. They are, at least occasionally, the privileged witnesses of rare acts of quiet heroism or Christian generosity. It is one of the few consolations of an otherwise lonely and demanding vocation.

While on pastoral visitation in a rural parish in the west of Ireland, I came across an isolated hovel on the side of a mountain. At first I thought it was uninhabited. Such abandoned homes are not unusual in those parts. The windows were boarded up or blocked with cardboard. I was about to pass by, when I noticed a thin line of smoke curling up from the chimney. I knocked at the door and, after a pause, what sounded like a girlish voice called me in. Once inside, I could see nothing. It was pitch-black except for the faint glow of a dying fire in the hearth. I looked around to locate the owner of this ghostly voice. At last I found her. She was a tiny little creature, sitting on the hob, under the chimney and as black as the chimney itself. She must have been in her eighties in spite of her little girl's voice. I picked a little stool to sit on and we began to talk. It wasn't an easy conversation. I found it hard to find her wavelength. From what I could make out she was born retarded, which probably explained the little girl's voice. She was what was known in Irish as *Duine le Dia* ('one of God's people'). She had been cared for all her life by an older sister who had died a few years previously. When I asked her how she managed now, she replied grinning toothlessly, 'Johnny O'Hara comes every week with a bag of coal and a few groceries.' I knew this weekly Santa Claus only by reputation and that reputation wasn't great, at least in church circles. He was one of those who if he came to church at all, lurked on the fringes outside the door. He was, to use the local expression, 'one of the lads.' Only a short time before he had been the subject of a tirade from the local parish priest. I made a mental note to put a word in that defective ear, though I doubted it would have much effect. The latter was not given to revising his opinions of people.

I remember another unlikely good samaritan too, a journalist with a somewhat lurid Sunday tabloid. His regular mission of mercy was to a Dublin attic flat where a single mother and her baby were threatened with eviction.

Why attendance at Sunday mass should be the sole litmus-test of Christian practice, I have never understood. Priests, like accountants, have a fixation with figures. Mass-attendance, like baptisms, marriages and deaths, lend themselves to easy measurement. But a large measure of the Christian life is not so easily quantified. Christian charity by its nature is anonymous. It is a secret between the giver and the receiver. More often than not, even the beneficiary does not know who the donor is. Priests frequently receive sums of money, large and small, to be distributed to those in need, in envelopes slipped through their letter-box, without ever knowing where they came from. Church poor-boxes yielded tidy sums until church vandals deprived the poor of this valuable source of income. Nobody can be in any doubt that church-attendance figures are in steep decline and, more than likely, this trend is irreversible. But more than one observer has commented on the high level of concern, particularly among the young, for the poor and the deprived in society. Many volunteer to work with the poor on inner city projects here, or abroad with famine victims in the Third World. I confess to feeling justifiably proud when watching reports on French television on the plight of refugees in Rwanda, where the short interview invariably features a young Irish volunteer, cradling an emaciated child in her arms. At least for a small country a disproportionate number of Irish seem to be featured in such reports. If Catholic practice is in decline, there is no evidence that Christian practice is. Mass observance may be down, but gospel observance is certainly up.

Those who listen weekly to Christ's words and do not act on them are building on sand. 'I have never known you' will be Christ's final rejection.

'It is not those who say to me, "Lord, Lord", who will enter the kingdom of heaven, but the person who does the will of my Father in heaven.'

Suggested additional Bidding Prayers

We pray

– that our Sunday Mass will be reflected by the Christian charity of our lives.

– that we will always show solidarity with the less fortunate in our community.

– that we will enter the kingdom of heaven by doing the will of the Father.

Catechism of the Catholic Church

1970 The law of the gospel requires us to make the decisive choice between 'the two ways' and to put into practice the words of the Lord. It is summed up in the Golden Rule, 'Whatever you wish that men would do to you, do so to them; this is the law and the prophets.'

Tenth Sunday

Readings: Hos 6:3-6. Rom 4:18-25. Mt 9:9-13.

Introduction

It is often said that you can tell a lot about people by 'the company they keep'. Jesus was accused of keeping company with some very dubious types, like tax-collectors and sinners. Those who claim to follow Jesus should try to show his mercy to others.

'The company he keeps ' (Mercy)

For years the Irish population in Paris remained relatively static, somewhere in the low hundreds. It consisted mainly of embassy staff, semi-State bodies, OECD secretaries and of course, a sizeable scattering of 'au pairs'. There was also a small group of Irish nannies, most of them elderly and retired. Then sometime in the middle eighties the number of Irish increased dramatically and by the early nineties the figure had reached somewhere in the region of 10,000. From the chaplain's point of view, they were largely a trouble-free community, mostly highly-educated young people, like computer programmers, architects and bilingual secretaries.

But there was a proportionate growth in another Irish group, which did cause the chaplain some headaches. This was the Irish

prison population in French jails. Hitherto, these were very rare
birds such as an unfortunate tourist who had run foul of French
justice in some way or other and was lodged in prison for a couple of days to await his trial. The new inmates were mainly
members of the IRA who were apprehended on French territory
and charged with terrorist offences. There were one or two others charged with drug-smuggling. Because, for obvious reasons,
access to these prisoners was difficult and costly for their families, they sought the help of the chaplain. It didn't make it any
easier for him that they were invariably lodged separately in different prisons. For all I know, the prisoners themselves may
have thought I was a kindred soul. I made no effort to convert
them. Two subjects were never broached between us, politics
and religion. Politics in deference to me, religion in deference to
them. I would have been happy to discuss religion had they
raised it but I could never bring myself to take advantage of
such a captive audience. To visit them was a Christian obligation. 'I was in prison and you visited me.' There was no obligation to proselytise as well. Some people who got to know of my
prison work, suspected me of IRA sympathies and began to cold-
shoulder me. Not only have I an abhorrence of all kinds of violence but I have long come to the view that this global village of
ours would be a happier and safer place if we could rid it of all
nationalist aspirations, whether it be in Belfast or Baghdad,
Bosnia or Bylorus.

'Why does your master eat with tax collectors and sinners?'
the Pharisees asked Jesus' disciples. It was depressing to find
that, after two thousand years, such attitudes still persist. Later
followers have not always shown that friendship for sinners that
so characterised its Master. The church has often been more liberal with its condemnations than its concern.

Matthew must have been in later years the butt of many a jibe
about his collaborating past. The tax he collected then was for an
occupying power. There is more than a hint of it in the account
of his vocation he wrote in today's gospel. He relished Christ's
robust rejection of the Pharisees' sneers about the company he
kept. 'Go and learn the meaning of the words,' he told them,
'What I want is mercy, not sacrifice.' He was quoting the prophet
Hosea, who pulled no punches either:

What am I to do with you, Ephraim?
What am I to do with you, Judah?
This love of yours is like a morning cloud,

like dew that quickly disappears.
This is why I have torn them to pieces by the prophets,
why I slaughtered them with the words from my mouth,
since what I want is love, not sacrifice;
knowledge of God, not holocausts.

Suggested additional Bidding Prayers
We pray
– for God's mercy in spite of our failings.
– that we may be merciful to those who sin against us.
– that we will love sinners while abhorring their sin.

Catechism of the Catholic Church
589 Jesus gave scandal above all when he identified his merciful conduct towards sinners with God's own attitude toward them. He went as far as to hint that by sharing the table of sinners that he was admitting them to the messianic banquet.

Eleventh Sunday

Readings: Ex 19:2-6. Rom 5:6-11. Mt 9:36, 10:8.

Introduction
Recent clerical scandals have dismayed many Catholics. Some feel that the institution of the priesthood is itself in crisis. Today's gospel encourages us to pray that God will continue to provide priests for his church.

Strange vocations (Priesthood)
Twenty years ago the city of Saigon fell. The Communists swept in from the North and the Americans, the greatest power on earth, beat a hasty and undignified retreat. In the final twenty-four hours, they launched a massive evacuation of US personnel and Vietnamese sympathisers, flying a constant stream of helicopters from the embassy compound to a fleet of forty US warships standing out to sea. Panic set in on the streets of Saigon. Thousands of Vietnamese who felt compromised or had reason to fear the wrath of the invading communists, tried to flee. They crammed on to boats and barges along the Saigon River, with their few possessions and far too little provisions, and put to sea. Thus began the 'boat people'. Li Pinh was a twenty-

year old student, who managed to climb on to a boat, with seventy others, packed like animals. For days they drifted in the South China sea, quickly running out of food and water. Death and delirium began to take its toll. Just then they encountered a British freight-carrier, plying between Hong Kong and Singapore. They begged to be taken aboard but the captain refused adamantly, offering instead to give them supplies of food and fresh water. Li Pinh pleaded desperately with the captain. As a last resort he held up a new-born baby. A young woman had given birth on the boat. The captain relented. They were taken to Singapore, from where Li Pinh and others were eventually transported to England. Now, twenty years later, he is a parish priest in Manchester. 'I owe my life and my priesthood to that little baby,' he said, when he described his ordeal to me recently. I had simply asked him: 'How come a Vietnamese is a parish priest in Manchester?'

For who can say by what strange way
Christ brings his will to light.

There are others, too, whose paths to the altar were no less strange. There is Huu-Thu from Laos, a sixteen-year old who with his younger sister spent some years in a refugee-camp, before finally reaching Switzerland and the priesthood. His mother is a Buddhist. Or M'boya from Kenya, whose parents were Muslims. Or Thallapalli whose family belong to the caste of Untouchables in India. These I know because I shared a home with them in an international *convitto* in Rome. The fastest growing church today is that of Seoul in South Korea. Many of the older churches in France and elsewhere in Europe are served by priests from Africa and other recent missionary countries.

Those depressed in Ireland by the recent spate of clerical scandals should shed their insularism and take a global view of their church and its priesthood. Maybe what their jaded church needs now is a new infusion of blood. New priests unburdened by their Christian heritage. They see their priesthood with more gospel eyes. Conversion is a never-ending process. Yesterday's converts become tomorrow's missionaries. Thus is the church re-vitalised.

They could take heart, too, from Christ's calling of the twelve, recorded in today's gospel. The slightly less than 10% failure rate recorded there differs little from the present rate, magnified out of all proportion by media reports. Maybe as well, the growing scarcity of priests is God's deliberate way of

creating space for his other priesthood of all believers. A church
reluctant to avail of all that talent may now be forced to do so.
Nor will God leave us 'sheep without a shepherd', as long as we
continue to want such priests. All we have to do is ask. Jesus
gave his own assurance: 'The harvest is rich but the labourers
are few, so ask the Lord of the harvest to send labourers to his
harvest.'

Suggested additional Bidding Prayers
We pray
– that God will continue to provide priests for his church.
– that the church will exploit imaginatively the talent of the laity.
– that priests who have lost their vocations may continue to
serve the church.

Catechism of the Catholic Church
1578 No one has the *right* to receive the sacrament of Holy
Orders. Indeed no one claims this office for himself; he is called
to it by God. Anyone who thinks he recognises the signs of
God's call to the ordained ministry must humbly submit his desire to the authority of the church, who has the responsibility
and right to call someone to receive orders. Like every grace this
sacrament can be *received* only as an unmerited gift.

Twelfth Sunday

Readings: Jer 20:10-13. Rom 5:12-15. Mt 10: 26-33.

Introduction
The truth that God is at work in all the actions of his creatures is inseparable from faith in God the Creator. No creature
can attain its ultimate end without the help of God's grace. We
should always trust in God's providence while remembering
that he expects our collaboration in achieving good.

Two-a-penny (Providence) See also Seventh Sunday of Easter B
The golden age of the early Celtic monks have left their legends and their legacy scattered all over western Europe. Why
they left their bee-hive cells in Ireland and sought out her-
mitages in France and Germany, Switzerland and Austria, remains something of a mystery. Nothing seemed planned about
their itineraries. They put to sea in currachs, leaving God to

guide them to their destination. Their trust in providence was enormous. One such monk is reputed to have set out in a boat without oars, drifting with the currents of the ocean, trusting God to bring him safely to land. It must have tried the patience of the Almighty to pilot one who never heard that 'God helps those who help themselves.' His fate we do not know. He may well have ended up a savoury rarity for some ravenous shark. Or like so many of his contemporaries, he may have safely come ashore somewhere, to startle natives by his strange appearance and extraordinary beliefs. Their fearlessness and trust in God was legendary. Of these they left no doubt. Even after fifteen hundred years, their names are cherished and remembered in Luxeuil and Bobbio, Wurzburg and St Gallen, and hosts of other places from the coast of Brittany to the environs of Salzburg.

Providence is the virtue of the poor. The less you have, the more you trust in God. Not surprisingly, it's not strong currency in the present times. Welfare, rather than God-fare, is the last resource of today's deprived. It was once fashionable to explain the economic divergency between the northern and southern states in Europe by religious affiliation. Catholic Ireland, lumped with Latin countries, like Spain and Portugal, were providence-prone and poor. Protestant countries, like Holland and Germany, were industrious and wealthy. Such a theory conveniently overlooked the extraordinary divergency between northern and southern Italy or indeed France which has one of the world's largest economies. Recent natural disasters, strangely called 'acts of God', suggest that richer countries may have as much need of God's providence as their poorer neighbours. The self-reliant Dutch came within a hair's breath of annihilation when heavy floods undermined their dykes. The smuggness of the Japanese was rudely shattered when their quake-proof buildings collapsed in seconds with murderous consequences. The turbulence on the international money markets reduced the thriving economy of Mexico in a single day to a Third World country. Even 'In God we trust' stamped on the almighty American dollar did nothing to shore up that ailing currency. Strange that we should call our 'natural' disasters, man-made and otherwise, 'acts of God'

It is consoling to read in today's gospel that our heavenly Father keeps an eye on the 'two-a-penny' sparrow but his hands must be very full indeed today minding all the other threatened species we seem hell-bent on destroying. We were created in the

image of a creative God and we best reflect that image when we
are creative. Wilfully to harm or destroy any part of his creation
is to spit in the face of our Creator. Our selfishness and greed
threatens the survival of the world. We are called 'to declare
ourselves for God in the presence of men.'

Suggested additional Bidding Prayers
We pray
– that we will rid ourselves of our anxieties by trusting in God's
providence.
– that we will collaborate with God's providence by preserving
our environment.
– that we may see God at work in all the actions of his creatures.

Catechism of the Catholic Church
307 To human beings God even gives the power of freely
sharing his providence by entrusting them with the responsibility
of 'subduing' the earth and having dominion over it. God thus
enables men to be intelligent and free causes in order to complete the work of creation, to perfect its harmony for their own
good and that of their neighbours.

Thirteenth Sunday

Readings: 2 Kings 4:8-11, 14-16. Rom 6:3-4, 8-11. Mt 10:37-42.

Introduction
   We welcome Christ today in the Eucharist. We should ex-
tend the same welcome to all, especially to foreign immigrants
who live and work in our country.

'Come into the parlour' (Welcome)
   I have been to Africa only once. I was between jobs at the
time. Truth to tell, I had just left a job under a bit of a cloud and I
was feeling somewhat bruised as a result. Rather than feeling
sorry for myself at home and brooding about the unfairness of
life, I decided on impulse to visit a friend in Africa. It was one of
the wisest decisions I have ever made in my life. I returned a
new man. My friend, Jim, was a priest in Sierra Leone who was
in charge of a very large secondary school up-country in the
bush. He was there to meet me at the airport in Freetown when I

arrived and we drove for half a day along dusty tracks, weaving
and turning to avoid the potholes before we reached his school-
compound in the bush. For the next six weeks, he seemed to
have nothing more to do than entertain me. In fact, the reality
was the opposite. His school was the most prestigious in the
country. Everybody was vying to get their sons into it. All the
more remarkable as the country was 90% Muslim. On one occasion, he had to expel the son of the prime-minister for breaches
of discipline. There was constant tension between the native and
foreign teachers and incidents flared up at the slightest provocation. With all the problems he had to cope with, I could never
understand how he could devote so much time to entertaining
me. I thought I must have been a special case. He knew I was
having problems. Then one day a missionary arrived in from
one of the outlying villages where he was parish priest. He told
me how he loved to come in here every so often to get away
from his mission-station and his lonely life. All the other missionaries did the same. 'It's like coming home,' he said. 'There is
always a great welcome and Jim makes you feel he has nothing
else to do but look after you.'

All those pleasant memories of my one and only African sojourn came flooding back when I read Christ's instructions to
the twelve in today's gospel:

Anyone who welcomes a prophet because he is a prophet
will have a prophet's reward; and anyone who welcomes a
holy man because he is a holy man will have a holy man's reward.

More than anyone else I know, Jim deserves a holy man's reward. Though not quite the one Elisha gave the woman who
built a little room for him on her roof, where he could break his
journey when he passed.

There is a world of a difference between a kind thought and a
'cup of cold water'. We all feel kindly disposed towards others
except they seldom choose the right time to call. 'Oh! It's you!'
we say, opening the door, barely suppressing the word 'again'.
'You couldn't have caught me at a worse time.' We had been
watching TV when the door-bell rang. Or when we do bring him
in, we keep looking at our watch to make sure he doesn't out-
stay his welcome. We have no time because we have no welcome. It is amazing how much time we can make on those rare
occasions, when somebody of importance arrives on our doorstep.
'You're not going already?' we say, as the evening draws to
close and the whiskey-bottle is all but empty.

Nowhere is welcome more needed than in our world at this time. There are immigrants almost everywhere. France is flooded with North Africans and Portuguese. Germany has its large Turkish community who do the menial tasks that Germans are no longer prepared to do. The tenements of English cities are crammed with immigrants from the Carribeans and other former English colonies in Africa, largely replacing the Irish there and on the building sites. So many 'wet-backs' cross the Rio Grande every day that it is predicted that Spanish will soon replace English as the first language of the United States. Xenophobia has raised its ugly head everywhere. Turkish families have been burnt to death in their German flats. The National Front, with its undisguised anti-immigrant rhetoric, are winning votes all over France and its massive rallies are regularly followed by murderous attacks on innocent immigrants. We in Ireland don't have any immigration problem and it may be just as well, judging by the way we treat our own itinerants. Our 'hundred thousand welcomes' might not not survive that test.

We follow Christ who 'came unto his own and his own received him not.' He spent his early days with his mother and father, as a little immigrant family in Egypt, fleeing persecution in his own country. Our Christianity would be mockery indeed if we fail to welcome others and especially our immigrants.

Suggested additional Bidding Prayers
We pray
– that we will always be welcoming towards foreigners and strangers.
– that we will be protective of immigrants in our society.
– that our own young emigrants may find a welcome in their adoptive homes.

Catechism of the Catholic Church
2241 The more prosperous nations are obliged, to the extent they are able, to welcome the foreigner in search of the security and the means of livelihood which he cannot find in his country of origin. Public authorities should see to it that the natural right is respected that places a guest under the protection of those who receive him.

Fourteenth Sunday

Readings: Zech 9:9-10. Rom 8:9, 11-13. Mt 11:25-30.

Introduction

We are invited to come to Jesus in today's Eucharist where we will find rest from our labours and burdens. Only the humble and little children can put themselves and their problems in God's hands.

Mere children (Humility)

'Put your hand in the hand of the man from Galilee' was the refrain of a fairly recent pop-tune. Putting a hand in somebody else's is the characteristic gesture of a child. Only to parents will a child give its hand unquestioningly. It implies complete trust. No amount of cajoling will entice it to take the hand of a stranger. Once outside the familiarity of the home, a child confronted with a big and frightening world becomes acutely aware of its own smallness and helplessness. Without father's hand it wouldn't dare venture out. Holding his hand there is nowhere it will not venture. The child is not only willing to be led, it positively wants to be led. The sad thing about growing up is that we lose our fathers or they lose us. In any event, we outgrow our need of them. And having lost the need for parents, God becomes very remote for us. Only children instinctively understand God-language. Every child's father is God to him. And God to every child is his Father. Thus is God revealed to 'mere children.'

Growing up means becoming more independent. Or rather ceasing to be dependent. We exchange a child's dependence on people for an adult's dependence on things, like money, alcohol and drugs. And things are notoriously fickle. The world of an adult is stress-ridden and anxiety-plagued. There is no escape from tension. Drugs may provide temporary relief but can never reach the underlying cause. Contentment is a quality of the soul. A state of harmony between a creature and his creator, a child and his father. Adam and Eve unfortunately grew up. They lost their innocence. The original sin was Adam's pride, his ambition to 'go it alone'. It has tainted our nature ever since.

It has left us all 'labouring and over-burdened'. Labouring under illusions of grandeur and burdened with conceit. The heaviest load we have to carry is the load of our own unfulfilled ambitions, the burden of our own ego. We've grown too big for our boots. Only humility can restore our lost innocence and our lost paradise. The humility to accept our creature-status, our child-status. We must learn to want to be led. We must trade childish pride for child-like humility. We must 'put our hand in the hand of the man from Galilee', if we ever hope to find our way home. Jesus invites us to do just that:

Come to me , all you who labour and are overburdened, and I will give you rest. Shoulder my yoke and learn from me, for I am gentle and humble in heart, and you will find rest for your souls. Yes, my yoke is easy and my burden light.

Suggested additional Bidding Prayers
We pray
– for the grace of humility.
– for those in authority that they will exercise their power as a service for others.
– for those who have the care of others that they may always act with gentleness and humility.

Catechism of the Catholic Church

2779 ... Humility makes us recognise that 'no one knows the Son except the Father, and no one knows the Father except the Son and anyone to whom the Son chooses to reveal him', that is, 'to little children'. The purification of our hearts has to do with paternal or maternal images, stemming from our personal and cultural history, and influencing our relationship with God ...

Fifteenth Sunday

Readings: Is 55:10-11. Rom 8:18-23. Mt 13:1-23.

Introduction

We celebrate Christ who came to sow the seed of God's word in the world. The fate of that seed depends on the type of soil it was sown in. We have all received the seed. Whether it bears fruit will depend on how we receive it.

All in the family (Harvest)

What was sown along the path

Matt came to a bad end. His body was fished out of the Thames one morning a couple of years ago. Nobody knew for certain what had happened. There was talk about an 'underworld killing' and a 'gangland vendetta'. Those who knew him back at home in Ireland were not really surprised. He was always a cold fish. Even as a young lad there was a vicious streak in him. When he twisted your arm he made sure it hurt. His first protection-racket began in the primary school. The others bought him off with sweets, pencil-sharpeners and apples. He was afraid of nobody. Flogging held no terrors for him.

What was sown on rocky ground

Concepta was different, very different. From the very beginning she was very religious. At school she was the nuns' favourite. I think they hoped she would enter the convent. She didn't. She got a job in the civil service instead. She never married. She became very active in her parish church as a lay reader and eucharistic minister. If ever they ordained women, she would have been one of the first. Then one day all that changed. They say she had a terrible row with the parish priest. She has never darkened the church-door since.

'What was sown among thorns'

Pat was the golden-boy of the family. He was confident, able and ambitious. At school he was a natural leader. Maybe it had something to do with being the eldest. Everything he touched in the business world thrived. He had both the head and the stomach for it. Luckily for him, heart did not enter into it. Because he hadn't any. Whatever feelings he had for people have long since been choked to death by his greed for money.

What was sown on good soil

Bridget was the youngest. People said there was no go in her at all. It was no surprise to anybody that she was the one who stayed at home. She was always very easy-going. She married a local lad who turned out to have a bit of a problem with the drink. She has had more than her share of troubles since her last child was born retarded. And looking after her bed-ridden father doesn't help either. Still, she never complains. She wouldn't think of herself as a very religious person but her children, husband, father and neighbours are all reaping the harvest of her goodness.

Listen, anyone who has ears!

Suggested additional Bidding Prayers

We pray

– that the word of God for us will not fall on stoney ground.

– that the word of God will not be choked by our material greed.

– that the word of God sown in us will blossom into eternal life.

Catechism of the Catholic Church

546 Jesus' invitation to enter his kingdom comes in the form of parables, a characteristic feature of his teaching. Through his parables he invites people to the feast of the kingdom, but he also asks for a radical choice: to gain the kingdom, one must give everything. Words are not enough, deeds are required. The parables are like mirrors for man: will he be hard soil or good earth for the kingdom?…

Sixteenth Sunday

Readings: Wis 12:13, 16-19. Rom 8:26-27. Mt 13 24-43.

Introduction

We are reminded by today's parable that we are all sinners. It would be presumptuous of us to correct others. We can best persuade others to follow Christ by living the gospel in our own lives.

Weeding out (Judgement)

As any gardener knows, weeding can be the greatest threat of all to the life of the young seedling. At first, the problem is one of identification. The weeds must be left until the seedling can be clearly recognised. Even then, removing the weeds may pose an even greater threat. It might sever the seedling's root system. Often the weed brings the seedling away with it.

In the case of human beings it is an even more hazardous operation. 'Weeding-out' has no history of success which doesn't seem to curb people's passion for it. Fifty years after Hitler's final solution, the horrendous weeding out of six million Jews in concentration camps, the Bosnian Serbs are attempting the brutal policy of 'ethnic cleansing'. Race, religion, colour, sex, politics are still considered ready-reckoners for identifying society's weeds. Increasing power over nature provides new and sinister instruments for weeding out. The unborn child, the seed of life is threatened with abortion. At the other end of life, euthanasia is proposed as the final solution for the new Jews, the old, the maimed, the incurables and the burdensome. Right through life, the weeding-out continues remorselessly. The handicapped are institutionalised, the delinquent are penalised, the deviant are ostracised and the poor are patronised.

Weeding out is not confined to faceless bureaucracy. We all try our hand at it. We like to think our judicious weeding-out prevented many great personal calamities. We are very sharp at spotting the undesirables, the troublemakers, the misfits. We may admit reluctantly to lapses in our watchfulness but never to mistakes.

One shudders to think of the people who might have been weeded out if men had got their way and God himself had not chosen to intervene. Probably most of the saints in the calendar. Peter, after his triple denial in the crucifixion crisis should have been weeded out for failing the leadership test. Strange isn't it, that Christ never weeded out Judas? The church did not always show her master's tolerance. Galileo could testify to that. The spirit of the Inquisition lives on. Excommunications and anathemas may be out of fashion but old habits die hard.

The lesson of the parable of the weeds is so uncompromisingly simple and so widely ignored. To the question 'Do you want us to go and weed it out?' the answer is a categorical 'No'. And the reason is self-evident. Only God has eyes sufficiently discerning and fingers sufficiently gentle for this job. Weeding-out is God's prerogative. Life would be so much better for everybody, if only we would leave it to him.

Suggested additional Bidding Prayers
We pray
– that we may resist the temptation to interfere in other peoples' lives.
– for all those who have been ostracised in our society.
– for those minorities in the world who are deprived of their civil rights.

Catechism of the Catholic Church
827 ... All members of the church, including her ministers, must acknowledge that they are sinners. In everyone, the weeds of sin will still be mixed with the good wheat of the gospel until the end of time. Hence the church gathers sinners already caught up in Christ's salvation but still on the way to holiness.

Seventeenth Sunday

Readings: 1 Kings 3:5, 7-12. Rom 8:28-30. Mt 13:44-52.

Introduction

Solomon prayed for the gift of discernment. It is something we all need. All things have a value. If we over-value them, we de-value God. We need the spirit of detachment which allows us to let go of our most prized possessions when they come between us and God.

The price of a pearl (Detachment)

There is no greater indictment of the quality of life than the sight of an old man clinging on desperately to his holding. To him, this miserable patch of grass and bog is his only insurance against abandonment. But hanging on is not the answer. It only sows bitterness and frustration in sons whose best years are squandered in waiting. Sons who in turn never learn themselves from the mistakes of their fathers. Love alone can guarantee security and care in one's declining years. Possessions provide only the illusion of security.

Elderly farmers are not the only ones who hold on to things for security. Others have their own holdings from which only death can separate them. It may be property and wealth, status and prestige or power and influence. It may even be an awful lot less – trivial comforts and an easy life. It may be a sixteen-hour day or the thankless responsibility of high office. Or a reputation we can no longer live up to. There is nothing more pathetic than an ageing beauty-queen who refuses to accept the ravages of time.

'Ask what you would like me to give you,' God said to Solomon. 'Give your servant a heart to understand how to discern between good and evil,' he replied. It is the kind of gift we all need. Possessions come in many forms. It is not so much these possessions that we should rid ourselves of, as the demon of possession itself that should be exorcised. Poverty has become a dirty word in the world we live in. We should not let an Ethiopian famine or a Rwanda disaster make us forget that poverty is also a Christian virtue. It is no accident that Christ began his Sermon on the Mount with 'Blessed are the poor in spirit, for theirs is the kingdom of heaven.' Or that the only condition for his followers is that 'they leave all things'. Or that the

rich young man should have failed all because he failed this one
test, 'for he had great possessions'. Or that the pearl in today's
parable could only be bought by 'selling everything he owns'.

The trouble with most people is that they want it both ways.
All this and the good life too. But they can't have it both ways.
There is a pearl for everyone. And there is a price for everyone to
pay. A price tailored to each's individual circumstances.
Detachment is that price. To be able to walk away from what we
cherish most without so much as looking back with regret. Our
tragedy is not that we cannot find the pearl but that we are unwilling to pay the price.

Suggested additional Bidding Prayers
We pray
– for the gift of discernment between good and evil.
– for the gift of detachment lest we become possessed by material
things.
– for addicts everywhere that they may be released from their
addiction.

Catechism of the Catholic Church
546 Jesus' invitation to enter his kingdom comes in the form
of parables, a characteristic feature of his teaching. Through his
parables he invites people to the feast of the kingdom, but he
also asks for a radical choice: to gain the kingdom one must give
up everything ...

Eighteenth Sunday

Readings: Is 55: 1-3. Rom 8:35, 37-39. Mt 14: 13-21.

Introduction
Today we recall Christ's pity for the hungry multitudes who
followed him. But he did not simply feel pity for them, he took
practical steps to feed them. The Eucharist today should inspire
us to take practical steps to help feed the starving millions in the
world.

Feeding the hungry (Waste) See also Seventeenth Sunday Year B
My father dug a pit at the end of the garden which served as

a rubbish dump. Every day I emptied a bucket of ashes into it, the remains of yesterday's fire. Though it wasn't very deep, it seemed to be a bottomless pit. It never overflowed. But then, apart from the ashes, I can't remember anything else that was thrown into it. It just wasn't a throw-away age. There was always another use found for everything. Clothes were handed down to the next in line and when that line petered out, they began a new life as dusters and mops. Or if the colour was right or near enough, there was always a trousers to be patched or reinforced in some strategic area. We covered our copy books with the brown paper our groceries were wrapped in and cut-outs from cardboard boxes helped to reinforce the covers of our school books. They too had to be passed on. Newspaper was the most versatile of all and there was always a shortage of it. It was used to light the fire in the morning and wrap our lunch sandwich in. The bottoms of drawers were lined with it to keep out the damp and it was placed under the mattress to keep in the heat. When father brought his newspaper to the toilet it was not only to broaden his mind. The leftovers on the table, if there were any, were used to feed the dog and cat and a whole generation of mice thrived on what they in turn left over. I must hasten to add that, though I wasn't born with a golden spoon in my mouth, my father with his teacher's salary was regarded as a man of means.

How the world has changed in such a short time! Garbage-disposal is now a major industry and one of the few which continues to boom even during a depression. Even the remotest farmhouse in rural Ireland now has its brightly coloured garbage-bin on the side of the road waiting for the weekly collection. One of the more pathetic sights in cities is that of an old woman rummaging in a garbage-bin for something to salvage. Worst of all are the television pictures of people scavenging in rat-invested city dumps for the wherewithal to support their families. 'The scraps which fall from the rich man's table.' Whole shanty-towns have sprung up on the outskirts of Rio de Janeiro, and elsewhere in the Third World, on the site of these dumps. If we are to believe the commercials, the wide variety of cat and dog food we buy to feed our pets would provide a nourishing diet for these unfortunate creatures.

We should 'take pity on them' as Christ did when he multiplied the loaves and fishes, recorded in today's gospel. John provides us with a few extra details. It appears that it was a small

boy who produced the five loaves and two fish. It has been suggested that others too among the five thousand, shamed by the
little boy's generosity, produced their hidden hoard. When
shared around, it proved more than enough to feed them all. If
so, it would have been no less a miracle. 'Pick up the scraps left-
over,' Christ said, 'so that nothing gets wasted.' This garbage
collection was not intended just to protect the environment.
Presumably, there were other hungry mouths to fill when that
crowd got home.

The message for us is clear. Our garbage condemns us. If we
had shared our bread with the hungry of this world, we would
have no waste to dispose of.

Suggested additional Bidding Prayers
We pray
– that God will give us the grace of sharing our surplus with the
needy.
– that we will convince our government to increase its Third
World aid.
– that we will not pollute our environment with our waste disposal.

Catechism of the Catholic Church
1335 The miracles of the multiplication of the loaves, when
the Lord says the blessing, breaks and distributes the loaves
through his disciples, prefigure the superabundance of this
unique bread of his Eucharist.

Nineteenth Sunday

Readings: 1Kgs 19:9, 11-13. Rom 9: 1-5. Mt 14: 22-33.

Introduction
We are called to a world of faith. The gospels set out the
ideals we should aim at. In spite of our many falls we should
never water down these ideals to what is more easily attainable.

Walking on water (Ideals)
None of us remember now what must have been one of the
greatest achievements of our lives. Our very first steps. Since
then we have re-lived the same experience with our own children.

A mother's eyes keep aloft her child attempting these first totter-
ing steps. Her outstretched arms encourage, ready to catch her
baby when it falls. As fall it does. But that baby's world will
never be the same again. Its first ideal has been born. Never
again will it be content to grope about on all fours in that safe
myopic world of pots and pans and table-legs. It has climbed the
mountain and seen the promised land. A vertical world of un-
limited horizons. We may not have performed again on cue
when mother summoned in the neighbours to witness this historic moment. But the goal was now in sight.

A similar but less momentous occasion I do remember, is the
day I learned to swim. It was the 'dead man's float'. Holding my
body stiff with outstretched arms and taking a deep breath, I lay
back on the water. Father held me with his strong hand beneath
my back. Slowly he withdrew it. I sank momentarily beneath the
water and then re-surfaced and remained afloat. I had mastered
my fear. It was an unforgettable moment. Ever since, I always
prefer swimming on my back. I may not always know for sure
where I'm going but my gaze is firmly fixed upon the skies.

Those faltering steps of Peter on the water mimic so closely a
baby's first attempt to walk upright. Of all the apostles, Peter's
impulsiveness is infant-like, if not occasionally infantile. Seeing
Jesus walk upon the water, he cries out, like children do: 'Let me
try too.' 'Come,' Jesus said, as most indulgent parents would.
One foot out, he tests the water, solid as the ground. Eyes fixed
on Jesus, he begins his weightless walk. Until he realises the
enormity of his feat. Then looking down, he sees the windswept
waters swirling round his feet and he begins to sink. Jesus put
out his hand at once and held him. 'Man of little faith,' he said,
'why did you doubt?'

His first steps, his first fall. But there would be no going back
now. He had taken his first few steps into the world of faith
where all was possible.

We too are called to this world of faith, the world of the spirit.
'Be ye perfect,' the gospel tells us, 'as your heavenly Father is
perfect.' The demands it makes seem impossible, its ideals unattainable. Mired as we are in the mud of daily living, we are
asked to raise our eyes to higher things. The happiness we are
promised will make us walk on air, if not on water. Like the
child on all fours on the kitchen floor we are encouraged to
stand up and attempt to walk. 'Come,' Jesus calls us like Peter in
the boat. And when we start to sink, he reaches out his hand and

holds us, clucking like a mother to her child. 'Men of little faith, why do you doubt?'

Suggested additional Bidding Prayers
We pray
– for the courage to take our first steps into the world of faith.
– that our lives will be inspired by the ideals of the gospel.
– for the grace to start again after every fall.

Twentieth Sunday

Readings: Is 56:1, 6-7. Rom 11: 13-15, 29-32. Mt 15: 21-28.

Introduction
We should never despair of God's help. The insistent pleas of the Canaanite woman should inspire us to bring our problems to the Master's table where we will find an answer to our prayers in the Eucharist.

The Master's table (Communion) See also Eighteenth Sunday B
My mother took me to the local draper to buy me a suit. I was getting ready for my First Communion. I tried on several suits and my mother made me walk up and down while she and the draper discussed the relative merits of each. Eventually, one was chosen to the satisfaction of both. I was delighted too, as it was the one I had set my heart on. They began to haggle over the price, while I waited impatiently to get back to play with my friends. It was then I noticed that the atmosphere had changed. It appears that we had an outstanding account in that shop and the draper decided to use this occasion to settle it. My mother offered to make a small deposit but the draper would have none of it. It was all or nothing. I was ashamed to hear my mother pleading with him, though I knew, God love her, she was doing it all for me. It was all in vain. We left the shop empty-handed, my mother squeezing my hand to ease my disappointment, while I fought hard to hold back tears, more of shame than disappointment. She found a piece of material somewhere and the local tailor ran up a suit just in time. It was nothing out of the ordinary while the draper's son, who was my friend and classmate, looked like Little Lord Fauntleroy. Looking at my First Com-

munion photo now, all I now recall about that special occasion, is the incident in the draper's shop.

It puts me in mind of the way the Canaanite woman kept pleading with Jesus to cure her little girl. Her insistence was matched only by Christ's indifference. 'He answered her not a word.' Even his disciples were dismayed by his lack of compassion. 'Give her what she wants,' they pleaded. The woman dropped to her knees. 'Lord,' she pleaded, 'help me.' When at last he spoke to her his words sounded brutal. 'It is not fair to take the children's food and throw it to the dogs.' But a child's pain can make a mother eloquent. 'Even the dogs eat the crumbs that fall from the master's table,' she replied. It was enough. Her prayer was answered.

I remember, when I was an altar-boy, a man who came to Holy Communion every morning. The strange thing about this man was that I never saw him outside the church but he was drunk. I was too young then to realise that he was an alcoholic. He wasn't the type we would expect to find at the altar-rails every morning. But he was the type God expects to find there. And he knew that. He pestered heaven with his pleas for help.

Christ knows our failings and our weaknesses. He knows our troubles better than we do ourselves. Others give us a helping hand when we are in trouble. He gives us his whole body so that we might borrow his whole might in carrying our burdens. 'This is my body which is given for you,' he said. It is sad to see how many of us let this help go a-begging. The real tragedy is that just those people who most need it seldom take it. Christ doesn't send anyone away hungry. Like the Canaanite woman and that alcoholic, we too should come for 'the crumbs that fall from the Master's table.'

Suggested additional Bidding Prayers
We pray
– that we will never spurn Christ's generous offer of his body in Communion.
– for all those, and particularly the young, who have drifted away from receiving Communion, that they will return to the Master's table.
– for priests and ministers of the Eucharist.

Catechism of the Catholic Church
1384 The Lord addresses an invitation to us urging us to re-

ceive him in the sacrament of the Eucharist: 'Truly, I say to you, unless you eat the flesh of the Son of Man and drink his blood, you have no life in you.'

Twenty-First Sunday

Readings: Is 22:19-23. Rom 11: 33-36. Mt 16: 13-20.

Introduction

We celebrate today Christ's choice of Peter, in spite of his shortcomings, to be the rock on which he founded his church. We pray for our present pope that he will be given the strength to face the challenges of the modern world.

The Rock (Papacy)

'How many divisions has the Pope?' Stalin retorted dismissively when an aide suggested his policy might encounter opposition from the Vatican. That former seminarian should have known church history better. The Soviet empire he so brutally created was one of history's briefest, while the papacy, though still maligned, continues to thrive as it prepares to enter its third millennium. Ironic too that a Polish pope contributed in no small measure to the Russian empire's demise.

The Pope, it seems, has more divisions than Stalin ever dreamt. It was as Christ promised Peter on whom he built his church. The gates of the Soviet underworld, with all its terror and secret agents, could not hold out against it.

The Pope and his powers is a subject much debated, even among Catholics, while papal claims are generally dismissed outside the church. The old Latin dictum, *Roma locuta est, causa finita est* ('Rome has spoken, the case is closed'), is not so readily accepted, particularly in recent times. To judge by the media, it would appear that every papal statement is greeted only with controversy. But probably it was always so, since Paul first resisted Peter 'to his face' over the circumcision of early Christians. It certainly was so, a little over a hundred years ago, when the First Vatican Council promulgated the doctrine of papal infallibility. Some eighty bishops, some of them Irish, left in protest before the decree was passed. John Henry Newman wrote at that time about Pope Pius IX: 'It is not good for a pope to live twenty years. It is anomaly and bears no good fruit; he becomes a god, has no one to contradict him, does not know facts, and does cruel things without meaning it.' Those strong words of that saintly man will not, I suspect, hasten his canonisation, though a later pope made him a cardinal. The fears of some in 1870 that Catholics would be deluged with dogmas as 'plenty as blackberries', never materialised. Papal infallibility has very rarely been used. Even the recent encyclical of the present strong-minded Pope did not invoke his infallibility. It is not the infallibility of the Pope we need to fear, but the infallibility of those many lesser popes through whom his words are filtered down to us.

Our world is torn asunder by ideas and ideologies. Unlike other times, it has no central philosophy that compels assent. Well-meaning people are ranged up equally on opposite sides of the moral divide, making sometimes strange bedfellows. Those who are anti-abortion are pro-war, those for euthanasia are against capital punishment. Passions flare easily and danger-ously. Fanaticism is no substitute for conviction, nor intimida-tion for persuasion. Yeats might well have had in mind our world rather than the Second Coming, when he wrote his fa-mous lines:

Things fall apart, the centre cannot hold,
mere anarchy is loosed upon the world ...
... the best lack all conviction
while the worst are full of passionate intensity.

Governments are too busy currying favour with the electorate to provide leadership. So often tainted themselves by corruption, they are least suited to give lessons in morality. The world needs a conscience. If the papacy did not exist to play that role, it, or something like it, would have to be invented. The UN is subject to too many sectional pressures to fill that need. As Newman wrote: 'Demos is the greatest tyrant of all.'

Our church is founded on a Rock, a light-house to pilot us through troubled waters. Let us be grateful for it. Life is too short and too precious to be spent bickering among ourselves. We should share in the wonder of it all like St Paul:

How rich are the depths of God – how deep his wisdom and knowledge – and how impossible to penetrate his motives or understand his methods!

Suggested additional Bidding Prayers

We pray
– for the Pope, that he may wisely guide the church in this secular age.
– for harmony between the Pope and preachers of the gospel in the church.
– for theologians who courageously explore the frontiers of truth.

Catechism of the Catholic Church

881 The Lord made Simon alone, whom he named Peter, the 'rock' of his church. He gave him the keys of his church, and instituted him shepherd of the whole flock. The office of binding and loosing which was given to Peter was also assigned to the college of apostles united to its head. The pastoral office of Peter and the other apostles belongs to the church's very foundation and is continued by the bishops under the primacy of the Pope.

Twenty-Second Sunday

Reading: Jer 20:7-9. Rom 12:1-2. Mt 16:21-27.

Introduction

We are reminded in today's gospel that suffering is part and parcel of our human condition. The acceptance of suffering is demanded of all those who wish to follow Christ.

Carrying a cross (Suffering) See also Fifth B and Twelfth C

The homily I am writing now – or one very like it – I delivered once on the RTÉ series *Outlook*. Ireland was a single channel area then and that late-night religious programme had a surprisingly large audience. Besides, it was transmitted just before the nightly news and as a result netted quite a few otherwise unwilling viewers. That I gathered from the letters I received, not all of which were fan-mail. On that occasion, a woman wrote to me. She was the mother of four young children, one of whom was handicapped. Her husband had left her some time previously for another woman and was not paying her any child-support. Her life was a constant struggle trying to hold on to a badly-paid job and look after her young children. All this, and much more, she poured out in her letter to me. My talk, then as now, was a commentary on Christ's injunction to his disciples in today's gospel: 'If anyone wants to be a disciple of mine, let him renounce himself and take up his cross and follow me.' She bitterly resented the smuggness of someone like me, with the comfortable life that I led, lecturing people like her about accepting suffering. Her punch-line certainly shattered my smuggness. 'The heaviest cross you have ever carried,' she wrote, 'was probably your golf-bag.' I was, in fact, though she couldn't have known it, a very keen golfer at that time. I replied to her, as I always did to all the letters I received, complimentary or otherwise. Apart from her trenchant criticism, I was very impressed by the quality of her writing. She was a natural born writer. I told her so, suggesting that she try to publish something, a somewhat inane suggestion, given her circumstances. But it did do wonders for her self-esteem, as she told me in another letter, regretting the bitterness of her remarks in the earlier one. The moral of this story is that those who have no crosses to carry should be the last to encourage others to do so. The trouble about preaching the gospel is that a preacher must never dilute its message, just because he doesn't practice it himself. Having thus prefaced my homily, I now propose to do just that.

With the rising standard of living of our world, our tolerance of suffering has diminished enormously. Certainly we've all become softer compared to previous generations. Pain or discomfort of any kind is something to be avoided at all costs. We bombard the doctor with all sorts of trivial complaints. Our bathroom closets are full of pills for all sorts of ills, real or imaginary. Unused medicines are so extensive, that campaigns are regularly launched to have them collected and sent to the disease-ridden Third World. We try to take the pain out of living. We long for a trouble-free existence. A sort of Utopia, where we can have comfort without effort, roses without thorns, happiness without tears. In short, the sort of life, that every commercial promises us. In religion, we have been chipping away for some time now at anything that smacks of suffering either here or in the hereafter. 'Nobody is bound to the uncomfortable' would seem to be our moral bottom-line. Self-denial, abstinence, sacrifice are dismissed as weird practices from an ignorant and superstitious past.

It's a long way from the world the gospel was written in. It's a long way too from the world our parents grew up in. But they probably had a vision of life far closer to reality than ours. Suffering for them was part and parcel of living. The great myth of modern life is that perfect health, like perfect happiness, is attainable. But perfect health, as Ivan Illich once told doctors, is not the absence of pain, but the ability to cope with it. And, it is precisely this ability that we are fast losing by our dependence on drugs that mask the symptoms rather than cure the disease.

Maybe the older people were too fatalistic, too pessimistic, too prone to accept suffering as the will of God. But at least they knew that you can't take the cross out of Christianity any more than you can take the pain out of living. As St Rose of Lima said: 'Apart from the cross there is no other ladder by which we may get to heaven.' Crosses are burdens you carry on your shoulders (golf-bags excluded!) not just pretty ornaments you wear round your neck.

'Get behind me Satan!' Christ strongly rebuked Peter when he tried to dissuade him from heading towards Jerusalem, where his cross and crucifixion awaited him. 'The way you think is not God's way but man's.' St Paul has the same message for us: 'Do not model yourselves on the behaviour of the world around you.'

Suggested additional Bidding Prayers
We pray
– for the grace to take up our cross and follow Jesus.
– that we will accept the sufferings that come our way.
– for all those who suffer and are sick, especially those whose illnesses are terminal.

Catechism of the Catholic Church
618 The cross is the unique sacrifice of Christ, the 'one mediator between God and men'. But because in his incarnate divine person he has in some way united himself to every man, 'the possibility of being made partners, in a way known to God, in the paschal mystery' is offered to all men. He calls his disciples to 'take up (their) cross and follow (him)', for 'Christ also suffered for (us), leaving (us) an example so that (we) should follow in his steps.' In fact Jesus desires to associate with his redeeming sacrifice those who were to be its first beneficiaries.

Twenty-Third Sunday

Readings: Ez 33: 7-9. Rom 13:8-10. Mt 18: 15-20.

Introduction

Today's gospel reminds us that we have an obligation to correct those who do wrong. We are all in need of correction at some time. It is incumbent on parents and all those who have others in their care to administer such correction.

Casting a blind eye (Permissiveness)

Recent disclosures about a paedophilic priest in Ireland, which made worldwide headlines, shocked and dismayed many Catholics. It was its political consequences, causing as it did the downfall of a government, that attracted international interest in the story. Cases of child-abuse and worse, even by priests, are no longer regarded in many places in today's world as front-page stories. But the quaint medieval image of Ireland abroad as a country where the actions of a priest could bring down a government was newsworthy. Reaction in Ireland was altogether different. Old hardened priests with lifelong experience of dealing with sinners and their sins, with all their sordidness, were known to have broken down and wept. A priest who betrayed his sacred trust with the most innocent of all victims, a child, was beyond their comprehension. What angered people most of all was that the story might never have come to light if the priest had not been charged by the police. And that despite the fact that his superiors knew about his child abuse aberrations for years. How many victims might have been spared had those superiors taken appropriate action.

One would think that those who preach the gospel had never heard that gospel where Christ said to his disciples:

If your brother does something wrong, go and have it out with him alone, between your two selves. If he listens to you, you have won back your brother. If he does not listen, take one or two others along with you; the evidence of two or three witnesses is required to sustain any charge. But if he refuses to listen to these, report it to the community; and if he refuses to listen to the community, treat him like a pagan or a tax-collector.

One thing is sure. The local community where that priest abused his many victims with impunity was the last to be told. One

wonders whether Christ had anything as heinous as child-abuse
by a disciple in mind, when he gave them those instructions.

It was a tragic irony that one who probably preached against
the permissiveness of our age should have been guilty himself of
one of the grossest forms of it. This permissiveness with all its
tragic consequences, is symptomatic of the times we live in.
From bishops to bosses, politicians to policemen, parents to
teachers, 'passing the buck' is rampant. They want the privileges
of power without accepting the penalties. We all shy away from
problems, cast a blind eye, shirk responsibility. And when the
scandal leaks out, as inevitably it does, we always make the
same excuse. We claim we didn't know. But such ignorance in
those of us who exercise authority is no excuse. What the Lord
told Ezekiel, applies equally to us: 'I have appointed you as sen-
try to the House of Israel.' And he went on to spell it out plainly:
'If you do not warn the wicked man to renounce his ways, then
he shall die for his sin, but I will hold you responsible for his
death.'

President Truman had a card on his desk in the White House
with the words inscribed on it in bold capitals, 'The buck stops
here.' It would sit as well on a teacher's desk in the classroom as
in the headmaster's office; in the priest's parlour as in the bishop's palace. It would fit indeed anywhere people are 'their
brother's keepers.' But nowhere would it fit better nowadays
than on the kitchen mantlepiece, with its four simple words
pointing straight at us like an accusing finger. For those of us
who have others in our care, our main concern should not be to
be popular but to help. And we help most by accepting our responsibility.

Suggested additional Bidding Prayers
We pray
– for those in authority that they will accept the responsibility
they are entrusted with.
– for ourselves that we will act responsibly with those entrusted
to our care.
– for those who have gone astray through the permissiveness of
society.

Catechism of the Catholic Church
2526 So-called moral permissiveness rests on an erroneous
conception of human freedom; the necessary precondition for

the development of true freedom is to let oneself be educated in the moral law. Those in charge of education can reasonably be expected to give young people instruction respectful of the truth, the qualities of the heart, and the moral and spiritual dignity of man.

Twenty-Fourth Sunday

Readings: Eccles 27:30-28:17. Rom 14:7-9. Mt 18:21-35.

Introduction
   We cannot celebrate today the Lord of compassion and love, unless we show forgiveness to those who have wronged us. We should forgive others as Christ forgives us.

Let byegones be byegones (Forgiveness) See also Fourth Lent C
   She slipped upstairs to find a few more playthings. Her neighbour had just left her two little ones with her to mind and, with her own two, there wasn't enough to go round. They had started squabbling already. Rummaging in the toy-box, she came across an old photograph. She looked at it, daydreaming for a moment. Just long enough for one of her little charges to toddle out the front door which had been left slightly ajar. The little body was found later in the pond at the bottom of the garden. She went to pieces. While she was being treated in a psychiatric hospital, the mother of the dead child came to see her, the worst of her grief now over. Her forgiveness helped enormously to set her on the road to recovery. But she was never the same again. She could never forgive herself for that moment's neglect.
   There is a young couple in Paris, with whom I am very friendly. They have two little children. Since they don't have a car, they occasionally call on my services to ferry them somewhere or other. I am always delighted to do so. Once the two little ones are firmly strapped in the back seat, I dangle the keys in front of the parents and ask: 'Now, which of you is going to drive?' They are both excellent drivers. I just couldn't take responsibility for them. If anything were to happen, God forbid, I would never be able to forgive myself.
   Forgiveness is a very hard thing. 'Forgive and forget', we are told. If only we could forget, forgiveness would come easy. But the scars of old hurts fester on, refusing to heal. And our resent-

ment grows each time we remember the rejection, the insult, the injury. Our resentment wells up again, as if it was only yesterday. Byegones refuse to be byegones. The closer the friendship, the deeper the hurt. The only forgiveness we can muster, is usually reserved for strangers. Our lives are strewn with broken friendships. And all because we couldn't find it in ourselves to forgive. 'Shake hands and make up' we were told, when we fought as little boys in the school playground. That lesson seems to have disappeared with our schooldays.

No wonder we ascribe forgiveness to God alone. 'To err is human, to forgive is divine.' We subscribe wholeheartily to the Psalmist when he says:

It is he who forgives all your guilt,

who heals every one of your ills,

who redeems your life from the grave,

who crowns you with love and compassion.

'May God forgive him!' we mutter to ourselves, recalling for the umpteenth time some ancient hurt. We could spare ourselves that prayer. What God would like to know is will *we* forgive him.

Swift, with all his satire, was closer to the truth than we care to admit:

We have just enough religion to make us hate,

but not enough to make us love one another.

How else explain those murderous wars between those who claim allegiance to their God? An expert recently claimed that, of all the thirty wars being fought at present in the world, none were against foreign aggressors. All the belligerents were compatriots, separated only by their religion. It is certainly true of former Yugoslavia, where Muslims, Orthodox and Catholic are locked in fratricidal war. Or Palestine, where Abraham's children, Jews and Arabs, nurture ancient wrongs. Such wars will last as long as we refuse to forgive.

'As we forgive them', we like to pray. Thus, we are passing sentence on ourselves, as long as we withold forgiveness.

Forgive your neighbour the hurt he does you,

and when you pray, your sins will be forgiven.

If a man nurses anger against another,

can he then demand compassion from the Lord?

Suggested additional Bidding Prayers
We pray
– for the grace to forgive those who have wronged us.
– for reconciliation among warring parties.
– for reconciliation among feuding families and neighbours.

Catechism of the Catholic Church
2843 Thus the Lord's words on forgiveness, the love that
loves to the end, become a living reality. The parable of the mer-
ciless servant, which crowns the Lord's teaching on ecclesial
communion, ends with these words: 'So also my heavenly
Father will do to every one of you, if you do not forgive your
brother from your heart.' It is there, in fact, 'in the depths of the
heart', that everything is bound and loosed. It is not in our power
not to feel, or to forget, an offence; but the heart that offers itself
to the Holy Spirit turns injury into compassion and purifies the
memory in transforming the hurt into intercession.

Twenty-Fifth Sunday

Readings: Is 55:6-9. Phil 1:20-24, 27. Mt 20:1-16.

The dole-queue (Unemployment)
I hear them every other day, loudhailers blaring out the slogans. The sound has become almost as common in Rome as the
never-ceasing scream of the police-sirens. My little room, where
I am writing these homilies, is on the fifth floor of a building
overlooking the Forum. Protest marches start usually from
Piazza Republica, wind their way down via Cavour, before
swinging right into Piazza Venezia. By the time they reach
where I stay, they are in full formation and in full throat. It is difficult to distinguish one protest from another. They all seek better wages, better pensions, better conditions or shorter hours.
They carry trade-union banners or red flags. Police march in
front and behind and riot-police in full gear are discreetly stationed
in side-streets along the route. A single helicopter circles contin-
uously overhead. They all seem to pass off peacefully. What
they achieve, apart from traffic-jams and the frustration of com-
muters, I have no idea. But they are now as much a part of the
political system in any democracy as the ballot-box.

One thing has changed though, since trade unions started about one hundred and fifty years ago. Workers then were at the bottom of the heap, shamelessly exploited, grossly underpaid and legally unprotected. They were hired and fired at will by employers and until trade unions organised them into strong disciplined movements, they were their own worst enemies, under-selling each other in their fight for jobs. They have come a long way in a hundred and fifty years. They are now the privileged ones, with jobs and wages and pensions. Now there is another group at the bottom of the heap, the unemployed, which has grown dangerously large in recent years. They range across a wide spectrum of society, young and old, men and women, the educated and the uneducated. They include the young, newly-arrived on the the job-market and the middle aged made redundant. For them, life offers only the bleak prospect of a place in the dole-queue. They have no voice. They exercise no pressure. They have no trade union because they have no trade, no workers' union because they have no work.

Tackling the problem of unemployment has become the main preoccupation of governments, if for no other reason than the crippling costs of welfare payments. Their best efforts are hampered by the sectional interests of the salaried majority. Employers insist on profit: employees demand security. The driving mechanism of each is self-interest. Helping the unemployed threatens both. The gospel is fundamentally at odds with such a world. You cannot serve the God of all and the mammon of some.

What is needed is generosity on the scale shown by the master of the vineyard in today's gospel. The parable presents a cameo of our society. First we have the employer, then the unions, and finally the dole-queue. A wage-settlement is agreed between employer and workers – one denarius a day. Work begins with stable industrial relations. But the dole-queue persists. The good employer takes imaginative and generous measures to help the unemployed, cutting his profit margins to the bone. The unions complain. In our world, they would probably have called a lightening strike and let the remaining grapes rot. But it is not our world and as Isaiah puts it in the mouth of God: 'My thoughts are not your thoughts, my ways not your ways.' It would be foolish to suggest that the measures taken in this parable would solve our unemployment. But there is no doubt that it can only be solved by such generosity from all parties.

Suggested additional Bidding Prayers

We pray

– for the unemployed that they will speedily rejoin the ranks of wage-earners.

– for employers that they will give priority to maintaining employment in their enterprises.

– for the government that they will use energy and imagination in creating employment for its citizens.

Catechism of the Catholic Church

2433 Access to employment and to professions must be open to all without unjust discrimination: men and women, healthy and disabled, natives and immigrants. For its part society should, according to circumstances, help citizens find work and employment.

Twenty-Sixth Sunday

Readings: Ez 18:25-28. Phil 2:1-11. Mt 21: 28-32.

Introduction

In today's gospel Jesus warns the chief priests and the elders that prostitutes and tax-collectors are making their way into the kingdom of God before them. It is a warning to us that our religious affiliation gives us no exclusive rights to the mercy of God.

Members only (Exclusion)

It is hard to believe now that until the early nineteen-hundreds bishops in Ireland were chosen only from the ranks of the aristocracy. Of course, there was a good economic reason. They had to be self-supporting. The people were too poor to pay them. But it was equally true in wealthy countries like France and Italy. There too Rome's first requirement in a bishop was that he was from the ranks of the nobility. Indeed, it was customary for titled families, where the eldest son succeeded, to destine the second son for the church or the army. The great mass of the lower clergy, parish priests and curates, were excluded from bishoprics. Some of the trappings of aristocracy still survive in the church. Some at least of those 'princes of the church' retain their bishop's 'palaces', like to be addressed 'Your Lordship' and offer their hand to have their ring kissed rather than for a friendly shake.

One of the last aristocratic appointments in Ireland was a member of the wealthy Dunboyne family. He was appointed Bishop of Cork, where he served with moderate success for twenty-three years. When his brother, Lord Dunboyne died, he abandoned the church, became a Protestant and married to insure an heir to the family. Ironically, one whose distinguished lineage Rome had deemed a priority should now consider the continuance of this line his priority. Ironic too that he should fail to produce an heir. Rome had lost a bishop while Dunboyne gained no heir.

The beginning of the end of the aristocratic world, which began with the dawn of history, came in the wake of the French Revolution. It decreed the abolition of hereditary titles and made all citizens equal in the eyes of the law. The world of the common man was brought into being and though it took another hundred years to come to fruition, the process was irreversible. Now, what titles remain are largely honorary. But old habits die hard, and not only in the church. A new elite has come to replace the old. Aristocrats have given way to plutocrats. Money occupies the place of lineage. The old exclusive world of privilege never really died. It only changed hands. The modern rich have all the trappings of the old nobility, save the titles. They provide themselves with security-guarded palatial homes, chauffeur-driven limousines, exclusive clubs, and whatever else is needed to protect them from contamination from the common herd.

The need for exclusivity seems deeply inbedded in human nature itself. It has invaded even the sanctuary. 'How odd of God/to choose the Jew,' Belloc wrote playfully. The Jews were very happy to exploit this divine oddity, excluding not only the rest of the world from God's favour, but even the Samaritans who failed their rigid test of orthodoxy. Jesus did not bandy his words when he told their chief priests and elders, 'Prostitutes and tax-collectors are making their way into the kingdom of God before you.' From the Jews as the chosen people to Calvin's elect, to our own 'outside the church there is no salvation', exclusivity has always been a feature of religion. With the diminishing numbers of church-goers, and religion no longer a mass phenomenon, we may be more than ever tempted to claim exclusive rights to God's mercy. Jesus' warning to the Jews has a special relevance for us today. St Paul puts it simply: 'Always consider the other person to be better than yourself.'

Suggested additional Bidding Prayers
We pray
– that we will never use our religion to exclude others.
– for the courage to challenge all attempts in our communities to exclude others.
– that we will 'always consider the other person to be better than ourselves'.

Catechism of the Catholic Church

546 Jesus' invitation to enter his kingdom comes in the form of parables, a characteristic feature of his teaching. Through his parables he invites people to the feast of the kingdom, but he also asks for a radical choice: to gain the kingdom one must give everything. Words are not enough, deeds are required.

Twenty-Seventh Sunday

Readings: Is 5:1-7. Phil 4:6-9. Mt 21:33-43.

Introduction

The church is the choice vineyard of the Lord. Here we grow to maturity in the sunshine of God's grace. We pray that we may never be soured by bitterness or disillusionment.

Sour grapes (Growth)

He was a cultivated man, fluent in several languages. Grace and nature had endowed him with formidable talent. As a university professor he had gained recognition in his field. I came to know him on his frequent visits to Paris. At first I was flattered that he should seek out my company when in that city. I suppose it was a sign of my own mediocrity that I should be so easily impressed by those of superior status. Or maybe it was that I had been fortunate in my earlier life to have encountered people steeped in literature and history whose wide learning made them open-minded and humble. One was my father. Another was a priest who taught me in secondary school. I think I owe my vocation to him. As a teenager he was my ideal of what an educated man should be, broad-minded, tolerant and self-effacing. I had assumed my distinguished Paris visitor would be all that and much more. Soon I became disillusioned. I came to dread his visits and seek to be absent when he called. He was

one of the most negative persons I had ever met, hyper-critical of
everyone and everything. Either he was deeply-flawed by nature
or some earlier experience in life had soured him. The only thing
that seemed to have blossomed in him was his bitterness.
Isaiah's song brought him to mind:

My friend had a vineyard
on a fertile hillside.
He dug the soil, cleared it of stones,
and planted vines in it.
In the middle he built a tower,
he dug a press there too.
He expected it to yield grapes,
but sour grapes were all that it gave.

Since then, my earlier idealism has given way to a more realistic
appraisal of the value of education. Education, like travel, does
not always broaden the mind. I have met other 'sour grapes'
whose academic achievements seem only to have confirmed
their prejudices and reinforced their narrow-mindedness.

Looking at the neat rows of vines on terraced hillsides in
France or Italy, I have always been struck by how labour-inten-
sive vine-growing is. We have nothing comparable in Ireland.
Nothing is left to chance. The carefully pruned branches are
meticulously interwoven through strands of wire kept taut by
closely-spaced stakes. The ground between the rows is kept
hoed, no weeds are allowed to rob the soil of nourishment.
Grape-picking is done by hand. It must be the only area in agriculture untouched by modern machinery. Little seems to have
changed since biblical times. The sun provides the secret of success. A vintage year is a long season of summer sun. Grapes
fully ripened by the sun produce the best wine. Otherwise sugar
must be added to sweeten the grapes. The more sugar added,
the more alcoholic the wine and the poorer the quality. The great
enemy is frost, either late in spring or early in autumn.

It is no surprise that the vineyard provides the favourite
metaphor for religious growth in the bible, both in the Old and
the New Testaments. Our religious growth is the product of
careful nurturing by ourselves and others and the warm sunshine of God's grace. Grace builds on nature. Life's frost can
make us bitter. Frost-bitten branches must be pruned to let the
vine grow and flourish. Otherwise, it will yield only sour
grapes. Religion, no less than life, has its share of such. Book-
burning bigots like Savanarola, a far cry from his sweet-tem-

pered founder, St Francis, both products of the same country
and the same vineyard.

'Finally, brothers, fill your minds with everything that is
true, everything that is noble, everything that is good and pure,
everything that we love and honour, and everything that can be
thought virtuous and worthy of praise.'

Suggested additional Bidding Prayers
We pray
– that we may grow in wisdom, in tolerance and in humility.
– that we will never become soured by life's disappointments.
– for our parents, teachers and others who have nurtured our
faith by word and example.

Catechism of the Catholic Church
755. 'The church is a *cultivated field*, the tillage of God. On that
land the ancient olive tree grows whose holy roots were the
prophets and in which the reconciliation of Jews and Gentiles
has been brought about and will be brought about again. That
land, like a choice vineyard, has been planted by the heavenly
cultivator. Yet the true vine is Christ who gives life and fruitfulness to the branches, that is, to us, who through the church remain in Christ, without whom we can do nothing.'

Twenty-Eighth Sunday

Readings: Is 25: 6-10. Phil 4: 12-14, 19-20. Mt 22: 1-14.

Introduction
By baptism we have been invited into the kingdom of God.
Our eucharistic celebration today should recall that invitation
and alert us to how we are responding.

'Bread and circuses' (Heaven)
I suspect that our notion of heaven derives largely from what
we regard as most desirable in this world. Such was always the
case. Every age re-invents heaven to mirror its own time. What
is depicted tells us more about conditions here than in the hereafter. Whatever else it represents for me now, it is certainly not a
marriage feast. Like most priests, I have had more than my share
of wedding receptions in this world, with their invariable

menus of turkey and ham, to have any desire for more of the same in the next. Yet, there was a time in my life when food came high on the list of desirables. The smell of a fry from the professor's dining-room in my boarding-school days was enough to transport me to another world.

Such was the bleakness of the lives of most people in biblical and other times, when food was very basic and very scarce, it is not surprising that Jesus compared the kingdom of heaven to a royal wedding feast. There was of course a political agenda behind those royal banquets. They helped to insure that the heir to the throne would be accepted and loved by his poorer subjects. Caesars and senators in ancient Rome were accustomed to sponsor gladiatorial contests and other bloody spectacles for much the same reason. Cynical Romans were well aware that their acquiescence in, if not allegiance to, the ruling junta, was being bought with 'bread and circuses'. Vestiges of the same still survive today as richer countries vie with each other to host the Olympic Games or the World Cup.

There was nothing hidden about the parable Jesus addressed to the religious hierarchy of his time. They were his prime target and they knew it. (Already they had plans in the pipeline to rid themselves of this rabble-rousing rabbi.) They and their likes were too preoccupied with the pursuit of privilege and power to accept the invitation to the wedding-feast. Others had their 'farms' and their 'businesses', their shady deals and worldly transactions. They did not take kindly to being told to abandon their dubious practices. They rejected and maltreated the prophetic messengers sent to warn them that the feast was ready. But they have now long since gone and paid the price of their infidelity.

But the story and the story-teller goes on choosing in every age a new audience. Certainly those executives in Roman collars who run their local churches like regional subsidiaries of a giant international company are now being targetted. But they are not alone. It would be comforting to think that we are too low down to be included. Or worse, that we are part of that great unwashed at the crossroads who finally fill the wedding-hall. It would also be very naïve. Our baptism placed us in the first place on the guest list. Our profession of faith every Sunday confirmed it. Our preoccupation with this world suggests we might not make it to the wedding.

It used to be thought that heaven was the better of the two

options on offer when we die. The reality is quite different. The offer is made now. Death only freezes for eternity the choice we make here. We have already received our invitations. We have been tagged with an RSVP. We are already making our responses by the priorities we choose here and now.

Suggested additional Bidding Prayers
We pray
– for the courage to respond positively to the invitation to the Lord's wedding feast.
– for the tenacity to withstand the allurements of the world.
– for the strength to overcome our preoccupation with material wellbeing.

Catechism of the Catholic Church
1024 This perfect life with the Most Holy Trinity – this community of life and love with the Trinity, with the Virgin Mary, the angels and all the blessed – is called 'heaven'. Heaven is the ultimate end and fulfilment of the deepest human longings, the state of supreme definitive happiness.

Twenty-Ninth Sunday

Readings: Is 45:1, 4-6. Thess 1:1-5. Mt 22: 15-21.

Introduction
Christians are called to live in a pluralist world. It presents them with huge challenges. Only the depth of their convictions will enable them to survive in a secular society.

'Render to Caesar…' (Church / State)
No sooner had the Berlin Wall fallen, marking the end of the Cold War, than another ominous divide in our world made its appearance. This new division is between the Muslim world and what was once the Christian West. The Muslim world has experienced an extraordinary growth in fundamentalism. Many countries there have imposed or are seeking to impose the law of the Koran as the law of the state. Algeria in North africa, just off the southern tip of Europe, is presently the scene of a murderous East-West conflict. Some European countries feel threatened, particularly France, with its large Muslim population and

close historical ties with Algeria. Already controversy has broken out there, with Muslim demands that their schoolgirls be allowed to wear the veil in French public schools. Strange how people so often adopt the attitudes and strategies of their adversaries. Muslim fundamentalism in Arab countries has been matched by a noticeable 'move to the right' in western countries. Not surprisingly, this is most apparent in France where the extreme right-wing National Front have made extraordinary gains in recent elections. Even the more moderate mainstream parties are calling for tighter immigration laws. The signs for the future are ominous, to say the least.

The clash between religion and the secular state is not new. The history of the Christian West is largely a history of this conflict. For the first few centuries of its existence, the Christian religion was fiercely persecuted by the state, leaving in its wake, a bloody trail of martyrs. All that changed with the conversion of the emperor Constantine. Soon Christianity became the state religion. Now the boot was on the other foot. The high point of the power of religion came at Canossa in the high Middle Ages when an excommunicated emperor knelt in the snow and humbly submitted to a pope to regain his imperial crown. In the Caesar-God contest, the first round went decidedly to God. All throughout the Middle Ages the church extended its sphere of influence into the secular domain. With the break-up of Christianity in the sixteenth century the process began to reverse. The French Revolution marked a decisive turning point, this time in favour of the state. Napoleon made the point dramatically, when he took the imperial crown from the pope and placed it himself on his own head. Ever since the state has been clawing back the ground once usurped by the church. And understandably, the church has ceded its former influence reluctantly. The boot has changed feet once more.

Today's gospel, with its famous 'Render to Caesar the things that are Caesar's and to God the things that are God's' has a particular topicality in our world. And perhaps nowhere more than in Ireland, where controversy has flared over proposed divorce and abortion legislation. While the principle enunciated by Christ in the gospel is clear and unambiguous, its application in particular circumstances is quite another matter. The *Catechism of the Catholic Church* points out three circumstances where citizens are obliged in conscience to refuse obedience to the civil authorities. They are when the laws are 'contrary to the moral order, to the fundamental rights of persons and to the teachings of the gospel.' Once more, the principle is clear. However, its application is not so simple, as the decision by the Irish Supreme Court in the famous X case revealed. Invoking the constitutional rights of persons, that decision left the legal position regarding abortion, in the eyes of many, in a worse state than before.

The complexity of these issues often render them unsuitable topics for the pulpit. What the preacher can and must do, is advise believers on the obligation of Christian behaviour in all circumstances. No matter how deeply they hold their convictions or how warmly they espouse their causes, they must never resort to violence. And that includes intimidation in all its forms. Muscular crusades, whether modern or medieval, cause irreparable harm. The end never justifies the means. We live, even in Ireland, in a world of pluralism. There are others whose principles and beliefs differ radically from ours. The state must also take cognisance of them. Our only resort is persuasion. Persuasion is always a gentle art. We best persuade by living our Christian lives to the full, remembering always that 'the anger of man works not the justice of God.'

Suggested additional Bidding Prayers
We pray
– for harmonious relations between church and state in seeking the common good.
– that each will recognise the legitimate concerns of the other.
– that Christians and citizens will always act with restraint and tolerance.

Catechism of the Catholic Church
2242 The citizen is obliged in conscience not to follow the directives of civil authorities when they are contrary to the demands of the moral order, to the fundamental rights of persons or the teachings of the gospel. Refusing obedience to civil authorities, when their demands are contrary to those of an upright conscience, finds its justification in the distinction between serving God and serving the political community. 'Render therefore to Caesar the things that are Caesar's, and to God the things that are God's.' 'We must obey God rather than men.'

Thirtieth Sunday

Readings: Ex 22:20-26. 1 Thess 1:5-10. Mt 22:34-40.

Introduction

Today we celebrate the great commandment of love. We should rid ourselves of all prejudice particularly against those who differ with us by race, nationality, religion or colour.

Suspect number one (Prejudice)

A bomb had just gone off in Boulevard Montparnasse. A few people were killed and many others were injured. Terrorism had raised its ugly head in the French capital. The authorities reacted swiftly. Suspects were rounded up. Paris was and is the nerve centre of an international web of terrorist groups. It is here they make contact, exchange information, do their cross-dealing. It is probably why it is one of the most incident-free cities in the world. Nobody in their senses would dream of fouling the nest. It was common knowledge that the perpetrators of this atrocity would be severely dealt with, if not by the police, by one or other of the terrorist organisations. I had been taking my evening stroll in Jardin du Luxembourg when the bomb went off a short distance on the other side of the garden. The first I became aware that something had happened was the constant wail of sirens of police cars and ambulances that raced to and from the scene for the next few hours. Only later when I watched the evening news did I learn the full horror of what had happened and realise how close I had been to the scene.

The fun-loving city of Paris changed complexion overnight. There were police everywhere. People were constantly stopped and interrogated. People were frisked and searched going in to shops, cinemas and restaurants, which were compelled to employ special security staff for the purpose. Police manned all Métro entrances, demanding to see identification papers. I had been living a number of years in Paris and gone everywhere without an identity card. I had never even bothered to apply for a *carte du séjour*. My Irish passport then was bulky and in any case I was always afraid of losing it, so I never carried it on me. I did now while I began the long and tortuous hassle with French bureaucracy to obtain a *carte du séjour*.

As far as I can remember now these high security measures remained in force for a couple of months. Certainly, they lasted long enough for me to learn something I had never realised before. My white face was my passport. At every checkpoint I encountered I was never stopped, while every coloured person before and after me were held and interrogated lengthily. And often, ironically, by coloured officers who form a sizeable percentage of the Paris police force. I mentioned my discovery to a coloured friend. He looked at me in disbelief. 'All that changed for me,' he said, 'was that before the bomb, I was stopped and questioned every other time. Now I am stopped and questioned every time.' He opened my eyes to the existence of racial prejudice in a city as liberal and as cosmopolitan as Paris. Now I see it all the time.

Prejudice is blind. Those who practice it most are often least aware of it in themselves. Ireland must be the country with proportionately the least number of coloured people in the world. The few coloured stars on our World Cup soccer team are hardly likely to arouse our prejudice. Nor do the Olympic athletes or an O. J. Simpson do so in the United States. When it comes to national prestige, they are net contributors. We have to look elsewhere for signs of prejudice. The way we treat our itinerants is a case in point. The attitudes of our emigrants abroad, like the Irish in South Boston, is another pointer to the latent prejudice in the Irish at home. There is a lot of soul-searching we need to do. We more than most should identify with immigrants, whatever their hue or colour. Many of our race in foreign lands were widowed by the loss of their homeland and orphaned by lack of status in their adopted country. It should make us more receptive to words the Lord spoke to Moses:

> Tell the sons of Israel this, 'You must not molest the stranger or oppress him, for you lived as strangers in the land of Egypt. You must not be harsh with the widow or the orphan; if you are harsh with them, they will surely cry out to me, and be sure I shall hear their cry; my anger will flare and I shall kill you with the sword, your own wives will be widows, your own children orphans.'

Suggested additional Bidding Prayers
We pray
– for all those in our society who are victims of prejudice.
– that God will open our eyes to our own prejudices.
– that we will always find a place in our hearts and our homes for strangers.

Catechism of the Catholic Church
1935 The equality of men rests essentially on their dignity as persons and the rights that flow from it. Every form of social or cultural discrimination in fundamental personal rights on the grounds of sex, race, colour, social conditions, language or religion, must be curbed and eradicated as incompatible with God's design.

Thirty-First Sunday

Readings: Mal 1:14-2:2, 8-10. 1 Thess 2:7-9, 13. Mt 23:1-12.

Attracting attention (Appearances)
There were about fifty of us under the same roof. It was an international residence attached to one of the pontifical universities in Rome. The majority were priests, ranging in age from late twenties to sixty plus. There were a small group of seminarians and the rest were lay students. We represented almost twenty nationalities, from all five continents. What intrigued me most were the clerics, priests and seminarians. I had spent the previous twenty years living on my own, largely isolated from clerical circles. It was a new experience for me to live in an almost exclusively clerical environment. A sizeable minority wore clerical dress. The others were indistinguishable from the laity. The breakdown did not seem to follow any recognisable pattern. It wasn't a question of age, though many of the seminarians and some of the younger priests wore the clerical collar. Nor was there a clear geographical division. Most of them – whom I later regarded as the *sanior pars*, when I got to know them better – wore 'civvies'. They came from places as disparate as South Korea and Brazil, Kenya and Australia. The clerically-dressed were almost exclusively confined to Argentina, Switzerland and oddly enough, the United States. As I got to know them better I came to realise that they also represented a different mindset. They had a conservative, almost pre-Vatican II vision of the church.

Clerical dress, at least in my view, has always been a non-issue. For a large part of my priestly life, I worked in France where the clergy wear lay clothes. Prior to that I worked in the secular world of publishing and television, where it was customary for priests to dress like other employees. Wearing the collar there would be frowned on as an attempt to pull rank. Besides, being an historian, I was always aware of the wide range of clerical attire down through the centuries, from the powdered wigs and frilly cuffs of the *ancien régime* clerics in France to the peasant garb of penal priests in Ireland. Let history judge, but for me our finest hour was those times of persecution when priests were disguised as others, rather than those decadent times like our own when, it would seem, others are often disguised as priests.

That there are solid arguments in favour of a distinctive clerical dress goes without saying. Perhaps the strongest is that the priest in the parish should be easily recognisable by those who seek his help. The other argument that clerical dress is a sign is more questionable. The problem is, a sign of what? If I lived the gospel, like Mother Teresa of Calcutta or Abbé Pierre in France, I would feel no embarrassment wearing a habit or a collar. But a sign works both ways. Recently I was taking a stroll in Piazza Navona. There were three young Franciscan friars in their brown robes and sandals just ahead of me on the pavement. It is not an unusual sight in Rome. They stopped at a cash-dispenser, fished out their credit cards from the deep folds of their habits and withdrew some money. Most ordinary people nowadays do the same. And so do I. But in this case the clash of symbols deeply disturbed me. Rome is full of down-and-outs who sleep in doorways or on the pavements. What kind of impression would a sight like that make on them? What would that beggarman, St Francis, have thought?

But the strongest argument of all is today's gospel where Christ castigates the scribes and Pharisees who did 'not practise what they preach'. 'Everything they do is done to attract attention,' he said, 'like wearing broader phylacteries and longer tassles, like wanting to take the place of honour at banquets and the front seats in the synagogues, being greeted obsequiously in the market squares and having people call them Rabbi.' He could well have been describing the world where I first started life as a priest. The collar was very much a symbol of power and privilege then and provoked a good deal of anticlericalism. I remember my sister, the mother of a few young children, returning home from the butcher's, furious. She had to queue for ages. A priest joined the end of the queue and when the butcher spotted the clerical collar, he called him up to serve him immediately.

It didn't pacify my sister when I told her that the priest was probably embarrassed by this special treatment and did not refuse because he did not wish to hurt the butcher's feelings. 'He doesn't have a dinner to cook and children to mind and feed like me,' she retorted.

Coincidentally, that is exactly how St Paul describes his priestly work among the Thessalonians: 'Like a mother feeding and looking after her own children.' Whatever clothes we priests wear – and I am still of two minds about it – we must follow the teaching of Christ: 'The greatest among you must be your servant.' Otherwise, we will earn the curse Malachi threatened on the priests who strayed from the right way and become 'contemptible and vile in the eyes of the whole people.' Some might say we have reached that point already.

The Psalmist has got it right:
O Lord, my heart is not proud
nor haughty my eyes.
I have not gone after things too great
nor marvels beyond me.

Suggested additional Bidding Prayers
We pray
– that priests and religious may be distinguishable by the quality of their lives.
– that we may never judge people by appearances.
– that we may always spurn privilege as unworthy of the gospel we profess to believe.

Thirty-Second Sunday

Readings: Wis 6:12-16. 1 Thess 4:13-18. Mt 25:1-13.

Introduction
At some time we are all afflicted by grief at the loss of a loved one. The period of mourning can be long and difficult. St Paul reminds us that as Christians we have the hope of the resurrection and that should not grieve like others who have no hope.

A time for tears (Grief)

The strange thing about it is that people never really regarded them as being very close. Even in their younger days they rarely went anywhere together. Of course, he was a good deal older than her, which probably explains why they never had children. In any case, as far as appearances went, they seemed more like a man and his housekeeper than husband and wife. He was a gruff sort of man and the older he got the gruffer he became. Neighbours found him off-putting. Nobody ever really got very close to him. But he was one of them and they all turned out for his funeral. Everybody was very kind. They called to the house and offered sympathy. The women made tea and sandwiches. The men helped with the funeral arrangements and contacted relatives. And all that time she remained very composed. Even at the graveside her grief was scarcely noticeable. Some people even said it was probably a great relief to her. He must have been a very difficult man to live with.

But it wasn't like that at all. It was only in the following days and weeks and months, in the privacy of her empty house that she really broke down and wept. In fact, it took the best part of a year before she managed to pull herself together again. At first, she used to sit in a chair for hours on end unable to do anything. Every time she turned round she expected to see him sitting there reading the newspaper. Whenever a door slammed or a floorboard creaked she thought it was himself pottering around upstairs. There were even times when she thought she heard him cough or call. And each new realisation of her loss crushed her.

That this should surprise us is itself surprising. After all she had shared more than forty years of her life with him. She could scarcely remember now that time in her life before she knew him. Even if their love was never very demonstrative, it was nonetheless very real for all that. They had grown in to each other. The man who was her 'other half' was not at all the man the neighbours saw.

We have a great reputation in Ireland for attending funerals. No matter who you are you can be certain of a decent send-off. Our presence is a great comfort to the bereaved. We crowd out their sorrow at a time of great grief. We mourn with great dignity. Not so the Italians. They applaud the deceased as the coffin is carried through the streets. And the graveside can often be a scene of unrestrained emotion with the next-of-kin screaming hysterically. From what I have seen on television, it seems much

the same in the Arab world. I suspect the Irish were the same
with their keening women, before the English 'civilised' us.
Psychiatrists tell us that it is better to let it all out rather than bottle it up.

However we grieve – and grief at the death of a loved one is
inevitable – we should remember the advice of St Paul and
'comfort one another with thoughts such as these':

> We want you to be quite certain, brothers, about those who
> have died, to make sure that you do not grieve about them,
> like the other people who have no hope. We believe that
> Jesus died and rose again, and that it will be the same for
> those who have died in Jesus: God will bring them with him.

Suggested additional Bidding Prayers
We pray
– for all those who grieve that the Lord may wipe away their
tears.
– that those who grieve may find hope in the resurrection.
– for the souls of the faithful departed that they may rest in
peace.

Catechism of the Catholic Church
1687 .... The death of a member of the community ... is an
event that should lead beyond the perspectives of 'this world'
and draw the faithful into the true perspective of faith in the
risen Christ.

Thirty-Third Sunday

Readings: Prov 31:10-13, 19-20, 30-31. 1 Thess 5:1-6. Mt 25:14-30.

Introduction
Today's gospel, on the penultimate Sunday of the church's
liturgical year, recalls the judgement on the Last Day. We write
the book of evidence for that judgement on ourselves now.
There will be no surprises then when all will be revealed.

Book of evidence (Judgement)
They called it the 'trial of the century'. A black American
football star was accused of brutally murdering his wife and her
alleged lover. The trial was beamed all over the world on cable

TV. Trial by television had finally become a reality. For many viewers the final frontier between fact and fiction disappeared. Real life became a soap-opera. Soon it became apparent that what was really on trial was the American judicial system. What surprised most non-American viewers was the length and thoroughness of the pre-trial selection of the jury. That process itself lasted longer than most trials. The fate of the accused lay in the hands of these twelve people. Not surprisingly, both the prosecution and defence attached enormous importance to the selection of these jurors. It was almost as if they were selecting two opposing football teams. Detective agencies were employed to investigate the lives of each of the proposed jurors to find if there was anything there which might prejudice the case in favour of one side or the other. Commentators openly described them as pro-defence or pro-prosecution jurors. Only when both sides were satisfied that the jury was packed at least slightly in their favour, was the trial at last allowed to get under way. But even then, the composition of the jury continued to dominate the proceedings. Within twelve weeks, half of them were already dismissed, as evidence emerged of possible bias towards one side or the other. The objections against them were not that they were not impartial but that they were playing for the other team.

If that represents the present state of the jury system, it may be just as well that the trial we all have to face some day will not be a trial by jury. Our verdict will be handed down by the judge alone, who will base his decision on the book of evidence. That book we write each and every day of our lives. For people of my age or older, that book is almost complete. But nobody can be sure when the last page is written. 'Times and seasons', as St Paul points out, are illusory. 'The Day of the Lord is going to come like a thief in the night.' Rather than gamble our eternity on some hoped-for last minute conversion, we decide our fate at every present moment.

The witnesses, we know them well. The most important live with us and work with us. Your wife and children should be well-disposed, if not decidedly partial. But it is not always so. Your secretary may be another story. It didn't help her that she was a spinster, plain and middle-aged. You never missed an opportunity to put her down. You knew she looked after her invalid mother. She told you on the one and only morning she arrived a few minutes late for work. 'You are not paid to bring your problems to work with you, Miss,' you snarled at her. But *you* did. Every time you had a quarrel with your wife, you took it out on her. And when you had a confrontation with your teenage son who had arrived home drunk the previous night, she had to bear the brunt of it. If she sniffled all the time into a Kleenex, it wasn't that she suffered from a chronic cold. Your sarcasm hurt her deeply. She couldn't complain. She couldn't risk her job. She was too old and her mother too dependant. The other hostile witnesses, 'the least of his brethren', I pass over in silence. But *he* won't.

The matter of 'talents' will dominate the book of evidence. You were born into a good family, loving and Christian. Nothing was spared in your education. Religion played an important and largely a benign role in your early formation. Family background assured you a comfortable position in life. You were blessed with an agreeable wife to whom, with you, God entrusted a couple of children. Five talents chosen at random! And what have you got to show for them? Your name inscribed on the roll of honour in your local golf club and a fat bank account! If you can't do better than that, you may be needing those Kleenex you so despised your secretary for, in that place 'where there will be weeping and grinding of teeth'. She won't be needing them anymore.

Suggested additional Bidding Prayers.
We pray
– that we may use the 'talents' God gave us in the service of our neighbour.
– that we may always 'be faithful in small things'.
– that God will welcome us into eternal happiness on the Last Day.

Catechism of the Catholic Church
678 Following in the steps of the prophets and John the Baptist, Jesus announced the judgement of the Last Day in his preaching. Then will the conduct of each one and the secrets of the heart be brought to light. Then will the culpable unbelief that counted the offer of God's grace as nothing be condemned. Our attitude to our neighbour will disclose acceptance or refusal of grace and divine love. On the Last Day Jesus will say: 'Truly I say to you, as you did it to one of the least of these my brethren, you did it to me.'

Our Lord Jesus Christ, Universal King Years A and B

Readings: Dan 7:13-14. Apoc 1:5-8. Jn 18:33-37.

Introduction
On the last Sunday of the church's year we honour Christ the
King. It is a timely reminder to us that we must always remain
loyal to Christ and to his gospel.

'God save the King' (Loyalty)
When Louis XVI was condemned to death, he made one last
request to the revolutionary government. He asked for the services of a priest to help him in his last moments. Most French
priests had fled Paris or gone into hiding. The one Louis asked
for by name was an Irish priest, Abbé Edgeworth, who had been
confessor to the King's sister. Death stalked the streets of Paris
and priests were the favoured targets of the venom of the revolutionary mobs. 'The few honest people who continue faithful to
their God and king keep silence and weep daily over the ruins of
the altar and the throne,' Edgeworth wrote to a friend in Ireland,
a short time previously. When the King's message reached him,
he was asked would he be willing to offer his services. Acceptance
would almost certainly entail his own execution. Without hesi-
tation Edgeworth replied, 'A King even in chains has the right to
command.' When he met the King that night in his prison cell,
Louis broke down 'Forgive me,' he said, 'I have lived so long in
the midst of my enemies, that the sight of a loyal subject moves
me deeply.' Edgeworth spent the night with the King in prison
and, after celebrating Mass early next morning, he accompanied
the King to the guillotine. After the King's execution, he turned
to descend the scaffold, only to find that it was surrounded by
twenty or thirty thousand armed revolutionaries. Trusting to
providence he approached the first line which, to his surprise,
opened up before him, as did the second and third. By the time
he came to the fifth line he was lost in the crowd and made good
his escape. He was a witness that day, not only to the execution
of a king but to the death of an era, half as old as time itself.
While kings continued to cling on to their thrones in some countries for almost another century, the advent of democracy was
irreversible.

By the end of the First World War, the remaining thrones in
Europe were toppled. Ironically, it was just at this time 1925, to

be exact that the church decided to institute the Feast of Christ the King on the last Sunday of October. Honouring Christ under the title of king seemed oddly out of tune with the times. Nationalism was the dominant ideology of the period. People were encouraged to give their allegiance to a flag, the symbol of the new nation states. From time immemorial they had professed their loyalty to a person, their king. Loyalty was the virtue *par excellence* associated with kingship. High treason, the betrayal of your king, was then the most odious of crimes. It seems strange to us today to read of people sentenced to be executed on the orders of their sovereign, going to their deaths declaring, 'God save the King.' Loyalty loomed large in the hierarchy of virtues and permeated all areas of peoples' lives. They were loyal to their clans, their families and their friends. Their wars – and they were many – were conflicts of loyalties. Above all, their relationship with God was, like the people of Israel, defined in terms of loyalty.

We in the modern world have little cause to mourn the passing of kings. History shows little that was edifying about their lives or their reigns. But few would dispute that the virtue of loyalty may have largely gone with them. How else explain the alarming incidence of marital breakdown in our time, except in terms of infidelity? Loyalty commands little respect there or else here. If people are not loyal to their God, they are scarcely likely to be loyal to anyone. We must make Christ king in our lives.

'"I am the Alpha and the Omega," says the Lord God, who is, who was, and who is to come, the Almighty.'

Suggested additional Bidding Prayers
We pray
– that we may always remain loyal to Christ our King.
– that husbands and wives may always remain loyal to each other, and children to their parents.
– that we may always remain loyal to the Mass and the sacraments.

Catechism of the Catholic Church
680 Christ the Lord already reigns through the church, but all the things of this world are not yet subjected to him. The triumph of Christ's kingdom will not come about without one last assault by the powers of evil.

Year B

First Sunday of Advent

Readings: Is 63:16-17, 64:1, 3-8. 1 Cor 1:3-9. Mk 13:33-37.

Introduction

The liturgy begins and ends its year with a reflection on death. The significance of death at the beginning of the year may not be immediately evident. What is death, an end or a beginning? Is it, as the world thinks, obsolescence, or as the Christian believes, a new birth? We could hardly make a better beginning to the liturgical year than by placing our lives in this perspective.

Potter's Clay (Death)

Strange, isn't it, that the church should begin its year in November? It is a time of fallen leaves and souls in purgatory. Nature reeks of death in Advent. Not even the faintest rumours of Spring in the air. While nature is steeped in death, the liturgy would have us start again. The season is not ill-chosen as death puts our lives into their true perspective. By making death our starting point we will have no illusions about life. We can look reality in the eye and face our tomorrows in hope. We are waiting for our Lord Jesus to be revealed. Life is a vigil, a time of waiting which only ends with death and the advent of the day of the Lord.

Everything we touch in our lives bears within it the seeds of obsolescence. The more we advance technologically, the shorter-lived become our creations. In the course of an average life-span, we preside over the obsequies of hundreds of thousands of material things, all of which were a part of us for a time. We've scarcely become attached to our car, with all its whims and moods, when it needs replacing. A suit of clothes is barely broken in to the irregularities of our contours before it is consigned to the rag bin. A shoe that finally accepts our bunions, is well on the way to the garbage heap. The consumer society is technologically so sophisticated that it mass-produces disposables with a built-in obsolescence. A popular American TV series began each episode with a shot of a tape-recorder being switched on delivering a message beginning: 'This tape will self destruct within four seconds.' If the squeak in our shoes or the rattle in our cars could be translated, it would probably be the same message.

Knee-deep in obsolescence, it is not surprising that the notion colours our attitudes towards people. We speak of redundant workers and obsolete professions. We scarcely raise our eyebrows at the suggestion of relegating people to the scrap-heap. We accept as inevitable, perhaps even desirable, the rationalisation of man-power and personnel pruning. If we are a little perturbed at plans to dump the over forties, it is only because we have reservations about the cut-off mark. Retirement in our world is not a matter of relieving the elderly of their burdens but of relieving the company of dead weight.

We are pilgrims on a journey. Death is our home-coming. If there is any high point in our lives, it is surely towards the end as we come in sight of home. The evening of our lives should combine the satisfaction of a long road travelled with the expectation of a better life to come. 'Lord, you are our Father; we the clay, you the potter, we are all the work of your hand.' If the potter builds obsolescence into the clay vessel he fashions, it is not to increase the turnover of creation. Our durability is contingent only on the will of our maker. When he chooses to recall us, 'evening, midnight, cockcrow or dawn,' is not for us to know. Life-users, like road-users, must stay awake. Advent is a lay-by where we take stock of our position, consult our maps, and ready ourselves for the coming of the day of the Lord.

Suggested additional Bidding Prayers
We pray
– that God will put our lives in his perspective this Advent.
– that we will respect the elderly as pilgrims on their way to the Father.
– that we will ready ourselves this Advent for the coming of 'the day of the Lord'.

Catechism of the Catholic Church
672 According to the Lord, the present time is the time of the Spirit and of witness, but also a time still marked by 'distress' and the trial of evil which does not spare the church and ushers in the struggles of the last days. It is a time of waiting and watching.

Second Sunday of Advent

Readings Is 40:1-5, 9-11. 2 Pet 3:8-14. Mk 1:1-8.

Introduction

John the Baptist's role was to stage-manage the greatest event of all time – the coming of Christ. He prepared the way by raising expectations. Once Christ had arrived, there only remained for John to disappear gracefully from the scene. For us the message is clear. Make way for Christ and then give way to him.

Giving way (Precursor)

Since the extraordinary events that took place behind the Iron Curtain, there has been growing suspicion that all was not as it appeared. There is mounting evidence to show that these 'spontaneous' revolutions were stage-managed from Moscow by the KGB to replace the hardliners with moderates in these Communist regimes. 'The best-laid schemes of mice and men gang aft a-gley' and, at least in some countries like Czechoslovakia and East Germany, the whole communist party was swept away. In others, notably, Romania and Bulgaria, the party structures remained intact. It raises the question of to what extent we are all manipulated in a media age.

In the West, management of public events has given birth to an enormous public relations industry. No US president would dare leave the White House without the benefit of their expertise. A mini army travels ahead of him, entrusted with the task of stage-managing his reception at the various stop-overs along the presidential route. They organise reception committees, alert the media, smooth out protocol problems, arrange the control of protesters. If need be, they will even hire a flag-waving crowd. Often it is not so much a matter of 'making straight his path' as greasing it.

It is perhaps somewhat unjust to place the Baptist in such dubious company but he does share some similarities with these backroom boys. His role, like theirs, was to prepare an event. Like them too, he sought to ensure a good reception. And there the similarities end. No flag-waving crowd would suffice for John. He demanded nothing less than a change of heart. The party machine proved more than uncooperative. Like the politicians they were, they resented any unaccredited prophet messing around with their constituents. Both church and state were more than a little unnerved at the prospect of the Messiah arriving just then. *Plus ça change!* As Isaiah predicted, his was a voice crying in the wilderness. It was a daunting undertaking but John was equal to it. With enormous moral courage, he castigated the religious hypocrisy of his time. Moral courage exacts a heavy price, then as now. John paid the ultimate price, his life. He gave the lie to those of us who seek to justify our timidity with the plea, 'what is one voice against so many?' He is proof, if proof be needed, that individuals create their own world. We are not playthings of history, formed by the times we live in. We cannot wash our hands so glibly of the world's evils.

Once Christ made his appearance, John's mission was completed. It was his finest moment. Idolised by the people, his name on every lip, he pointed to a stranger on the fringe of the crowd and said: 'This is the lamb of God who takes away the sins of the world.' With that, he slipped gracefully into oblivion. That moment is beautifully immortalised in the Mass, when the priest raises the host and invites the people to receive Christ.

Like the Baptist, our mission in life is to make way for Christ and then give way to him. And there's the rub. We do so like to hog the limelight. There is a teenage daughter who refuses to go to Mass anymore because mother never stops on about it. And mothers are by no means the chief offenders. More miracles of grace are bungled by somebody blundering into another's life at the wrong moment. God does not need our fussiness to implement his will. Like John the Baptist, our role is to point out Christ to others and then leave them free to become acquainted.

Suggested additional Bidding Prayers
We pray
– that we will prepare the way for Christ in the lives of our families and friends.
– that we will not alienate the young by our fussiness.
– that we will know when it is best for us to retire, to make way for others and for Christ.

Catechism of the Catholic Church
523 St John the Baptist is the Lord's immediate precursor or forerunner, sent to prepare his way. 'Prophet of the Most High', John surpasses all the prophets, of whom he is the last. He inaugurates the gospel, already from his mother's womb wel-

comes the coming of Christ, and rejoices in being 'the friend of the bridegroom', whom he points out as 'the Lamb of God, who takes away the sin of the world'. Going before Jesus 'in the spirit and power of Elijah', John bears witness to Christ in his preaching, by his baptism of conversion, and through his martyrdom.

Third Sunday of Advent

Readings: Is 61:1-2, 10-11. 1 Thess 5:16-24. Jn 1:6-8, 19-28.

Introduction

Paul urges the Thessalonians to be happy always. The problem is to know how. The world is full of experts on happiness and also of unhappy people. Paul offers his own blueprint – prayer, gratitude and a generous response to the Holy Spirit.

Best wishes (Happiness)

Happy Christmas! At this time of the year these are probably the two most used words in all languages. We may already have wished some people that; we have certainly written it on our Christmas cards. It would seem that we have almost a complex about it. With so many well-wishers, we are almost obliged to be happy at Christmas. We certainly work hard at it. Spending money we can ill afford, exchanging gifts that rarely satisfy, indulging ourselves to saturation point. 'Christmas comes only once a year', we say, topping up our glass for the umpteenth time. If we cannot be happy, we can certainly be merry! There is a quiet desperation about the whole business. 'How did the Christmas go?' we ask each other, a week later. 'Not bad,' is the invariable reply, scarcely concealing our disappointment.

'Be happy at all times' would seem a very tall order from St Paul, particularly from a man who was at the receiving end of more than his share of the world's nastiness. But he does strike a universal chord. The search for happiness is relentless. Our right to pursue it is enshrined in constitutions. It is the common goal we all share, mystic and addict, hermit and *bon viveur*, saint and sinner. If religion has any claim on our lives, it is because it promises happiness. 'The opium of the people,' Marx dismissed it contemptuously. 'Pie in the sky when you die,' taunted his atheistic followers.

Paul's recipe is deceptively simple. Prayer and gratitude. Pray constantly and for all things give thanks to God. Thousands have taken him literally and dedicated themselves to a life of prayer in monasteries. Buddhists, Hindus, Muslims and others have reached the same conclusion independently. We should not dismiss the witness of so many lives so casually. The ragged army of Marx's followers are re-opening churches to alleviate the misery of half a century of indoctrinated atheism. There is a spiritual famine in the West too. The crowded pubs and the empty church tell their own story. We are drowning our sorrows instead of solving our problems. We have exchanged a good time for true happiness. 'Seek ye first the Kingdom of God.' Prayer gives life its direction and problems their perspective. It gets priorities right and gives what money cannot buy, peace of mind. The dreary stragglers emerging from church in the evening may compare very unfavourably with the gay crowd leaving the pub a few hours later. The reality is certainly the reverse.

We are hugely concerned in the modern world with rights, civil rights for minorities, for racial groups, for women. This concern is the glory of our age. 'We shall overcome,' is our proud new anthem. We might do well to temper our ardour with a little gratitude. We do, after all, have the right to protest. A large part of the world has yet to achieve that. Gratitude is the point from which all protest should begin. If we do not start out grateful for what we have got, we will not end up happy, no matter what we get.

Look at Mary. Think of the young girl with her premature pregnancy, her first delivery in sordid surroundings, her forced flight out of the country with her baby. Think of the woman who spent her life in the obscurity of a backward village, whose only intrusion into the limelight was in middle age to watch her only son executed as a dangerous revolutionary. And read again her Magnificat, today's responsorial psalm.

'God who is mighty has done great things for me.'

Suggested additional Bidding Prayers
We pray
– that we will discover the gift of prayer this Advent.
– that we will learn to be grateful for all God's gifts.
– that our happiness will lead others to Christ.

Catechism of the Catholic Church
2633 When we share in God's saving love, we understand that every need can become the object of petition. Christ, who assumed all things in order to redeem all things, is glorified by what we ask the Father in his name. It is with this confidence that St James and St Paul exhort us to pray at all times.

Fourth Sunday of Advent

Readings 2 Sam 7:1-5, 8-12, 14, 16. Rom 16:25-27. Lk 1:26-38.

Introduction
The greatest revolution of our time is undoubtedly the women's liberation movement. Their right to vote was only conceded in this century. Much still remains to be achieved. Many would consider the church's emphasis on women's traditional role of motherhood and home-minder as hostile to women's rights. Be that as it may, the sins of the church should not be visited on Mary. Her *fiat* could in no way have compromised the rights of her sex.

Solitary boast (Annunciation)
The emancipated Ms of the Western world might well ponder the plight of her veiled sisters in the Arab world and wonder why. Or she might reflect upon the vast female labour force of the Dark Continent. The sari-clad Hindu girl may personify the mysteries of the East but there is nothing mysterious about her status in the Indian sub-continent. The 'inscrutable Asians' might divulge little, but there is nothing secret about the traditional roles assigned to their women-folk. The high-flying, fast-driving, loose-living girl is a phenomenon unique to the West. Her liberal world was fashioned out of christendom. It is deeply permeated with its ethos. If women are less discriminated against in this culture than elsewhere, perhaps we should look to the Christian religion for an explanation. Women who have fought long and hard to win a modicum of civil liberties for their sex in the teeth of a hostile church, can hardly be expected to warm to the notion that their emancipation has Christian roots. That battle may be too recent to allow for sober reflection. Nevertheless, it merits investigation.

Mary has played a unique role in civilising Western society.

When men were compelled to honour Mary as the mother of their God, they learned thereby to respect their own mothers, wives, sisters, daughters. The cult of Mary may have suffered at the hands of a patriarchal church, but there is no escaping the implications of the Annunciation. Mary is 'our tainted nature's solitary boast'. The miraculous Madonna, so beloved by the Latins, or the anaemic, willowy, plaster statue that filled so many niches in our childhood, scarcely do justice to the sturdy peasant girl chosen to play such an awesome part in the salvation of humanity. Artists have not often been kind to her, obliterating the glories of her womanhood out of an exaggerated reverence for her holiness.

The spare lines drawn by the gospel artist are the only authentic expression we have of her. Our earliest picture comes from Luke and the person outlined there bears little resemblance to the figure that has been foisted on us for centuries. She is not seated in her boudoir deep in contemplation, only to be disturbed by the fluttering of an angel's wings against her latticed window. More likely, she was bent over a washing tub or a cooking pot, like any other teenage girl of her class, when God's message reached her. Fear gripped her at the prospect of an unmarried pregnancy. The only bells that accompanied the first Angelus were bells of alarm. She was deeply disturbed. It could not have been easy for her to accept conception in such exotic terms. It would have been well-nigh impossible for others – even those who loved her most – to accept such an explanation of her pregnancy. Tongues would wag in Nazareth. Her engagement to Joseph seemed certain to be broken. It was a frightening prospect for a girl still in her teens. The loneliest part of all was that there was nobody to whom she could confide her terrible secret. Then, as later, she was left alone to ponder all these things in her heart. For all his fine words, the angel had placed a terrible responsibility on such young shoulders. Her answer to his unprecedented challenge was extraordinarily courageous, a blind leap in the dark: 'Let what you have said be done to me.'

Suggested additional Bidding Prayers
We pray
– that Mary's courage will inspire us to meet the challenges in our Christian lives.
– that we may never dishonour Mary by discriminating against her sex.
– that we will show a special concern for single mothers.

Catechism of the Catholic Church

488 'God sent forth his Son', but to prepare a body for him, he wanted the free cooperation of a creature. For this, from all eternity God chose for the mother of his Son a daughter of Israel, a young Jewish woman of Nazareth in Galilee, 'a virgin betrothed to a man whose name was Joseph, of the house of David; and the virgin's name was Mary'. The Father of mercies willed that the Incarnation should be preceded by assent on the part of the predestined mother, so that just as a woman had a share in the coming of death, so also should a woman contribute to the coming of life.

The Season of Christmas

First Sunday of Lent

Readings: Gen 9:8-15. 1 Pet 3:18-22. Mk 1:12-15.

Introduction

All the great religions have desert roots. God is more easily experienced in the desert than anywhere else. For us, Lent should be a sojourn in the desert where, stripped of our usual preoccupations, we can better discover God and re-evaluate life's blandishments.

Children of the desert (Inner Life)

Some years ago I went on a pilgrimage to the Holy Land. For two weeks I followed with the other pilgrims in the footsteps of Christ. We visited Bethlehem, Nazareth and Jerusalem. We climbed the Mount of Beatitudes and Mount Tabor where he was transfigured. I swam in the Sea of Galilee and even in the Dead Sea (which was not a very pleasant experience). I walked from Jerusalem to Jericho, looked into Jacob's Well, stood on the site in Cana where Jesus changed the water into wine and climbed Calvary where he was crucified. Everywhere we went, we took our gospel with us and read the appropriate passage. It was a moving experience. I still have vivid memories of it all. But the strongest impression I have retained is that of the desert where Christ spent forty days before starting his public life. Of the two weeks, we spent a day and a night in the desert.

It is not surprising that the three great world religions, Judaism, Christianity and Islam, were all born in the desert. It was through the desert that Moses led the Israelites from slavery in Egypt to the Promised Land. It was from that desert that John the Baptist came to herald the Messiah and soon after Jesus followed to proclaim himself Messiah. After my visit there, I came to realise the significance of the desert. The desert is a purgatory man must pass through to reach paradise. What is impressive about the desert is its sheer aridness. There is no vegetation, no bird life and, apart from the odd tiny lizard, almost no animals. The silence is almost total. In that bleak landscape, nothing comes between man and his God. One either discovers God or succumbs to despair. It is no wonder that those Bedouins who ply the salt trade following their caravans across the desert are deeply religious. No life thrives here except the inner life. It is not surprising that it was the Desert Fathers who created that great institution dedicated to fostering the inner life, Western monasticism. It has so profoundly marked Christianity that we are all now, in a sense, children of the desert.

Living now as many of us do, in built-up areas, piled high on top of each other in high-rise apartments, bombarded day and night with the roar of city traffic and the blare of electronic music, we are in danger of losing our desert roots. And with that our inner life. We need to create a time and a space to nurture our spiritual lives. Lent is such a time. The Spirit drove Jesus out into the wilderness and he remained there for forty days. Like Jesus, we should let the Holy Spirit lead us out into the desert this Lent where we can confront the devils that haunt our lives, and like him too, triumph over them.

Suggested additional Bidding Prayers
We pray
– that the Spirit may lead us out to a desert this Lent where we will encounter God.
– that God will help us to triumph over the devils that plague our lives.
– that this Lent will be an opportunity to nurture our inner lives.

Catechism of the Catholic Church
538 The gospels speak of a time of solitude for Jesus in the desert immediately after his baptism by John. Driven by the Spirit into the desert, Jesus remained there for forty days without eating; he lives among wild beasts, and angels minister to him. At the end of this time Satan tempts him three times, seeking to compromise his filial attitude toward God. Jesus rebuffs these attacks, which recapitulate the temptations of Adam in Paradise and of Israel in the desert, and the devil leaves him 'until an opportune time'.

Second Sunday of Lent

Readings: Gen 22:1-2, 9-13, 15-1. Rom 8:31-34. Mk 9:2-10.

Introduction
Lent is a time for making sacrifices. Few of us like Abraham will be asked to sacrifice an only son. We have lesser Isaacs in

our lives – those obsessions which dominate our lives and distance us from God. Now is the time to identify them and, if necessary, be prepared to sacrifice them.

Off the drink (Making Sacrifices)

The Chernobyl nuclear disaster in Russia will be long remembered. The number of its victims continues to grow. Hundreds have already paid with their lives, many of whom struggled heroically to control the radiation. One of these was a Russian helicopter-pilot, sent in to extinguish the smouldering giant, bombarding it with sand. It was David against Goliath. The radiation was intense at that closeness, and from his exposure the pilot inevitably contracted leukemia. To save his life a bone marrow transplant was urgently needed. A worldwide appeal was launched for a donor. Hospitals were contacted. Their computers were scanned and their records scoured in an effort to locate a suitable donor. The name of a French woman was found. She was approached. She agreed to donate bone marrow anonymously. It was now a race against the clock. She was operated on in France. A plane stood by to fly the bone marrow to the United States where the Russian pilot had been flown for his life-saving operation. In spite of a successful operation the pilot died shortly afterwards, from lung failure. The woman's sacrifice seemed to have been all for nothing.

Sacrifices, such as hers, cannot be measured in human terms. Even the pilot's heroic efforts probably contributed little or nothing towards stopping the spread of the deadly radiation. Sacrifice, like prayer, is an end in itself. True, there are parents who make huge sacrifices for the welfare of their children. The net results in human terms may not amount to much but there is no denying the efficacy of their sacrifice. Sacrifices never fail. In the world of the human spirit they are mountain peaks conquered on our pilgrimage towards God.

Lent is the season traditionally proposed by the church for making sacrifices. As children, we were trained to give up sweets or sugar in our tea. The more stalwart among us graduated as adults into 'going off the drink' or cigarettes. It is no longer *á la mode*. Some suggested it was anti-social and inhibitive. It made us irritable. Others thought it more practical to make a contribution to the Third World. That is to confuse charity with sacrifice. Christ already gave his answer to Judas on that: The poor you have always with you.

If there was anything wrong with our old Lenten sacrifices, it was probably that we set our sights too low. We were not made of the stuff of Abraham. We were not prepared to 'sacrifice our Isaacs'. We all have our 'Isaacs'. It is the only child we are not prepared to sacrifice. It may be as little as an office perk, a special project, a status symbol or a seat on the board. Whatever it is, we have inflated its importance in our life. We clutch on to it as if our lives depended on it. It is what gives us our ulcers and steals our night's sleep. It makes our homes tense and our work intolerable. It poisons our relationships. It makes for us some very dubious friends and very certain enemies. If we are to follow Abraham up the mountain this Lent, we must be prepared to sacrifice this Isaac. Only then will the Lord say to us as he said to Abraham: 'Because you have done this, because you have not refused me your son, your only son, I will shower blessings on you.

Suggested additional Bidding Prayers
We pray
– that God will give us the strength to make sacrifices this Lent.
– that God will help us to identify the vice that most corrupts us.
– that God will give us the grace to triumph over that vice.

Catechism of the Catholic Church
1438 The seasons and days of penance in the course of the liturgical year (Lent, and each Friday in the memory of the death of the Lord) are intense moments of the church's penitential practice. These times are particularly appropriate for spiritual exercises, penitential liturgies, pilgrimages as signs of penance, voluntary self-denial such as fasting and almsgiving, and fraternal sharing (charitable and missionary works).

Third Sunday of Lent

Readings: Ex 20:1-17. 1 Cor 1:22-25. Jn 2:13-25.

Introduction
God gave Moses the commandments, all of them couched in the negative 'Thou shalt not!' All spiritual progress begins with our readiness to say 'No!' Lent is above all the season for self-denial.

No smoking (Commandments)
Modern life is becoming more and more cluttered with No-

signs. *No smoking* is spreading like a rash out of control. It has invaded even our neighbour's car. He too has his problem with the proliferation of *No Parking* areas all over our towns and cities. *No overtaking* always seems to pop up just when we get stuck behind a slow-moving juggernaut. For all its idyllic appearance, the countryside is just as forbidding with its thriving crop of prohibitions. *No Trespassing* is growing abundantly all over the land and there is a fair yield of *No Fishing* and *No Shooting* in the remoter scenic regions. *No Dumping* is to be found here too but it does well in all types of terrain. The back-packing hiker will not have to venture very far before encountering his first *No Camping*. The prosecution-bearing species is also much in evidence.

The *Don'ts* (sometimes called the *Do Nots*) are another member of the same family. *Don't Walk on the Grass* is a favourite in city parks. *Don't Cycle on the Pavements* thrives on asphalt or cement. They are available in two varieties, the plain and the *Please*. We are familiar with the Don'ts from childhood. They were the very first prohibitions we were taught to recognise, almost from infancy. *Don't Cry, Don't Wake the Baby, Don't Cross the Road, Don't Talk to Strangers* were mother's favourites. School was a whole world of them. They were the backbone of our educational system. Teacher had a whole bagful, graded for every occasion. Some were simple admonitions like *Don't be Late* or *Don't be Long*. Others were more menacing like *Don't be Smart* or *Don't be so Stupid*. Each day we were showered with them. When we emerged from the school system as young adults, we were ready to face the world and its *Don'ts*. Since then life has fluctuated from an official reprimand *Don't Rock the boat* to a wifely pat, *Don't Worry*.

That nowadays much maligned negative has had a long and distinguished history in religion. (*Thou Shalt Not* was the biblical rendering of *Don't*). Adam's education, like ours, began with a Godly *Thou Shalt Not*. We still live with the consequences of his failure. When Moses came down from the smoke-wrapped Mt Sinai, he brought with him two tablets of stone, on which were carved ten *Thou Shalt Nots*. Since then, the Ten Commandments have formed the basis of every legal system in the civilised world. Many a fine and lofty declaration has been made since then, such as the English Magna Carta, the American Constitution and the French Rights of Man. They have all drawn their inspiration from the Decalogue, filling in the small print of its bold prohibitions. The *Don'ts* of the Decalogue have evolved into a charter of human rights.

Christ drove the money makers out of the Temple with 'Don't turn my Father's house into a den of thieves.' Those today who flaunt his commandments and frequent his church do the same. They too will earn his lash.

Suggested additional Bidding Prayers
We pray
– that we may learn to say No to sin.
– that we may reject the temptations we encounter in our daily lives.
– that we may nurture within us a spirit of self denial.

Catechism of the Catholic Church
2072 Since they express man's fundamental duties towards God and towards his neighbour, the Ten Commandments reveal, in their primordial content, grave obligations. They are fundamentally immutable, and they oblige always and everywhere. No one can dispense from them. The Ten Commandments are engraved by God in the human heart.

Fourth Sunday of Lent

Readings: 2 Chron 36:14-16, 19-23. Eph 2:4-10. Jn 3: 14-21.

Introduction
Lent commemorates the exile of the Chosen People, so poignantly evoked in today's Responsorial Psalm. Our lives on earth are a period of exile, through which we must pass to reach the Promised Land.

'Valley of tears' (Exile)
'By the rivers of Babylon
there we sat and wept,
remembering Zion.'
Like the Jews, the Irish too throughout their history have had their share of remembering and weeping. Even today, they can be found clustering together on the banks of the Hudson, the Thames, the Mersey, the Seine and the Rhine. History and geography have combined to forge a nation of exiles, a race of nomads. Down through the centuries the O's and the Mac's have continued to spread in waves across the world. Like the Jews

too, they brought with them their harps and their songs. The can be found today in Irish pubs in foreign cities, singing their songs and drowning their sorrows. The bright lights and the gay life of a modern metropolis do little to disguise their longing for home. Their music, like today's Psalm, reeks of nostalgia for the 'oul sod'. There is a 'Come back to Erin' motif in all their songs. And it was always thus. 'There is a grey eye that looks back on Ireland,' Columba wrote in Iona in the sixth century. A thousand years later, a Franciscan friar, fleeing from religious persecution, re-echoed the theme when he wrote, 'We fill the seas with our tears and the wandering winds with our sighs.'

The earlier Irish gave a spiritual dimension to their exile. The Celtic monks who left their beehive cells and took to the seas in currachs were making the ultimate sacrifice. Their self-imposed exile was 'white martyrdom', a *peregrinatio pro Christo*. They were steeped in the nomadic literature of the Old Testament. There was a literalness in their lifestyle that refused to compromise the Word of God. Spiritual exile for them could only be attained by physical exile.

They had to leave kith and kin to find God. They had to become wandering aliens in faraway places before they could reach the Promised Land.

Lent is a time of exile. It commemorates the exile of the Chosen People. It also serves to remind us that our earthly lives themselves are a form of exile in this 'valley of tears'. We do penance; we accept a certain deprivation. We put ourselves in the shoes of an exile; we share his tears. We put ourselves in the mood, preparing for Easter, the resurrection and the Promised Land.

Suggested additional Bidding Prayers
We pray
– that we will live our lives as a time of exile on our way to the Promised Land.
– that we will cheerfully suffer deprivation for the kingdom of God.
– that we will show a special concern for emigrants everywhere.

Catechism of the Catholic Church
540 Jesus' temptation reveals the way in which the Son of God is Messiah, contrary to the way Satan proposes to him and the way men wish to attribute to him. This is why Christ van-

quished the Tempter for us: 'For we have not a high priest who is unable to sympathise with our weaknesses, but one who in every respect has been tested as we are, yet without sinning.' By the solemn forty days of Lent the church unites herself each year to the mystery of Jesus in the desert.

Fifth Sunday of Lent

Readings: Jer 31:31-34. Heb 5:7-9. Jn 12:20-30.

Introduction

Christ points out to Nicodemus that the grain of wheat must die to yield a rich harvest. Life is a series of dyings and rebirths. Lent is a time of renunciation, of dying to oneself.

A little dying (Renunciation)

He was in his mid-thirties, with a wife and three children and a fourth on the way. He had what was called a cushy number, a good salary, reasonable prospects and pensionable. With any luck, he might someday become a regional manager. After that, who knows? The problem was that he was bored to death with it. Deep down, he believed he should be out on his own. He asked my advice. I told him to go for it. But then advice costs nothing. He had a mortgage on his house, his car belonged to the company and we were in the middle of a huge recession. There was no shortage of *advocati diaboli*, his wife included. In the end, he took the plunge. Now, we meet occasionally and reminisce about those decisive days. He smiles and wonders why he took so long to make up his mind. From the vantage point of a successful company, it is easy to look back and dismiss the agony of indecision, the nail-biting and sleepless nights. But I remember – and so does he – it was a Calvary then.

In the course of an average lifetime, we all die several times. As Oscar Wilde put it:

And he who lives more lives than one,
More deaths than one must die.

The child has to die to become an adult, the single have to die to become married, the old have to die to become retired. Life comprises a series of deaths. As Christ said to Nicodemus: The seed must die. Death is the ultimate renunciation. At all the major milestones in our lives, we cross an abyss without a safety net.

The adolescent flies the nest of home to create its own niche; the newly married plunge into a void to found a family; the old retire from active life to end their days. It was always thus. To be born, we had to die. To die we have to be born. The womb was our first tomb. The tomb will be our last womb. We enter this world crying: we never leave it without a whimper.

Life is a series of dyings. Those who best master the art of living must be well practised in renunciation. We cannot go forward to the new unless we are prepared to renounce the old.

'Anyone who loves his life loses it;
anyone who hates his life in this world
will keep it for eternal life.'

Lent is the season when we are invited to practice renunciation. What we give up then may be small. But it does involve a little dying. These tokens augur well for the greater renunciation the Christian life demands of us.

'Unless a wheat grain falls on the ground and dies it remains only a single grain; but if it dies it yields a rich harvest.'

Suggested additional Bidding Prayers
We pray
– for the grace to renounce what corrupts our lives.
– that we may learn to accept all the traumatic changes life thrusts upon us.
– that by dying to self, we may be born to eternal life.

Catechism of the Catholic Church
1438 The seasons and days of penance in the course of the liturgical year (Lent, and each Friday in memory of the death of the Lord) are intense moments of the church's penitential liturgies, pilgrimages as signs of penance, voluntary self-denial such as fasting and almsgiving, and fraternal sharing (charitable and missionary works).

Passion Sunday   page 44
Easter Sunday   page 47

Second Sunday of Easter

Readings: Acts 4:32-35. 1 Jn 5:1-6. Jn 20:19-31

Introduction

Belief and doubt are natural bed-fellows. Belief thrives in a climate of doubt. Certainty is anathema to faith. By submitting to the test, Christ endorsed Thomas' approach. We should never be afraid to question our faith.

Doubting Thomas (Belief) See also Second Sunday of Easter A

It is commonplace nowadays, should anything extraordinary occur, to call for a public enquiry. Irangate followed Watergate almost as a matter of course. *L'Affair* looms threateningly on the French political calendar. Train crashes, plane crashes, stock market crashes, nuclear disasters, oil-tanker spills, toxic waste disposals, acid rain, industrial pollution – the list is endless – all send newshounds sniffing out the culprit to allay public alarm. Had the events surrounding the crucifixion and resurrection of Jesus Christ taken place in the last decade of the twentieth century, it might well have set the media screaming for a public judicial enquiry. The return to life of the dead would be a stupendous event in any age, and the public would be well justified in demanding that the facts be brought out into the open. It would make a fit subject for a public judicial enquiry!

About Christ's death there could be no doubt. It was a public execution. Besides, it was a brutal, drawn-out business. He was beaten and beaten badly. A lesser man could have died from these injuries alone. He had multiple injuries to his head from a crude thorn-spiked crown battered into position. Weakened by hours of torture and considerable loss of blood, he was forced to carry a backbreaking gibbet over a lengthy distance and up a steep incline. When it appeared that he might give way under the strain, a bystander had to be dragooned into sharing his load. He was fastened to it by driving nails through his hands and feet and was left suspended for some hours. Finally, a spear was driven through his side to remove any possibility of survival. Numerous witnesses could be called and they would all agree. The soldiers who carried out the execution, the women and his mother who remained to the end, Joseph of Arimathea and the others who removed the dead body and placed it in the tomb, all could testify to his certain death.

The resurrection is a different matter, as the enquiry would quickly discover. The witnesses are few and their evidence scarcely bears scrutiny. Prosecuting counsel would have a field day. The women who first circulated the story would be first to take the witness stand. Under cross-examination they would admit that the body was no longer in the tomb. Asked to describe what they saw in the tomb, the prosecution would elicit the information about the angels. The loud titters provoked would oblige the judge to threaten to clear the court-room. Mary Magdalene's evidence could scarcely be more unhelpful. Given a choice, the defence would probably have been well advised not to have called her at all. Lingering eloquently, in the time-honoured fashion, over the details of her unsavoury past, the prosecution would have demolished her as a credible witness, long before she was interrogated as a witness for the resurrection. Her evidence would go from bad to worse when forced to admit that she mistook Jesus for the gardener. How could she possibly have mistaken for somebody else a person as notorious and as striking as Jesus, the prosecution would ask, adding with obvious innuendo, a person whom she claimed to have known intimately.

Peter's turn would come next, to be followed by John. Here the prosecution could change tactics, choosing to rely on a psychiatric report on the two men, to discredit them as witnesses. Both had been deeply traumatised by the events of the last few days. They had gone into hiding, huddling in fear in a small room, awaiting the policeman's knock as the witch-hunt inevitably turned to rounding up the followers. In these circumstances they were ready to accept any old wives' tales as they obviously did when the women duly reported. The empty tomb had more rational and obvious explanations than what they proposed.

Finally, the two disciples who claimed to have encountered Jesus on the road to Emmaus would be called. Under cross-examination, they would be forced to admit that after several hours spent in his company, they had failed to recognise him, until they spotted some vaguely familiar gesture when this 'stranger' broke bread.

The case for the prosecution is by now almost wrapped up as Thomas, the final witness, is sworn in. Quietly, he recounts how he had stubbornly refused to believe any of the reports that Jesus was risen. The judge begins to listen with renewed interests in a now hushed court-room. At last, a cool level-headed witness. Thomas held out against the mounting pressure of his associates who believed, as he saw it, what they wanted to believe. He could accept only tangible proof, nothing less than touching the wounds of the risen Jesus. There is a gasp in the court-room when he informs them that, a week later, he did just that. In the end, it all came down to Thomas' evidence. As a result the enquiry was forced to bring in an inconclusive verdict.

For two thousand years, Thomas has got a bad press. In fact, the derogatory expression 'doubting Thomas' is now common currency in most languages. Thomas is long overdue a reappraisal. That his demand for proof was not inordinate is twice underlined in today's gospel. Firstly, Christ himself submitted to the conditions laid down by Thomas and secondly, the event was recorded – when so many others were not – 'so that you may believe that Jesus is the Christ, the Son of God.' We who believe today are indebted in no small part to the tenacity of Thomas.

Suggested additional Bidding Prayers
We pray
– that we may believe in the risen Christ, in spite of our doubts.
– that we may continue to probe the mysteries of religion in search of new insights.
– that we may never fear to submit our religion to intellectual enquiry.

Catechism of the Catholic Church
644 Even when faced with the reality of the risen Jesus the disciples are still doubtful ... St Matthew relates that during the risen Lord's last appearance in Galilee 'some doubted.' Therefore the hypothesis that the resurrection was produced by the apostles' faith (or credulity) will not hold up. On the contrary their faith in the resurrection was born, under the action of divine grace, from their direct experience of the reality of the risen Jesus.

Third Sunday of Easter

Readings: Acts 3:13-15, 17-19. Jn 2:1-5. Lk 24:35-48.

Introduction
Our age has been described as the 'death-of-God'. If that is true, it underlies our failure as witnesses. We proclaim, 'Christ

has died, Christ is risen, Christ will come again.' Our lives, like those of Peter and the first disciples, should bear witness to it.

God is dead (Witness)

There is a very clever cartoon film. It shows an unprepossessing type, an ordinary Joe, walking down the street with an aerosol paint can. He comes to a wall and begins to spray. The camera zooms in to capture his contribution. On the wall he has traced:

God is Dead.
Bill.

While still focused on the wall, Bill, the little cartoon character, moves out of shot, obviously in search of another wall to autograph. Suddenly, there is a flash of lightning, followed by a prolonged roll of thunder. The wall begins to shake. The camera zooms out and shows the earth shaking. The wall begins to crack and tumble down. The scene continues for several moments. When the earthquake finally subsides, the camera zooms in again. There is very little of the wall left. A few blocks remain standing, miraculously, those containing Bill's cryptic message. But two blocks have been disturbed. The camera zooms in further to frame the message, which now reads:

Bill is Dead.
God.

The age we are living in has sometimes been described as 'the death-of-God' age. Different periods in history have been given different names. The period when the great cathedrals like Notre Dame were built is sometimes described as 'The age of faith.' By comparison, God in our time has become a very minor figure in many people's lives and hence the expression 'God is dead'. There are very few plausible explanations of why this should have happened. God figures less in our everyday lives than in those of a Parisian of the twelfth or thirteenth century. The huge advances of science and technology in recent times have made us less and less dependent on God. Sickness and disease were the great scourges of the Middle Ages and for the medieval there was no medicine worth talking about. The sick had nowhere to turn to for a cure except to God. People believed in and looked for miracles. Now, people go to their local G.P. in search of such miracles. Their hope and belief is centred on his medical powers and they are less and less dependent on God. In this sense, God is, in fact, for many, dead.

But God is not and cannot be dead. As Pontius Pilate discovered on that momentous Easter, there is no tomb large enough or strong enough to hold God. Jesus Christ broke out of his tomb and even if this century and our age wishes to bury God a second time, it is not going to succeed. Every time he is buried, he rises again. Since the eighteenth century, generations of writers and philosophers have confidently predicted the demise of religion and yet it continues if not to thrive, at least to survive. It is now more alive than ever.

For forty or fifty years, people have placed tremendous faith in technology. But now the world is threatened with an AIDS epidemic and medicine is suddenly powerless. The God we seek is not in modern medicine. Its limitations drive us back to the God of the gospels, Jesus Christ. In any event, science will never produce what everybody really wants, happiness. There is no evidence to show that the higher our standard of living becomes the happier we are. Suicide rates continue to soar, particularly and tragically among the young. Terrorism has assumed draconian proportions. Science has conferred awesome powers of death and destruction on the single individual. A single human being with a bomb in his hand in a large modern airliner can hold the world up to ransom. The great superpowers with all their sophisticated weaponry are powerless against the taking of hostages.

If God is dead or dying or not so prominent in the world we live in, it is due to the failure of our witness to him. Somebody once said that 'the tragedy of Christianity is not that it has failed but that it has never been tried.' An exaggeration, no doubt, but there is a large element of truth in it. Every Sunday we repeat 'Christ has died, Christ is risen, Christ will come again.' It trips lightly off our lips on Sundays. It is something else altogether to go out and live it for the rest of the week, to live our belief. The key word in today's readings, used by Peter and Christ, is 'witness'. Its Greek original is 'martyr'. The witness demanded of the early Christians often involved giving their lives. We are not called to die for what we believe but we are called to live it. Christ rose from the dead on that first Easter Sunday, and 'to that fact', like Peter, 'we are the witnesses'.

Suggested additional Bidding Prayers
We pray
– that we may boldly proclaim the truth of Easter in our lives.

– that our witness will lead others to the risen Christ.
– that we may never lose hope in God's healing power.

Catechism of the Catholic Church

2044 The fidelity of the baptised is a primordial condition for the proclamation of the gospel and for the church's mission in the world. In order that the message of salvation can show the power of its truth and radiance before men, it must be authenticated by the witness of the life of Christians. 'The witness of a Christian life and good works done in a supernatural spirit have great power to draw men to the faith and to God.'

Fourth Sunday of Easter

Readings: Acts 4:8-12. 1 Jn 3:1-2. Jn 10:11-18.

Introduction

For too long we have restricted the notion of a 'practising Catholic' to those who attend Sunday Mass. Practice, for a Christian, is a much more all-embracing concept. It is the quality of the service they provide in their daily lives.

Hirelings (Service)

Some years ago I went to the Holy Land with a group of French pilgrims as I was living in Paris at that time. One of my friends there was a Palestinian Arab from the West Bank. He was a *persona non grata* in Palestine and could not return. When he heard I was going there, he asked me to look up his family. I telephoned his family from my hotel in Jerusalem and told them that I knew their son in Paris. They were thrilled to hear from me and insisted on driving in to Jerusalem to meet me and bring me to their home where they had a sumptuous meal prepared. My friend's brother-in-law, who took me in charge, was a Muslim priest and the Prodigal Son hardly fared better than I did on that occasion. After a marvellous day, he drove me back to my hotel and just before taking his leave, he asked me not to hesitate to ask him if there was anything special I wished to do while I was in Palestine. And he added: 'You have come to us from our brother in Paris and while you are here, you are our brother.' I mentioned that I would like to purchase some leather goods in the Arab Souks in Jerusalem and would appreciate his advice.

He immediately offered to bring me on my shopping trip. In one of the Arab bazaars, I found something which took my fancy and, as was the custom, as I thought, I began to bargain with the proprietor. He was a dour, unbending person. He quoted a price and, to my astonishment and in spite of all my efforts, he refused to budge from it. I even pretended to leave but he remained unmoved. In the end I did leave without purchasing. *Mea culpa!* We all have our prejudices. Mine are *á la Shakespeare*. I turned to my Muslim friend and remarked: 'That merchant must be a Jew?' 'No,' he replied, 'he is a Christian.'

Two criteria are sometimes invoked in assessing Christians. Most often, attendance at Sunday Mass: much less frequently, the quality of service in our lives during the rest of the week. Most people are now employed in what is called the service industry: teachers, doctors, nurses, etc., etc. As was the case of that Christian Arab, it is not always easy to recognise those in the service who are Christians. Practising Christians who serve others should be recognisable as such. Christian service differs from ordinary service. Others give service because they are paid to do so. We do so for that reason too but, more importantly, because we are followers of Christ. Our service is measured not by the amount of money people are willing to pay for it but by their need. Otherwise, we could be described in the terms of today's gospel as 'hirelings', hired people. We give what we are paid for and nothing more.

People's needs do not carry price-tags: their problems cannot be scheduled. Sickness does not have office hours: pain is not nine-to-five. How often have we returned bruised and hurt because people would not take the care and the time to understand our need? There are those who glory in the title of civil servants who are neither civil nor servants. Everybody has experience of queuing up for hours in government offices to fill up lengthy forms. For those with little education, it is a daunting experience: for illiterates, it is a nightmare. Those of us who work in such offices should be particularly sensitive to their needs. Otherwise we are mere hirelings instead of good shepherds.

The level of practice of our religion should be judged by the quality of the service we give others. People should be able to say to us that we are Christian traders, Christian secretaries, Christian teachers, Christian doctors etc. For as Peter says in today's reading: 'For of all the names in the world given to men, this is the only one by which we can be saved.'

Suggested additional Bidding Prayers
We pray
– that we will be sensitive to the needs of others in our community.
– that others will recognise us as Christians by the quality of our service.
– for all those who work in the service industries, that they may see Christ in those they serve.

Catechism of the Catholic Church
754 The church is, accordingly, a sheepfold, the sole and necessary gateway to which is Christ. It is also the flock of which God himself foretold that he would be the shepherd, and whose sheep, even though governed by human shepherds, are unfailingly nourished and led by Christ himself, the Good Shepherd and Prince of Shepherds, who gave his life for his sheep.

Fifth Sunday of Easter

Readings: Acts 9:6-31. 1 Jn 3:18-24. Jn 15:1-8.

Introduction
Too often we are content to accept the minimal demands that membership of a church demands. It may seem a lot in a world where many are turning in their membership cards. Today's readings make it clear that we are called to be disciples of Christ, not mere members of his church.

False prophets (Discipleship)
Most critics suggest that the brilliance of Oscar Wilde's plays was only surpassed by that of his conversation. He was a superb *raconteur* whose conversational offerings were heavily laced with irony. He had a penchant for parables, recounting them in the style of the gospel narrative. He is reputed to have recounted the following:

One day, a certain man walked down the street. It was the first hour and the people were not yet assembled in the market place. The man sat down by the wayside and, raising his eyes, he began to gaze up to heaven. And it came to pass that another man who was passing that way, seeing the stranger, he too stopped and raised his eyes to heaven. At the second and third hour, others came and did likewise. Soon word of this wondrous happening spread throughout the countryside and many people left their abodes and came to see this stranger. At the ninth hour, when the day was far spent, there was a great multitude assembled. The stranger lowered his eyes from heaven and stood up. Turning towards the multitude, he said in a loud voice: 'Amen, amen! I say unto you. How easy it is to start a religion!'

To start a religion, as Oscar Wilde so wittily pointed out, may not be difficult, but to insure its survival is quite another matter. People are very gullible. Futurists predict a growth in religious activity in the twenty-first century. For them it forms part of the leisure industry which is expected to expand dramatically. Whether one should greet this prediction with joy or apprehension is a matter for debate. A statistical increase in church membership is a very dubious gain. What counts for Christianity – indeed, what insures its survival – is not external but internal growth. What is required is not more members of the Catholic Church, but better disciples of Jesus Christ.

Membership and discipleship are worlds apart. Christianity has always suffered from a surfeit of members and a shortage of disciples. Humans are social animals and crave to be associated. In a world grown cold and depersonalised the churches offer a comfortable ambiance of friendship and security. Often the gospel is diluted to accommodate the prejudices and lifestyle of the parishioners. Few preached fearlessly enough, like St Paul, to risk their livings, let alone their lives. The radical Christ is transformed into a benign bishop and the collection plate registers members' approval. Too many withered branches remain unpruned.

St John tries gently to prod us into discipleship. 'My children, our love is not to be just words or mere talk, but something real and active.' You won't meet Christ in your Sunday liturgy, if you haven't rubbed shoulders with him in the office, in the factory or in the kitchen. You won't hear his message from the altar, if you were deaf to his call at your office desk. Jesus put it simply and bluntly: 'It is to the glory of my Father that you should bear much fruit and then you will be my disciples.'

Suggested additional Bidding Prayers
We pray
– that we will become true disciples of Jesus Christ.
– that we will never dilute the gospel by the quality of our lives.
– that we may become fruit-bearing branches of the True Vine.

Catechism of the Catholic Church

425 The transmission of the Christian faith consists primarily in proclaiming Jesus Christ in order to lead others to faith in him. From the beginning, the first disciples burned with the desire to proclaim Christ: 'We cannot but speak of what we have seen and heard.' And they invite people of every era to enter into the joy of their communion with Christ.

Sixth Sunday of Easter

Readings: Acts 10:25-26, 34-35, 44-48. 1 Jn 4:7-10. Jn 15:9-17.

Introduction

Love, in the words of the poet, is a many-splendoured thing. In the modern world, it is a much hackneyed term and bears little or no relation to the Christian commandment. It is never pleasurable. Its price is always pain.

Kind thoughts (Love) See also Fifth Easter C and Fourth Sunday C

People who have worked with handicapped children are agreed that it is a very rewarding experience. It seldom appears so to outsiders. I was once involved in preparing a class of handicapped children for their First Communion. One can never be sure whether these little ones are ready for the sacrament. It is sometimes so difficult to know what they think, what they understand. There was as usual great excitement as the big day approached, not only among the children themselves, but also among their parents and teachers. Excitement can provoke adverse reactions in a mentally retarded child. One could sense a certain tension among the adults as we prepared to celebrate Mass in the gaily decorated classroom. Then the moment of Communion arrived. Their teacher stood beside each child as they were led in turn to the altar. The excitement proved too much for one child who became difficult. It was a little girl and she refused to open her mouth. Finally, her teacher persuaded her. I placed the sacred host in her mouth. Suddenly, the child spat it out again. Before I could react to this extremely embarrassing situation, the teacher stooped down, retrieved the host and swallowed it herself.

This incident has etched itself on my memory as a perfect example of love, Christian love. Christ's commandment to love one another can seem so easy and so attractive. In modern times the word love has been monopolised by the romantic novel and TV soap-opera. It is glamourised. The word may be spelled the same; the reality is utterly different. Christian love does not come easy. It is as demanding and as difficult as swallowing what was rejected from another's mouth. Such love belongs to the realm of heroism.

In this media age it is often more comfortable to substitute a certain benevolent altruism. Almost daily, television bombards us with harrowing images of the victims of war and natural disasters. Right in our sitting-rooms we are confronted by the emaciated bodies of children wasting away from famine in Africa, maimed and crippled refugees fleeing war-devastated zones in Asia, shivering families, huddled over the remains of their homes, wrecked by earthquakes or hurricanes. We may even be moved to send a cheque or a postal order to the Red Cross, or Oxfam or the particular disaster fund which is very commendable. This minute contribution from our surplus does contribute something towards alleviating the sufferings of others but far more towards relieving our consciences. It makes us feel good. We are indulging in a sort of charitable voyeurism.

Charity, like sport, is in danger of becoming a spectator interest. Real sportsmen are players, not spectators. Christian love demands more than a distant, even though benevolent, solidarity with the world's huddled masses. Having kind thoughts and feeling sorry for the unfortunate can lull us into a dangerously false sense of spiritual well-being. There is all the difference in the world between a kind thought and a cup of water given with love. It is our nature to feel sorry for others less fortunate than us. It is not in our nature to drag ourselves out of the comfort of our armchairs to reach out a helping hand towards a suffering fellow-being.

'Love one another,' Christ said to the small chosen band of his disciples. Our love seems purest when focused on those most distant. Starving children on the other side of the world will soften the hardest heart. Our children's catechism may have defined our neighbour as 'all mankind' but in the older secular tradition it has always referred to the person next-door. Christ knew what we all learn by experience. So often it is our nearest associate who is the most unloveable.

Suggested additional Bidding Prayers
We pray
– that our charity begin at home, and that we may learn to love the less likeable of our neighbours.
– for those who work with the handicapped, that they will continue to find it rewarding.
– that by living the commandment of love we will bring Christ to others.

Catechism of the Catholic Church
2745 Prayer and Christian life are inseparable, for they concern the same love and the same renunciation, proceeding from love; the same filial and loving conformity with the Father's plan of love; the same transforming union in the Holy Spirit who conforms us more and more to Christ Jesus; the same love for all men, the love with which Jesus has loved us. 'Whatever you ask the Father in my name, he (will) give it to you. This I command you, to love one another.'

Seventh Sunday of Easter

Readings: Acts1:15-17, 20-26. 1 Jn 4:11-16. Jn 17:11-19.

Introduction
God plays a more active role in our lives than we give him credit for. Older generations liked to ascribe happenings in their lives to the will of God. Today's gospel suggests that we should trust more in God's providence

Casting lots (Providence) See also Twelfth Sunday A
Any casual breakdown of television programmes anywhere in the world would reveal a sizeable proportion of them devoted to games of chance. One of the more popular ones in France and in the United States and perhaps elsewhere, is a word game called 'The Wheel of Fortune' There is almost no country now without its national lottery with its regular draws on television nationwide. Their astronomical prizes are only dwarfed by their astronomical returns. This enormous expenditure on lottery tickets, particularly in times of recession, would be obscene, were it not in most cases a disguised form of taxation. Faith in God the Father may well be on the wane in the last decade of the

twentieth century but belief in Mother Luck was never more widespread. The wife of President Reagan of the United States revealed that her husband never made any important decision without consulting his stars. The star gazing public were not greatly perturbed by that revelation

From the account given in today's reading of the election of a replacement for Judas, it might seem that there is a certain scriptural precedence for such behaviour. Following Judas' betrayal and subsequent suicide, the apostles felt obliged to choose a successor. After having narrowed down the field to two candidates equally qualified, 'they cast lots' or spun the wheel of fortune. Taking today's reading as a primary historical document describing a major event in the life of the earliest church, I am at a loss to know why this practice was discontinued. It would be laughed out of court had the Archdiocese of Armagh decided to toss a coin between the two candidates reputedly in contention, to fill its See. If it was good enough for choosing a member of the twelve apostles, it should be good enough for choosing anybody, given of course, that the candidates are of equal merit. Perhaps we should go back to the ways of the Coptic Church in Egypt, when the last two names were placed on an altar and the winner was picked out by a child. The practice does in fact enshrine very sound theology. There is a time when God intervenes directly in our lives. What the world ascribes to chance, believers ascribe to providence.

The modern world is obsessed by games of chance and the predictions of astrology precisely because it has lost belief in God. But for a believing Christian, the toss of coin, as in today's reading, simply clears the way for the intervention of God. Look back on your own lives and you will discover there the enormous role that chance has played in making you what you have become. There are myriads of places along the road of life where we could have taken other turnings than those we took, and these in turn leading to countless others. Our paths were dotted with casual encounters, some of which altered the whole course of our lives. An older world, whose faith was more profound and more pervasive than ours, regarded these choices as 'the will of God'. In our time, it has become fashionable to scoff at that expression. We prefer to attribute it to chance or to our stars.

Today's reading from the Acts of the Apostles offers a model for those who wish to place their lives under God's direction. God has given us intelligent enquiring minds and he expects us to use them. Faced with important choices in our lives, we should use the best information available, seek the advice of those who have our best interests at heart and apply the best time honoured criteria. Then we should, like the apostles, pray long and hard about it. If after that there is still more than one choice on offer, you can toss a coin or spin a wheel. Why not? If it doesn't offend God's dignity it should not offend yours. Besides, whatever happens, you will be comforted by the belief that it was God's will. You are here because he created you and guided you. Your role, like that of Matthias, is to be a witness to his resurrection.

Suggested additional Bidding Prayers
We pray
– that we may come to place more trust in God's providence.
– that, through prayer, we will seek God's help in making important decisions in our lives.
– that the many who search the stars for guidance may return in belief to God.

Catechism of the Catholic Church
2748 In this Paschal and sacrificial prayer, everything is recapitulated in Christ: God and the world; the Word and the flesh; eternal life and time; the love that hands itself over and the sin that betrays it; the disciples present and those who will believe in him by their word; humiliation and glory. It is the prayer of unity.

Second Sunday

Readings 1 Sam 3:3-10, 19. 1 Cor 6:13-15, 17-20. Jn 1:35-42.

Introduction

The question of vocations is causing alarm in certain church circles. That there are noticeably fewer answering God's call to the ranks of the clergy and religious is beyond dispute. But, God is not neglectful of his church. We should pray for the enlightenment and imagination to better avail of the many he continues to call to the service of his gospel.

Endangered species (Vocation)

There is great concern in church circles about the crisis of vocations. The average age of the priesthood is rising steadily while the number of those entering the seminary continues to decline. Some speculate that if present trends continue, large areas of the church will be deprived of the services of a priest in the early years of the next millennium. Seminars are held to discuss the crisis. Surveys are commissioned. Reports are drawn up. The situation is found to be even worse than previously predicted. Priests are asked to preach about it. A day is designated as a special day of prayer for vocations. Recruitment is stepped up in the schools. Parents' committees are canvassed for support. The whole crusade is uncomfortably similar to a Save the Polar Bear campaign. The religious is classified as yet another of the planet's endangered species.

The problem about vocations is that the word itself has been high-jacked by the clergy. God calls everyone in some way or other. Even to the active service ministry, there is no evidence to support the view that there are now less vocations. Look at all those young men and women who volunteer to work in the Third World. Humanitarian societies have sprung up everywhere to help the less fortunate and they don't seem to suffer from 'a shortage of vocations'. If some religious congregation, that came into existence in the nineteenth century, is now in crisis, maybe it is because it did not evolve with the times. Some, inevitably, have outlived their usefulness. Vocations were never intended as a means of perpetuating the breed. Religious orders, as elsewhere among God's creatures, must adapt to survive.

There is no shortage of vocations. God does not nod when his creatures are in need. Somebody, like an Eli or a John the Baptist, is needed to mediate God's call. Thus, the boy Samuel was able to respond: 'Speak, Lord, your servant is listening.' Eli had given him an open ear. John the Baptist led Andrew to Christ, and it was through Andrew that his brother, Peter, became a disciple. If, today, God's calls seem to fall on deaf ears, it maybe that those of us who profess to be his disciples do not convincingly relay his message.

Suggest additional Bidding Prayers
We pray
– that the church will use imaginatively all those whom God calls to the service of the gospel.
– that God will attract more volunteers to work in the Third World.
– that those he calls to the priestly ministry will answer his call.

Catechism of the Catholic Church
1694 Incorporated into Christ by Baptism, Christians are 'dead to sin and alive to God in Christ Jesus' and so participate in the life of the Risen Lord. Following Christ and united with him, Christians can strive to be 'imitators of God as beloved children, and walk in love' by conforming their thoughts, words and actions to the 'mind ... which is yours in Christ Jesus', and by following his example.

Third Sunday

Readings: Jn 3:1-5, 10. 1 Cor 7:29-31. Mk 1:14-20.

Introduction
Christ promised Peter and the apostles that he would make them 'fishers of men' when he called them to preach his gospel. His promise remains true for those who preach his word each Sunday.

The few words (Preaching)
The American sociologist, Fr Andrew Greeley, was invited a number of years ago to give the keynote address at a major US conference of religious educators. Working on data from a survey he had carried out in Chicago, he listed the best or most effective religious educators on a scale of one-to-ten. Coming first

– and so far ahead of the other nine that it should hardly be included on the same league table – were Christian parents. In their role as religious educators of their children, mothers and fathers were the undisputed leaders in the field. That came as no surprise to anybody at the conference. One has only to reflect on one's own life, to realise that whatever religion we have, we owe in huge part to our parents and the early training we received at home.

Greeley then moved on to number two. There was a gasp of disbelief in the conference-hall when he announced the findings from his survey. The Parish Priest and his Sunday homily! But Greeley was adamant. That much-maligned Sunday sermon and its little appreciated author were the second most important religious educators.

Preaching has always had a bad press. The word itself is far more commonly used in its derogatory than in its literal sense. Even priests themselves prefer to refer to this part of their ministry as 'saying a few words' rather than 'preaching'. The word 'homily', with its homely ring, has all but replaced 'sermon'. There is a holier-than-thou odour that clings to preaching, which is as offensive to the listener as it is embarrassing to the preacher. Most, like Jonah, are reluctant preachers. Like him, too, they go in obedience to the word of the Lord.

When Christ began to recruit preachers of his gospel, he showed a marked preference for fishermen. It is not without significance. Fishermen are noted for two qualities, patience and hope. The results they achieve are rarely commensurate with the time they put in. But they persevere and they hope. Again and again they launch out into the deep and cast their nets. Simon and Andrew and the sons of Zebedee, James and John, had done their novitiate on the Sea of Galilee. 'Follow me,' Christ said to them, 'and I will make you fishers of men.' They left their boats and their nets for the life of an itinerant preacher. They were called to proclaim the good news, to preach the gospel. The long hours spent catching nothing in the Sea of Galilee would stand them in good stead.

Preaching is like fishing. When the priest casts out his line into a sea of souls on a Sunday morning, he never knows who might nibble at his bait. He has no way of knowing what his yield may be. He will never know what grace-filled words of his touched a soul in need. He can take comfort from Andrew Greeley's survey. It confirms Christ's promise to make him a fisher of men.

Suggested additional Bidding Prayers
We pray
– for preachers of the gospel, that God lend their efforts his grace to touch hearts.
– that God may enlighten preachers to open up the scriptures.
– that we may all find ways to help preachers in this important ministry.

Catechism of the Catholic Church
785 'The holy People of God shares also in Christ's prophetic office', above all in the supernatural sense of faith that belongs to the whole people, lay and clergy, when it 'unfailingly adheres to this faith ... once for all delivered to the saints', and when it deepens its understanding and becomes Christ's witness in the midst of this world.

Fourth Sunday

Readings: Deut 1:15-20. 1 Cor 7:32-35. Mk 1:21-28.

Introduction
Christ's teaching impressed his contemporaries 'because he taught them with authority'. The church, following its Master, must continue to impress the world by the authority of its teaching.

Distilled wisdom (Doctrine)
Sputnik was the first Russian word to become common currency all over the world. That little bleeping satellite, encircling the planet, heralded the arrival of the space age. For communist Russia, it marked a huge propaganda victory. Communism was triumphant. Marxist ideology seemed destined to conquer. A generation later, Russia was to make another contribution to the world's vocabulary, this time twins, *glasnost* and *perestroika*. They were to mark the virtual end of Marxism, one of the most powerful political creeds ever loosed upon the world. For the best part of a century, it held sway over half the world. Its adherents could be found from one end of the globe to the other. It rivalled the great world religions in the fervour and commitment of its believers. It brooked neither doubt nor dissent from its followers. No deviation from its doctrine was permitted. Then an insidious maverick made its appearance in the form of *glasnost*

and began to nibble at the foundations of the Soviet monolith. Suddenly, the whole edifice came tumbling down. Now, its altars are overturned, its priesthood despised, its doctrine reviled and its prophets discredited.

Had the communist leaders opened their Kremlin windows ever so slightly they might have sniffed the winds of change sweeping the modern world. Had their Sputnik trained its camera on Rome while it hovered overhead, they might have found a precedent for their present situation in Vatican II. *Glasnost* is a child of the media age. When the Council Fathers in Rome espoused the policy of transparency, the tremors were felt throughout the Catholic Church. Things would never be the same again. Gone were the old certainties. The catechism with its 'simple straightforward answers' was discarded. The casuistry of the moralists, so reminiscent of the Scribes and Pharisees, was repudiated. The laity came of age. Not all were able to adapt to their new-found freedom. There were casualties. For most, the bedrock of the gospel was enough.

A new church has emerged, pruned back to its gospel roots and guided as always by the Holy Spirit. Those who feared it might have dissolved into a mist of private opinions had not reckoned with the durability of the Master's doctrine. Two thousand years have passed and the church today is enriched with twenty centuries of distilled wisdom. It continues to cherish the insights of thousands of philosophers and theologians, saints and mystics. Christ remains its model, as he was that sabbath day in the synagogue of Capernaum. 'His teaching made a deep impression on them because, unlike the Scribes, he taught them with authority.'

Suggested additional Bidding Prayers

We pray

– that the church will continue to impress the world with the authority of its teaching.

– that the life of the church will bear authentic witness to the teaching of the gospel.

- that Christian teachers will always follow closely the model of their Master.

Catechism of the Catholic Church

888 Bishops, with priests as co-workers, have as their task 'to preach the gospel of God to all men', in keeping with the Lord's

command. They are 'heralds of faith, who draw new disciples to Christ; they are authentic teachers' of the apostolic faith 'endowed with the authority of Christ'.

Fifth Sunday

Readings: Job 7:1-4, 6-7. 1 Cor 9:16-19, 22-23. Mk 1:29-39.

Introduction
Sickness and suffering, especially in the young and innocent, is the mystery which most tries our faith. God is a caring God. Today's gospel invites us to bring our sick and suffering to him.

God's gentry (Sickness) See also 22nd A and 12th C
Eileen is a few months short of her third birthday. Most of her short life on this planet has been spent in hospital. She was born with a serious congenital defect. In fact, had she arrived a mere twelve months earlier she would probably not have survived. Luckily for her, medical technology had just made a breakthrough, which enabled the surgeons to operate on her. So far, she has undergone fifteen major operations, more than most people undergo in a lifetime. And in all likelihood, she has more ahead of her. It is a strange way to pass one's infancy, virtually on a surgeon's table. She has seen little of this world outside the operating room and the intensive care ward. Yet between operations, she is a bright, cheerful little thing, full of energy and chatter for her nurses. Her mother has been through purgatory for over two years, spending days at her bedside, in spite of having two other small children to mind. It does not make it any easier that the young family are in a foreign country and have to cope with a new language and an unfamiliar system. They have good cause to complain, life has treated them so unfairly. Yet far from being angry at what they might have considered an uncaring God, they are immensely grateful for Eileen's survival. They believe – notwithstanding the unquestioned skill of the surgeons – that Eileen's life is an answer to prayer. And they might well be right. Ever since her complicated birth, she has been prayed for by their little expatriate community at their Sunday Mass. There, she has become something of a mascot for a group only slightly older than herself. Each Sunday morning recent bulletins are passed around giving details on her weight, how she is being

fed, intravenously or otherwise, how long she was allowed play in the hospital nursery. It goes without saying, she has carved her own special niche in the prayer of the faithful. Many have gone to see her in hospital, giving her mother a much-needed break.

Nothing more threatens our confidence in a caring God than the sight of a suffering child. The arbitrariness with which sickness chooses its victims points the finger of suspicion at God. But when it numbers a child among them, it stretches our faith to the limit. How could God permit so innocent a creature to suffer so? It is a mystery which does not easily yield its secret to us. We use thought-patterns that often do little credit to our Creator. To describe a fellow-human as 'handicapped' because his physical or mental endowments do not conform to our narrow standard scarcely does justice to God the Father who made us all in his own image. There are no faulty creations, no nodding Creator. An earlier Irish spirituality had a deeper insight when it spoke of such a person as *duine le Dia* (one of God's people). The sick are God's special gentry. Their suffering is crucial to his plan of salvation. God is a caring God, and he gives the sick priority. The gospel leaves us in no doubt about that. 'He cured many who were suffering from disease of one kind or another.' Like Eileen's parents, we should bring our sick to him, 'crowding round his door.' By curing our sick, or at least by helping us to accept their sickness, he will cast out all those devils of doubt and disbelief that possess us.

Suggested additional Bidding Prayers
We pray
– for the sick, that a caring God will lighten their burden.
– for those who tend the sick, that they may bring to their patients Christian compassion.
– that God will heal our sickness and dispel our doubts.

Catechism of the Catholic Church
1501 Illness and suffering have always been among the gravest problems confronted in human life. In illness, man experiences his powerlessness, his limitations and his finitude. Every illness can make us glimpse death.

Sixth Sunday

Readings: Lev 13:1-2, 44-46. 1 Cor 10:31-11:1. Mk 1:40-4.

Introduction

The disease of leprosy is today well on its way to eradication. Yet the world has more lepers than ever, those whom society has marginalised. Following Christ's example, we are invited to 'reach out and touch' those untouchables and rid them of their leprosy.

Untouchables (Marginalised)

He was performing street theatre on a bridge over the Seine in Paris when I spotted him. He was a sight to behold. He was barefoot and wore a long, flowing saffron robe. He carried a staff from which dangled an assortment of objects with nothing in common except the vividness of their colours. In his other hand he held a large bunch of wild flowers. Around his neck hung a carved calf's head. Even without all this exotic gear, he was a striking figure, with his long black hair and thick bushy eyebrows. He entertained the crowd, gesticulating grandly and disclaiming boldly in a language few of them could understand. He was strangely reminiscent of John the Baptist. We were old friends and at a lull in the performance I invited him to join me at one of the outdoor cafes nearby. He laid down his belongings on the pavement while I ordered for both of us. A few minutes later, the waiter returned and informed us that the *patron* requested us to leave. I was dumbfounded. I immediately confronted the *patron*, pointing out that I was a Catholic priest and that my companion was one of Ireland's most prestigious artists. I added for good measure that that year was the bicentenary of the French Revolution when everybody was celebrating *Liberté, Egalité, Fraternité*. I was rewarded for my pains by being promptly told to 'Clear off!' And all this took place in the centre of Paris in 1989!

The world has a deep imbedded passion for categorising people. There is almost no country on earth without its minority. Race, religion, colour, language and a myriad of other traits are used as a basis for discrimination. It could be as little as the clothes you wear as was the case of my companion that day. All societies have their 'untouchables'. We proclaim loftily in our constitutions that 'we cherish all the children of the nation equally'. The reality is a very different story. Despite its much-vaunted liberalism, xenophobia is thriving in the Western world. There is deep-seated resentment of the Turks in Germany, the North Africans in France, the Muslims in Britain and the Puerto Ricans in New York. There is an alarming growth in electoral support for extreme right political parties whose avowed aim is to rid their countries of these 'impure' elements. Protesters of every colour, from the anti-nukes to 'crazy lefties', are subject to close police surveillance. The disease of leprosy is thankfully now well on the way towards complete eradication. Moral leprosy continues to thrive. We fill our pavements with a tattered mass of misfits, rejects and outcasts, those society has ostracised and disclaims responsibility for. We lump them together as the 'marginalised'.

The leper Christ met was denied association with the rest of society. He was condemned to living apart, ringing his bell and shouting 'Unclean! Unclean!' at the approach of a fellow human. Christ, flaunting all the laws and conventions of his society, stretched out his hand and touched him. His touch was contagious. The leper was cured. Christ's example invites us to do the same. We must reach out and touch the 'untouchables'. Only we can cure them. Only we can lift their contagion, because it was us who made them contagious.

Suggested additional Bidding Prayers
We pray
– for the marginalised, that Christians will welcome them into their communities.
– that we will, like Christ, reach out and touch the neglected ones in our societies.
– that God will cleanse us of the disease of discrimination.

Catechism of the Catholic Church
1947 The equal dignity of human persons requires the effort to reduce excessive social and economic inequalities. It gives urgency to the elimination of sinful inequalities.

Seventh Sunday

Readings: Is 43:18-19, 21-22, 24-25. 2 Cor 1:18-22. Mk 2:1-12.

Introduction

A Christian who takes refuge in nostalgia betrays his call. Our mission is to plough a new furrow, to 'make paths in the wild'. We must be future-orientated, looking forward to the Promised Land.

Good old days (Nostalgia)

Ironically, the more we advance technologically, the more nostalgic we become. We lapse into reminiscing about old times at the drop of a hat, or at least with every encounter with old friends. Nostalgia has proved a rich vein for TV programme makers. Each season has its own crop of revivals of old movies, like 'Gone with the Wind'. New serials are created each year from old classics like 'The Barchester Chronicles' or 'The Forsythe Saga'. Even the recent past has now become part of the 'Good old days'. The Elvis Presley empire continues to be a multi-million dollar industry. Frank Sinatra continues to pull in the crowds on his occasional tours.

Our penchant for looking back has many explanations. For some it is an escape from the drudgery of the present, or more importantly the dreadful uncertainties of the future. Most of us hanker after a lost innocence. Memories of our childhood fill us with warmth. It was the only time in our lives when we felt completely secure. The older we become the more we tend to indulge our nostalgia. There comes a point in everyone's life when there is more to look back on than to look forward to.

Occasionally wallowing in nostalgia is a pardonable lapse. Over-romanticising the past is a dangerous deception. Recalling the good old days 'when sex was dirty and the air was clean' is a gross misrepresentation of reality. Memory is highly selective. We remember the good times and bury the unpleasant. The summers of long ago were not all sunshine. Life in every age prior to ours was 'nasty, brutish and short'. War, disease, and poverty were endemic.

An old Russian proverb says, 'Look at the past and you lose one eye.' It distorts the present. We should respect time-honoured traditions and cherish the distilled wisdom of our ancestors. Mourning over a lost paradise is a dangerous illusion.

Christians look forward with hope towards the Promised Land.
We must strike out with courage. Isaiah expresses it well:

Thus says the Lord:
No need to recall the past,
no need to think about what was done before.
See, I am doing a new deed,
even now it comes to light;
can you not see it?
Yes, I am making a road in the wilderness,
paths in the wild.

Suggested additional Bidding Prayers
We pray
– that we may spend our lives looking forward with hope rather
than looking back with regret.
– for scientists, inventors, researchers, and all those pioneers of
the future.
– that God will guide us as we journey towards the Promised
Land.

Catechism of the Catholic Church
711 'Behold, I am doing a new thing.' Two prophetic lines
were to develop, one leading to the expectation of the Messiah,
the other pointing to the announcement of a new Spirit. They
converge in the small remnant, the people of the poor, who
await in hope the 'consolation of Israel' and 'the redemption of
Jerusalem'.

Eighth Sunday

Readings: Hos 2:16-17, 21-22. 2 Cor 3:1-6. Mk 218-22.

Introduction
We live in times of constant change. Our growth as persons
depends on our ability to cope with change. Christ's reminder is
timely for us: new wine needs new wineskins.

Heritage centres (Change)
Time, we are told, is the measurement of change. On that
computation, we who live in today's world have lived immeas-
urably longer lives than any of our ancestors. People now in

their nineties have seen transport develop from the push bicycle to the space shuttle. Their ancestors from time immemorial could conceive of no other form of transport than what was provided by the horse. The extraordinary changes in transport in our time can be mirrored in all the other facets of our lives. Our homes have become veritable centres of technology by comparison with those of our forefathers. Advances in communication have reduced our planet to a global village. Each day, in our own homes, we watch events taking place in far-away countries with strange sounding names, from Baghdad to Beijing, from Mongolia to Monrovia.

Change is the climate we live in and the greatest problem we have to cope with. We are in large part products of our environment. A constantly changing world makes enormous demands on our ability to adapt. Our growth and survival depends on it. As Cardinal Newman put it, 'To live is to change and to be perfect is to change often.'

Notwithstanding the enormous improvements in the quality of our lives, there is inevitably a debt side. There are casualties. Some will not, or can not, cope with change. All, to a greater or lesser degree, suffer from stress. Stress is often the result of our inability to change. Change is here to stay. The future promises a more accelerated rate of change.

The more we resist change, the more we stifle our growth as persons. Too often religion offers a refuge for the fearful. The growth of fundamentalism in all religions in recent times bears witness to this. The Lefebvrists, the followers of Ayatollah Khomeini and Paisleyism have all something in common. They play on fear, fear of change. Too often, people come to church to seek the certainties of the past. They were never meant to be heritage centres for the local community but power houses to 'renew the face of the earth'. Christ put it bluntly to his fundamentalist critics: 'New wine, new wineskins.'

Suggested additional Bidding Prayers
We pray
– that God will grant us the grace to adapt to the changing times we live in.
– that the Holy Spirit will always help to renew our lives and our faith.
– that those trapped in fundamentalism everywhere will be released from the prison of their past.

Catechism of the Catholic Church
794 Christ provides for our growth: to make us grow towards
him, our head, he provides in his Body, the church, the gifts and
assistance by which we help one another along the way of salvation.

Ninth Sunday

Readings: Deut 5:12-15. 2 Cor 4:6-11. Mk 2:23-3:6

Introduction
Attendance at Sunday Mass continues to decline. It forms
part of the change that modern society is undergoing. There are
no easy solutions. We should not easily discard the time-proven
Christian tradition of the Sunday obligation.

Observing tradition (Sabbath)
It all seems so recent and yet it belongs to a world beyond recall. On Sunday mornings the roads were black with people, all
making their way towards their church or chapel. For many
communities Sunday Mass was the social highlight of their
week. It was a time to dress up, to wear one's 'Sunday best'.
Most people walked, some carrying their shoes until they
neared the church. Others rode bicycles. Those with some pre-
tensions to grandeur came in their ponies and traps. But rain,
hail or shine, everyone came except the bed-ridden and the very
young.

Not to go to Mass was unthinkable then. It was a mortal sin
for which one risked eternal damnation. The Mass was in Latin,
incomprehensible to all. The sermons were long, cliché-ridden
and dull. Many said rosaries or read their prayerbooks while
Mass was going on. Nobody complained. Nobody expected
anything else. For almost everybody, the Mass on Sunday
crowned a week of work regulated by God and the seasons.

When change came it was gradual – some English and the
altar turned round. Many welcomed it. Some had misgivings.
Few were greatly disturbed. There were other changes outside
the chapel walls. Television had arrived, and transistors. Car
sales boomed. Parish boundaries were breached. The church
was no longer the focus of the community. Weekend leisure activities provided serious competition for the Sunday Mass. Big
business had other plans for the Sabbath.

Now, scarcely more than a generation later, there are almost no families without 'conscientious objectors', mostly among the young adults. Despite the best efforts of persuasive parents, the numbers of those refusing to go to Mass continues to rise. Making the Mass more meaningful is a laudable enterprise, but its effect on church attendance will be only marginal.

Our secular week has been shaped by the Jewish Sabbath and the Christian Sunday. It would be a pity to see it now de-sacralised. For the Christian the Mass, or the more aptly-styled Eucharist, is a communal act of gratitude to our creator. It is an obligation which we owe as creatures to our Creator. It never had any other justification in Christian tradition which adopted it from the Mosaic Law.

The Lord says this: 'Observe the Sabbath day and keep it holy, as the Lord your God has commanded you. For six days you shall labour and do all your work, but the seventh day is a sabbath for the Lord your God.'

Suggested additional Bidding Prayers
We pray
– that we will always remain faithful to the Sunday Mass.
– that God the Father will fill our hearts with gratitude for the blessings of creation.
– for those who have lapsed, that they may be once more restored to the practice of their faith.

Catechism of the Catholic Church
2175 Sunday is expressly distinguished from the sabbath which it follows chronologically every week; for Christians its ceremonial observance replaces that of the sabbath. In Christ's Passover, Sunday fulfils the spiritual truth of the Jewish sabbath and announces man's eternal rest in God. For worship under the Law prepared for the mystery of Christ, and what was done there prefigured some aspects of Christ:

'Those who lived according to the old order of things have come to a new hope, no longer keeping the sabbath, but the Lord's Day, in which our life is blessed by him and by his death.'

Tenth Sunday

Readings: Gen 3:9-15. 2 Cor 4:13-5:1. Mk 3:20-35.

Introduction

Evil is too well-documented by our daily papers to be dismissed as an out-of-date religious concept. It thrives precisely because we choose to ignore it. Like the Psalmist, we should recognise our complicity and seek forgiveness.

'Man's inhumanity to man (Evil)

In a celebrated speech, the former President of the US, Ronald Reagan, describe the USSR as the 'empire of evil'. How uncomplicated life would be if evil could be thus geographically confined. It would have all the simple charm of an old Western movie with its classical conflict between the good guys and the bad guys. That the system of government in the Soviet Bloc was corrupt we suspected for a long time. Aleksandr Solzhenitsyn had fleshed out its operation with spine-chilling detail in his *Gulag Archipelago*. Other courageous dissidents such as Vaclav Havel and Andrei Sakharov provided further witness. With the arrival of *glasnost* and the sudden collapse of the Iron Curtain, the full extent of the evil that permeated the system has come to light. But we should not leave this movie – as we did so often in our youth – cheered that the good guys had triumphed once more. And there is little cause for anybody, least of all an American President, to rub his hands gleefully at the demise of communist totalitarianism. Evil is not that easily routed. The serpent raises its ugly head elsewhere. Satan is alive and well, even within view of the White House itself, ravaging the streets of Washington with crack and cocaine.

It is heartening to discover how well the old maxims are vindicated by these extraordinary events. 'Power corrupts and absolute power corrupts absolutely.' No better personification of it could be found than Nicolai Ceausescu in Romania. Tragically for Romanians, his legacy seems destined also to fit the Shakespearean maxim: 'The evil men do lives after them.' His dreaded Securitate and omnipresent spies have left suspicions among neighbours and even within families that may take generations to eradicate. What never ceases to astonish about a Nazi Germany or a Stalinist Russia is how so many people, by all appearance 'simple, decent, ordinary people', can be got to connive at evil. This century alone has provided two lurid examples of it, on a scale hitherto unknown. Fear only partially explains it. Before fear can become a compelling factor there needs to be a general complicity on the part of a considerable section of the population. 'For evil to triumph, it is enough that good men do nothing.' Too many people looked the other way, as too many people everywhere look the other way. Yeats described it well:

The blood-dimmed tide is loosed, and everywhere
The ceremony of innocence is drowned;
The best lack all conviction, while the worst
Are full of passionate intensity.

It has become fashionable in our time to sneer at the doctrine of original sin. The penny catechism informed us that it left us 'prone to evil'. And our daily newspapers confirm it. Four times each day, morning, midday, evening and night, television chronicles in words and pictures 'man's inhumanity to man.' No generation was ever better informed than ours of the effects of original sin. The South American drug cartels, the Italian Mafia, Chinese repression and South African apartheid are only spectacular examples. Ours may be less newsworthy but nonetheless deadly. The Psalmist speaks for all of us.

If you, O Lord, should mark our guilt
Lord, who would survive?
But with you is found forgiveness:
For this we revere you.

Suggested additional Bidding Prayers
We pray
– that we may recognise evil in our society and have the grace to triumph over it.
– for the victims of evil everywhere, that they may be released from its tyranny.
– for forgiveness for the sins we have committed against others.

Catechism of the Catholic Church
401 After that first sin, the world is virtually inundated by sin. There is Cain's murder of his brother Abel and the universal corruption which follows in the wake of sin. Likewise, sin frequently manifests itself in the history of Israel, especially as infidelity to the God of the Covenant and as transgression of the Law of Moses. And even after Christ's atonement, sin raises its head in countless ways among Christians. Scripture and the

church's tradition continually recall the presence and universality of sin in man's history:

'What revelation makes known to us is confirmed by our own experience. For when man looks into his own heart he finds that he is drawn towards what is wrong and sunk in many evils which cannot come from his good creator. Often refusing to acknowledge God as his source, man has also upset the relationship which should link him to his last end; and at the same time he has broken the right order that should reign within himself as well as between himself and other men and all creatures.'

Eleventh Sunday

Readings: Ez 17:22-24. 2 Cor 5:6-10. Mk 4:26-34.

Introduction

Trees figure prominently in the story of salvation. The mustard tree in today's gospel symbolises our growth from a first encounter with the Word of God into a deeply-rooted believing and caring Christian.

'Only God can make a tree' (Growth)

Trees bring the four seasons into the heart of a great city: spring with its brave new foliage, the thick green leafy shade of summer, golden autumn transforming it into a gilded city and snow-covered in winter into a vast iced fairyland. 'Dear old dirty Dublin' has its own special charm, as that expression indicates. However, the warmth of its citizens is not quite matched by the elegance of its streets. But all that may well be changing, as some years ago the city fathers launched a vast scheme for tree-planting. I had an apartment in a southern suburb there shortly after the planting had commenced. Returning from work one evening, I was dismayed to discover that somebody had broken a branch of a tender young sapling just outside my window. The fractured limb, still hanging limply, was not completely severed from the tree. While I looked out my window in anger and dismay, an elderly neighbour emerged from his house carrying bandages, sticking plaster and short lengths of timber. He began to treat the broken limb, gently easing the damaged tendons back into place, binding up the wound, encasing it in solidly bandaged splints to support the fracture. For months I watched to see would the branch grow back again. One day new buds appeared and soon afterwards, my elderly neighbour came back to remove the bandages and splints.

It is surprising how much of the story of our salvation is peopled by these leafy giants. It was in a tree-filled garden that God placed our first parents, with permission to eat the fruit of all except of the tree of knowledge of good and evil. Perversely, they did and were expelled from there in fig-leafed disgrace. Noah and his extended family were saved by God from the waters of the flood in an ark specifically constructed from a gopher tree, and it was with a leaf of an olive tree in its beak that the dove reported the eventual subsidence of the waters. Out of a burning bush, God called Moses to set his people free and lead them to the Promised Land. The prophet Ezekiel proclaims, today as long ago, that God will make 'low trees grow' and the Psalmist assures us that 'the just will flourish like the palm-tree and grow like the cedar of Lebanon.'

But it is above all in the Christ-story of the New Testament that the theme of trees is most frequently invoked. Jesus is called 'the tree of life' and compares himself to the true vine of which we are the branches. Like trees, we are exhorted 'to go forth and bear fruit'. Today, the kingdom of heaven is likened to a mustard tree, whose seed is so tiny, yet matures into a giant. In the end, it was on the tree of the cross that our salvation was won.

Throughout, trees symbolise, as in today's gospel, growth and shelter. In the Middle East where Christianity has its roots, trees represent fertility in that near desert climate. A cluster of trees there forms an oasis with life-giving water. In its shade, nomadic man and beast find shelter from a relentless sun. In more Northern climes, they provide shelter too, from rain and wind. No Irish farmhouse is without its shelter belt. What country cyclist hasn't taken shelter under a tree from that sudden shower, that unpredictable squall? My elderly neighbour was being profoundly Christian when he doctored that injured sapling back to health. It was a sermon of gospel stature! The poet might well have included other preachers in his modesty when he wrote:

Poems are made by fools like me,
But only God can make a tree.

The priest at the altar, with arms outstretched, tree-like, prays for himself and his community that, deeply rooted in the gospels, they will grow into believing and caring Christians, stretching out their arms to offer shelter to the world's homeless.

Suggested additional Bidding Prayers
We pray
– that we may grow into deeply rooted and caring Christians.
– that we, the stewards of creation, may become more conscious and protective of our environment.
– that we may better develop our natural resources to feed the hungry and shelter the homeless.

Catechism of the Catholic Church

794 Christ provides for our growth: to make us grow towards him, our head, he provides in his Body, the church, the gifts and assistance by which we help one another along the way of salvation.

Twelfth Sunday

Readings: Job 3:1, 8-11. 2 Cor 5:14-17. Mk 4:35-41.

Introduction

Our lives are fear-ridden. Christ constantly seeks to dispel the fears of his disciples. We will only dispel our fears by learning to trust him more.

'Do not be afraid' (Fear)

One solitary memory has survived from my earliest childhood. Perhaps it was the trauma that etched it so deeply on my memory. Even some of the finer details linger on. I wore a single-piece knitted suit on that occasion which suggests that I was then no more, and possibly less, than two years old. I was with my mother in a crowded church, probably at Sunday Mass. At some point my mother left me, presumably to go to Communion. As soon as it dawned on me that my mother had abandoned me, I panicked. I bawled uncontrollably, refusing to be smothered into silence by a host of soothing women. Eventually, after what seemed to be an eternity – though it could have been no more than a few minutes – my mother returned. She took me in her arms, and still sobbing convulsively, I was carried out of the church and down to a sweet shop, where, with the help of a lollipop, my tears and fears were finally banished. It was my first experience of abandonment. I still melt with compassion every time I encounter, in a large department store, a crying child looking for its mother.

I have grown up since then but I have not outgrown my fears. In fact, they too have grown with me. We are fear-ridden animals, and most of our fears are self-inflicted. We are afraid of something all of the time and everything some of the time. And so I grow, afraid of the dark and its ghosts, afraid of dogs and their bites, afraid of failure and its punishment. No sooner had I out-distanced one, than I encountered another, even more chilling. The unconscious is inhabited by many-headed monsters with exotic names, who try to waylay us in our stressful moments. Fear stalks through our adult life, showing its fangs in every crisis. We can be haunted by all sorts of spectres, from the irrational to the impossible, from the unexpected to the improbable, from addiction to bankruptcy, from disgrace to dismissal. We are condemned to surviving battles without ever ending the war.

Christ reads us well. 'Do not be afraid!' he told Jairus, who feared his daughter dead. He said the same to Peter when he promised to make him a 'fisher of men', to his disciples as he launched them on their mission. Small wonder that he rounded on them when they disturbed his badly needed sleep during a storm, with the rebuke 'Why are you so frightened? How is it that you have no faith?' 'Do not be afraid,' God's messenger said, when he broke the news to Mary of her awesome pregnancy and when he persuaded Joseph to assume his responsibilities. When the child was born, the shepherds, first to hear the good news, were warned not to be afraid. Christ came to dispel fear as well as darkness. And, when he quit the tomb, the message he left there for his disciples was not to be afraid. Two thousand years later, when panic swept like a forest fire through the United States, a president tried to calm his people with the same message. 'You have nothing to fear,' Roosevelt told them, 'except fear itself.'

Inside each of us, their is a little lost child who is afraid of being abandoned. God does not sleep through our crises. Unlike my mother, he does not leave us, even momentarily.

Suggested additional Bidding Prayers
We pray
– that we learn to put our trust in God and overcome our fears.
– for all those who suffer stress, nervous breakdowns or are discouraged, that God will console them and dispel their fears.
– that Christians will bring to others Christ's words of encouragement.

Thirteenth Sunday

Readings: Wis 1:13-15, 2:23-24. 2 Cor 8:7, 9, 13-15. Mk 5:21-43.

Introduction

Healing forms part of the church's ministry. Many of our wounds are self-inflicted; not all of them are physical. Faith can cure them all, just as surely now as it did an old woman's haemorrhage in today's gospel.

'The hem of his garment' (Healing)

Some years ago, I lived in a presbytery just across the street from a doctor's surgery. The doctor had an excellent reputation and people queued up all day long to consult him. One morning there was an urgent knock on my door. When I opened it, the caller said: 'Come quickly, Father. A man has just dropped dead on the pavement outside.' Grabbing the sacred oils, I rushed out. Sure enough, a man was lying prostrate on the footpath. I anointed him conditionally, as there is a presumed interval between real and apparent death. A small group of people encircled the body. We were only a few yards from the door of the doctor's surgery. I was struck by the cruel irony of it. Had he survived these few extra yards, his life might have been saved by the doctor. As I straightened up, I made this observation aloud to the hushed bystanders. 'You have it all wrong, Father,' a woman replied. 'He was just on his way out from the surgery.' Whatever the doctor's recommendation was, he took it with him to the grave. Doctors, as they say, bury their mistakes.

In today's gospel, the woman with the twelve-year-old haemorrhage had undergone 'long and painful treatment under various doctors', without getting better. Of course, medicine then and up to quite recently, was fairly primitive. For most of history people prayed for real miracles to cure their infirmities. In the Middle Ages, death stalked everywhere, not least in pestilence-ridden cities. War was endemic and hygiene unknown. Town and country swarmed with the deformed, the maimed, the crippled and the blind. Death ran riot throughout Europe during the horrific period of the bubonic plague, aptly called the Black Death. Nothing stood between the individual and his eternity except God. The centre of every church was its shrine containing relics of the saints. People flocked to these shrines in search of cures. Many travelled great distances to Rome, to the

Holy Land, to Compostella, believing, like the woman with the haemorrhage, that it would suffice to touch an important relic to restore them to health. Compostella claimed to have such a relic, no less than the remains of St James, who had watched Christ raise the daughter of Jairus to life. One could hardly come closer to the healing power of Christ than that.

But the world has changed dramatically since then. In our own time cures have been discovered for almost every human ailment. We have all become fervent believers in the 'miracles of modern medicine'. Clinics have replaced churches for the stricken. The few relics that have survived serve as embarrassing reminders of our naïve past. But was it all that naïve? Christ claimed nothing else for these two miracles than the faith of the participants. 'Your faith has restored you to health,' he told the woman who was cured of her haemorrhage. All that separates us from her is the depth of our faith. Even modern medicine, in spite of its extraordinary successes, is rediscovering the importance of the patient's faith in his cure. Who knows? That man who went out the surgery door might not have stepped so abruptly into eternity, had faith in his doctor not faltered. That, like the doctor's prescription, is a secret he took with him.

Christ, now as then, can cure our sicknesses. All he needs is our faith. Of that, Lourdes is proof, if proof were needed. God does trail his coat in our shabby little world. With a little faith we could find it; with a little courage we could touch it. 'Do not be afraid,' he says to us, as he said to Jairus, 'only have faith.'

Suggested additional Bidding Prayers
We pray
– for parents who have lost a child, that God will fill the void in their lives.
– for those who are ill, that faith in Christ will help them recover their health.
– for all Christians, that they may have faith in the healing power of Christ.

Catechism of the Catholic Church
1509 'Heal the sick!' The church has received this charge from the Lord and strives to carry it out by taking care of the sick as well as by accompanying them with her prayer of intercession. She believes in the life-giving presence of Christ, the physician of souls and bodies. This presence is particularly active

through the sacraments, and in an altogether special way through the Eucharist, the bread that gives eternal life and that St Paul suggested is connected with bodily health.

Fourteenth Sunday

Readings: Ez 2:2-5. 2 Cor 12:7-10. Mk 6:1-6.

Introduction

As Christians, we are called to be prophets, like Ezekiel. Like him, we must stand up and speak out against the injustices of our time. We need not expect recognition for our prophecy.

Without honour (Prophecy)

At a certain period in my life, I grew a beard. It has been my constant companion ever since. But in the early days it did not win instant approval. At the time I was a regular contributor to a television series and when my little goatee made its first appearance on the little screen, it drew an angry response from a number of spectators. They claimed to have been former fans of mine but that now they would no longer follow my programmes. It was as if having altered my chin, I had in some way unbalanced my mind. It was strange that people, who surrounded themselves with the bearded images of their God and his disciples, should have found a bearded priest so unacceptable.

Most societies attach an inordinate importance to conformity which can sometimes, as in the case of my beard, reach down to the finer detail of an individual life. Observance of conventions is often rigorously insisted upon and those who step out of line can sometimes be severely ostracised. Beneath the charm of the rural town or village, there often lurks a lethal intolerance. Which helps to explain why the best of its young seem so eager to escape into the anonymity of the city. They are no places for a prophet, as Christ discovered in his home-town, Nazareth. Least of all, for the home-bred one. There, nobody is welcome who seeks to disturb the time honoured conventions. Truth and religion have long since been domesticated into a cosy conformism. Nobody is allowed question the reigning orthodoxy.

They call us aliens, we are told,
Because our wayward visions stray
From that dim banner they unfold.
The dreams of worn-out yesterday. (AE)

Little has changed since the return home of the Nazarene. Prophets still go unrecognised in their own times and in their own homelands. Some, like Martin Luther King and Mahatma Ghandi, had their voices silenced by an assassin's bullet, which conveniently could never be traced further than the manufacturer's tag. Others, like Andrei Sakharov, after a life-time of prison and persecution, die almost within sight of the promised land. Nelson Mandela might live to see it, after spending twenty-seven years in prison. His persecutors could scarcely have served him better. His prison silence resounded throughout the world. Prophets such as these often seem fated to receive the recognition abroad that they are denied at home. And those distant admirers who crown them with accolades, make sure to keep their own radicals on a tight leash. Prophets are uncompromising. Their demands are not negotiable. But their lives are expendable. Christ's hometown rejection foreshadowed his later condemnation and execution.

We are all called, by our baptismal anointing, to be prophets. 'The spirit came into me and made me stand up,' Ezekiel said. We too, like him, should stand up and speak out against the injustices of our time. It matters little whether people listen or not. What is important, as God explained to Ezekiel, is that 'they shall know there is a prophet among them'.

Suggested additional Bidding Prayers
We pray
– that we will have the moral courage to stand up and speak out against injustice in our society.
– for all those who are tortured and imprisoned for having the courage of their convictions.
– that we will always be tolerant of those in our communities who do not conform to our conventions.

Catechism of the Catholic Church
1273 Incorporated into Christ by baptism, the person baptised is configured to Christ. Baptism seals the Christian with the indelible spiritual mark (character) of his belonging to Christ. No sin can erase this mark, even if sin prevents baptism from bearing the fruits of salvation. Given once for all, baptism cannot be repeated.

Fifteenth Sunday

Readings: Amos 7:12-15. Eph 1:3-14. Mk 6:7-13.

Introduction
The virtue of poverty is an embarrassment in the affluent West. Without it, the gospel lacks authenticity. 'Take nothing with you,' Christ charged his first disciples. If we fail to heed his words, Christianity will continue to lose credibility.

A dirty word (Poverty)
Periodically, Irish newspapers publish a list of wills. The name and occupation of the deceased is followed by a figure denoting the value of his estate. Invariably, the editor will choose the priest who figures in the upper bracket, to headline the piece. Scarcely the epitaph Christ would have wished for one of his disciples. In Ireland, for almost two centuries, the priest has occupied a dominant – some might say, a domineering – position in society. As a result, he has come in for a fair share of criticism in literature and the media. James Joyce had many predecessors as well as followers. But traditionally, the people were more indulgent towards the short-comings of their pastors. Those who fell victim to the demon drink were more pitied than censored. Those who succumbed to the charms of the fairer sex were more gossiped about than condemned. The harshest criticism was reserved for the money-grasping priest. In this, the ordinary gut-reaction of the people – their *sensus fidelium* – mirrors accurately the gospel priorities.

Poverty, in the modern world, has almost become a dirty word. We are bombarded almost daily by the media with harrowing accounts of grinding poverty in the Third World. For over a decade, stories of the famine in Ethiopia and the Sudan have reached news saturation-point several times, forcing editors to curtail or withhold coverage for fixed periods. More recently, the Eastern Bloc is competing for attention, with their lengthening food-queues and empty shelves. The First World too has its poverty stories, with statistics showing the growing numbers living below the poverty line in the 'rich man's club'. No great city in the Western world would be complete without its poverty belt where the low or no income sector are confined in their poverty trap. The resulting plague of crime and drugs has obliged governments, in fluctuating bouts of enthusiasm, to declare war on poverty. Poverty, like disease, must be eradicated.

Small wonder if the *virtue* of poverty has become tarnished with the same brush. Unlike our ancestors, we are not given to making distinctions. In the popular mind, the virtue stands indicted like its demographic namesake. Even in economic terms, this is little short of disastrous. The reality will continue to ravage the Third World, as long as the First World fails to practise the virtue. They will remain poor, as long as we fail to share our largesse with them. In certain cases the situation is even worse. Recently, the story broke of an Italian shipping company dumping its cargo of dangerous toxic waste in an underdeveloped African state. Having plundered that continent for centuries to raise our standard of living, we now have the gall to fill its empty belly with our waste.

If the Christian West wishes to continue to preach the gospel in Africa and elsewhere, it badly needs to give a more authentic witness to it. If we wish to establish the kingdom of God on earth, we should remember that Christ began its charter with the words: 'Blessed are the poor in spirit, for theirs is the kingdom of heaven.' When he called his disciples, he made only one demand: That they leave everything to follow him. The only one who refused his call, the rich young man, did so because 'he had many possessions'. As he was sending them out to preach, his very first words, as recounted in today's gospel, were: 'Take nothing with you'. And the priest who left behind him as the fruit of his labours a tidy nest egg, failed spectacularly to carry out his Master's injunction.

Suggested additional Bidding Prayers
We pray
– that by practising poverty Christians may give a more authentic witness to the gospel.
– that Christians will strive to redistribute the riches of the world more equally.
– that we may eradicate poverty in our communities and in the world.

Catechism of the Catholic Church
943 By virtue of their kingly mission, lay people have the power to uproot the rule of sin within themselves and in the world, by their self-denial and holiness of life.

Sixteenth Sunday

Readings: Jer 23:1-6. Eph 2:13-18. Mk 6:30-34.

Introduction

Much of the vitality of the early church derived from its hermit tradition. More than ever, a group-obsessed world must discover a certain solitude if it is to restore its dynamism.

Some lonely place (Solitude)

According to the rag-trade, we come in three sizes: large, medium and small. For some garments, extra large is also available. Whatever our size may be, there is in each of us a little hermit seeking to escape. There are times when we yearn to take ourselves off 'far from the madding crowd'. When that expression was coined, the world was far more leisured and far less noisy than ours. Now, through all our waking hours, we are bombarded by man-made sound, screaming for our attention. We are the first of our race to be warned about dangerous levels of decibels. The walkman epitomises our age. From the solitary jogger in a city park to the country cyclist, all come 'wired for sound'. Be it Beatles or Beethoven, it hardly seems fair to our feathered friends, deprived of their two-legged audience. The new generation, it seems, is ready to face the world only when armed with a set of earphones. Our little hermit is threatened with extinction.

The hermit tradition is as old as religion itself. All the great religions, including our own, were born in the desert. It was out of the desert that John the Baptist came foreshadowing the Messiah. It was out of the same desert that Christ came to preach the kingdom. All during his hectic public life, he kept harking back to his hermit past. The early church, closer to its founder than ours, showed a marked bias for the hermit tradition. It even flourished far removed from its desert home in rain-swept Ireland in the sixth and seventh centuries. Sceilg Mhíchil never fails to intrigue the tourist, baffled how monks survived on that barren rock in the middle of an ocean. Some would see there the cradle of European Christendom. The wave of Irish monks who swept across Europe in the seventh century went first in search of solitude. Theirs was a voyage into the uncharted wilderness of their own being. This, above all, accounts for their extraordinary success as missionaries. The modern church paid its own compliment to the contribution of hermits when it chose St Thérèse, a convent-bound contemplative, as the patroness of the missions.

Those who seek God are more likely to find him in solitude. We cannot expect him to queue up for our favour or to elbow his way into our noise-cluttered lives. The poet had a point when he wrote:

A poor world this, if full of care,

We have no time to stop and stare.

Hermit, the lodger, might well in the end be the one who will save us from our own folly. We should lend him an ear each time he nudges us, because he is trying to tell us what Christ told his apostles:

You must come away to some lonely place all by yourselves and rest for a while.

Suggested additional Bidding Prayers

We pray

– that we may find a time and place in our lives for quiet reflection.

– that contemplative orders in the church will continue to thrive and to nourish the Christian life.

– for those living alone, those in solitary confinement, and for hermits everywhere, that God may fill their solitude.

Catechism of the Catholic Church

920 Without always professing the three evangelical counsels publicly, hermits 'devote their life to the praise of God and salvation of the world through a stricter separation from the world, the silence of solitude and assiduous prayer and penance.'

Seventeenth Sunday

Readings: 2 Kings 4:42-44. Eph 4:1-6. Jn 6:1-15.

Introduction

Miracles do happen. If they are missing in our lives, it may be because we have lost our childish sense of wonder. Today's gospel reminds us that, like the little boy's lunch-bag, God uses our tiniest efforts to work his greatest miracles.

Our little efforts (Miracles)

Progress always carries a price-tag. Chain-saws grind relentlessly through the Amazon rain-forest like a surgeon's scalpel threatening to puncture the planet's lungs. The architectural dinosaurs of the modern city not only scar the sky-line but also dwarf its inhabitants. We are being dangerously out-proportioned by our artificially-created environment. We could be reduced to a race of moral pygmies. One senses a growing feeling of inadequacy in ordinary people. Governments reach deeper into their lives and their pockets to pay for a progress that only too often diminishes them. Many feel that they are no longer in control and, worse still, that they no longer count. They badly need to recover a sense of the miraculous: the belief that though they themselves may not be able to perform miracles, they can contribute powerfully towards making them happen.

Today's miracle should help restore our lost confidence. 'There is a small boy here,' Andrew informed the others. And with this insignificant detail an extraordinary miracle began to take shape. The little lad calls for closer inspection. Presumably, in the manner of little boys, he had wormed his way to the front of the crowd where he caught Andrew's eye. He must have been close enough to overhear Jesus question Philip on the food situation. With all the innocence of a child he proudly displayed to Andrew the contents of his lunch bag – two fish and five barley loaves – and offered to share it. Most adults in a similar situation would have been more circumspect. One could, without exciting too much curiosity, slip momentarily behind a tree or a boulder and tuck in discreetly. Besides, nature has other calls which, like 'time and tide, wait for no man.' Conscience could easily be stilled with Andrew's observation, 'what is that between so many?' The little boy was obviously alone, not part of a family outing. It was an adult gathering, not the sort of place a little boy would choose to spend his day. More likely, he had spent his day fishing in the nearby lake and later came to see what the crowd were up to. And so he arrived with his catch of two fish and the five buns his mother had packed for his lunch.

That evening he would recount it all breathlessly to his mother. 'Imagine, Mother,' he would say, 'with the fish I caught and the buns you baked, Jesus fed five thousand people and there were baskets of it left over.' Mother might, as mothers do, have shaken her head in disbelief and packed him off to bed. But he would never forget as long as he lived that he had contributed to a miracle.

We should not forget either. Overwhelmed as we may be with the might of technological progress, we should always remember that it is with our little efforts that God chooses to make his greatest miracles. God and little boys together make a formidable combination

Suggested additional Bidding Prayers
We pray
– that in this technological world we may rediscover our belief in the miraculous.
– that God will continue to use our little acts of kindness to perform his miracles
– that individuals everywhere will recover confidence in their own efforts and in the power of God to transform the world.

Catechism of the Catholic Church
548 The signs worked by Jesus attest that the Father has sent him. They invite belief in him. To those who turn to him in faith, he grants what they ask. So miracles strengthen faith in the One who does his Father's works; they bear witness that he is the Son of God. But his miracles can also be occasions for 'offence'; they are not intended to satisfy people's curiosity or desire for magic. Despite his evident miracles some people reject Jesus; he is even accused of acting by the power of demons.

Eighteenth Sunday

Readings: Ex 16:2-4, 12-15. Eph 4:17, 20-24. Jn 6:24-35.

Introduction
We have become accustomed to famine-appeals and the plight of huge numbers of the world's hungry. There is another great hunger in the world, rarely alluded to in the mass media – God-hunger. Christ, the Bread of Life, alone can satisfy the famished souls of the world's affluent.

God-hunger (Communion) See also Twentieth Sunday A
History repeats itself. At least, certain historical events, though widely separated in time, often have features strikingly

similar. Historians attribute the proximate cause of the French Revolution to the chronic bread-shortage in Paris. What began as a simple demand for bread later evolved into a full-scale revolution for liberty, equality and fraternity. Two hundred years later, before the last bicentenary toast had been raised in Paris, another world-shaking revolution was in the making on the other side of Europe. The first inkling the West got of trouble brewing in the Soviet empire were the television pictures of lengthening bread queues in Prague and Bucharest and even Moscow itself. With a rapidity that took even seasoned political commentators completely by surprise, bread queues changed to mass rallies, toppling one regime after another. The Soviet regimes, like the *ancien régime*, had ignored the dictum cynically coined by the Romans two thousand years earlier: To keep the people happy, 'give them bread and circuses'.

TV revealed all, especially East Berliners pouring through a leaky Wall to gorge themselves on the bread and honey in the Promised Land on the other side. But the early euphoria was not destined to last. Soon, the more discerning were slipping back through their hole in the Wall, disillusioned at what they found there. The shops were full alright and so were the people. But for those who could see beyond the crass consumerism, there were long lines of soul-famished people. The well-upholstered West Berliner, wrapped in furs and dripping with pearls, was often just as hungry as his gaunt and thinly-clad cousin from the East. It may not be the hunger which provokes revolutions but it is just as lethal to individuals.

There is a great hunger too in the West, a hunger for God and his life-giving Bread. We should be slow to rub our hands in glee and gloat over the demise of atheistic communism. The Christian West is ailing too, less spectacularly, perhaps, but nonetheless alarmingly. With rapidly declining church attendances and fast disappearing priesthood, our needs are urgent. 'I am the bread of life,' Christ warns us as he warned the hungry crowd, 'He who comes to me will never be hungry: he who believes in me will never thirst.'

Suggested additional Bidding Prayers
We pray
– for those who hunger for God in the world, that we may lead them to him.

– for those whose lives are steeped in materialism, that they may rediscover the spiritual.

– for our young who no longer frequent the sacrament of the Eucharist, that they may find their way back to the altar.

Catechism of the Catholic Church

1391 Holy Communion augments our union with Christ. The principal fruit of receiving the Eucharist in Holy Communion is an intimate union with Christ Jesus. Indeed, the Lord said: 'He who eats my flesh and drinks my blood abides in me, and I in him.' Life in Christ has its foundations in the Eucharist banquet: 'As the living Father sent me, and I live because of the Father, so he who eats me will live because of me.'

Nineteenth Sunday

Readings: 1 Kings 19:4-8. Eph 4:30-5:2. Jn 6:41-51.

Introduction

Our world has experienced a dramatic erosion in belief in the after-life. Immortality remains a central tenet of the Christian faith. Christ's solemn message in today's gospel is reassuring, 'Everybody who believes has eternal life.'

Eternal life (Immortality)

In the early seventies I was invited to take part in a televised debate. The subject was the last things. A professional TV presenter acted as chairman, your humble servant was the invited expert and the audience of university students was live, articulate and irreverent. The other audience – the programme was going out at prime time – was conservative Ireland, clerical and lay, still frozen in its pre-Vatican II mould. I was caught in the eye of the storm. For forty minutes I battled heroically to defend the traditional wickets of heaven, hell and purgatory with what I thought was moderate success. Others thought differently, including my bishop who wrote expressing his disappointment that I 'had not stuck to the simple catechism answers'. With my ego bruised and my clerical prospects diminished, if not blighted, I was bloodied for a future that would hold few certainties.

Twenty years later it continues to run true to form. 'Eat, drink and be merry, for tomorrow you die.' So the jingle has it and so an increasing number of people believe. Recent polls show a surprising percentage of church-going Christians who do not believe there is a life after death. A survey of Irish university students carried out in 1987/88 shows that while 72% go to church weekly, only 59% believe in the after-life. One can trace this erosion of belief in the after life from the middle of the twentieth century. Limbo was the first casualty. The huge improvement in the infant mortality rate had much to do with that. For the better part of a thousand years, the Augustinian theory consoled countless numbers of mothers grieving the loss of their little unbaptised ones. Hell fell victim to its own lurid imagery. Nothing is more ephemeral than an image. Those who live by imagery will perish by imagery. Only 28% of those surveyed say they believe in hell. Hell's little brother crematorium, purgatory, was condemned to oblivion, and that despite the fact that a whopping 68% of the Irish students surveyed still believe in sin. Not surprisingly, heaven, albeit denuded of its winged and harmonious choirs, lingers on. The same survey shows that 56% continue to believe in it. A pleasure-bent age is loath to part with its Disneyland in the sky.

We cannot go on thus, nibbling at our faith with impunity. If some day the whole edifice of belief comes tumbling round our ears, maybe we have dislodged one brick too many. Christ warns us as he warned the Jews:

It is written in the prophets:
They will all be taught by God,
and to hear the teaching of the father
and to learn from it,
is to come to me ...
I tell you most solemnly, everybody who believes has eternal life.

Suggested additional Bidding Prayers
We pray
– that we will find in the gospel the words of eternal life.
– that we will find in the Eucharist the promise of eternal life.
– that we well live our lives here on earth in the shadow of eternity.

Catechism of the Catholic Church
1026 By his death and resurrection, Jesus Christ has 'opened'

heaven to us. The life of the blessed consists in the full and perfect possession of the fruits of the redemption accomplished by Christ. He makes partners in his heavenly glorification those who have believed in him and remained faithful to his will. Heaven is the blessed community of all who are perfectly incorporated into Christ.

Twentieth Sunday

Readings: Prov 9:1-6. Eph 5:15-20. Jn 6:51-58.

Introduction

As creatures, our attitude towards our creator is one of gratitude. The Mass is an act of thanksgiving. If we wish our young to continue to go to Mass, we should teach them above all to be grateful.

Vive moi! (Gratitude)

Two things intrigue me about grafitti-artists: when do they scribble on walls, and why? To judge by the sheer output of their work in a city like Paris, where there is hardly a single building which has escaped their attention, it must require the services of a veritable army of aerosol artists. On the thirty-kilometre train route from Charles de Gaulle airport to Gare du Nord every foot of the railway sidings in both directions is adorned. Even the trains themselves have not been overlooked. Yet nobody has ever seen one of them in action. More intriguing still is why they ply their art so liberally. Exhibitionism, whether in children or in adults, is almost always the expression of the need for attention. In the old days, when the art was in its infancy, messages were easily decipherable when schoolboys initialled their boredom on wooden desks and young lovers their love on trees. Adult contributions invariably took the form of crude political slogans. From its primitive days the art form now appears to have entered its abstract or illiterate phase. Their indecipherable scribblings defy my best efforts to interpret. Perhaps it is a reaction to the banalities of modern advertising. Be that as it may, one thing is sure: they are still screaming at passers-by for attention. And those that are legible almost invariably articulate a grievance or a grudge.

The Irish writer, Seán Ó Faoláin, must have found the solitary exception, which he later chose as the title of his autobiography. It read simply: *Vive moi!* (Hurrah for me!) That scribbler was a person after the Psalmist's own heart.

> I will bless the Lord at all times,
> his praise always on my lips;
> in the Lord my soul shall make its boast.
> The humble shall hear and be glad.

This is the sort of psalm St Paul urged the Ephesians to sing: 'and go on singing and chanting to the Lord in your hearts, so that always and everywhere you are giving thanks to God who is our Father in the name of our Lord Jesus Christ.'

Probably, the oldest and most authentic name given to the Mass throughout its history is the Eucharist. It derives from the Greek verb 'to give thanks' which in turn derived from Christ's gesture at the Last Supper as he took the bread and wine 'and when he had given thanks' he gave to his disciples. Hence, the Eucharistic Prayer always begins with, 'Let us give thanks to the Lord our God/It is right to give him thanks and praise.' It is a pity when the young ask their elders why they should attend Sunday Mass, we don't give them the simple truthful answer. They go to thank the Lord for their existence. The young may be careless but they are not ungrateful. Christ himself at the Last Supper was, as a good practising Jew, celebrating the feast of the Passover. Writing on the wall has a longer and more hallowed history than we generally credit it with. It was through the sprinkling of the blood of lambs on the walls of their houses that God chose to liberate the Jews from slavery. Their Passover and our Mass were born out of gratitude for our redemption.

Suggested additional Bidding Prayers

We pray
– that we will always be grateful for the gifts God has given us.
– that we will always express our gratitude by fidelity to the Sunday Mass.
– for all those who carry a grudge in life, that they may learn to be grateful.

Catechism of the Catholic Church

1328 The inexhaustible richness of this sacrament is expressed in the different names we give it. Each name evokes certain aspects of it. It is called:

Eucharist, because it is an action of thanksgiving to God. The

Greek words *eucharistein* and *eulogein* recall the Jewish blessings that proclaim – especially during a meal – God's works: creation, redemption and sanctification

Twenty-First Sunday

Readings: Josh 24:1-2, 15-18. Eph 5:21-32. Jn 6:60-69.

Introduction

We find some parts of the Christian message consoling; others are less palatable. We tend to tailor the gospel to fit our lifestyle. Christ was prepared to lose his disciples rather than compromise. Our commitment must be total. Like Peter, we have no other option.

'Hard sayings' (Commitment)

There is a programme on French television called *L'Heure de Verité* (The Moment of Truth). The US has a similar one called *Meet the Press*. A politician or prominent public figure is confronted for an hour in front of the cameras by a panel of experts/journalists on the main issues of the day. It is less a quest for truth than a ploy to force the interviewee into making damaging admissions. The public is led to believe that the politician is putting his reputation, if not his career, on the line. The journalists have raked through previous recorded statements of their victim to show his inconsistency and lack of credibility. But politicians have become very adept at deflecting this type of assault, claiming their previous statements are misquoted or taken out of context. For the public it is just another form of spectator sport. They are more interested in the performance of the politician than in the truth. His supporters are as confirmed in their support as his opponents in their opposition while the uncommitted remain more uncommitted than ever. Far from avoiding such confrontations, politicians actually seek them, on the assumption that, at least for them, all publicity is good publicity. What really frightens a politician is the whiff of a ballot-box. For them that is the real moment of truth. Here too they have become adept at confining it to its constitutional time-limit. Motions of censure in the French National Assembly are skilfully stage-managed to ensure the maximum exposure and the greatest suspense with the narrowest of victories for the government. No sitting politician ever wants to stand for election.

If politicians are nothing else, they are fairly representative of those who put them there. Unlike them, we do not have to face a regular scrutiny by public ballot to test our commitment. We can get by with a minimum of private conviction and a maximum of public profession, at least in the matter of religion. Recent surveys indicate that more Catholics in Ireland go to Mass on Sunday than believe in God. Other core-beliefs of the Christian faith fared even worse, some yielding remarkably low percentages. Recent voting patterns on divorce and abortion might well reflect more concern for our public image than our private conviction. In any case there are enough question marks hanging over our religious commitment to cause concern.

Surveys will never adequately reveal the true level of our commitment. Whatever can be gleaned from private conversation suggests a steady rejection of the 'hard sayings' of the gospel. It is symptomatic of our time. Modern people seek to tailor their religion to fit their lifestyle. There are many occasions when Christ could say to us, as he did to his disturbed followers: 'Does this upset you?' He was prepared to lose his followers rather than compromise the truth. 'After this, many of his disciples left him and stopped going with him.' At least they had what is so often singularly lacking in our religious conviction, honesty. And so too had Peter, who presumably did not find Christ's teaching any more palatable than the others. For him as for us, what other alternative have we? 'Lord, to whom shall we go? You have the message of eternal life ...'

Suggested additional Bidding Prayers

We pray
– that we may strengthen our commitment to the gospel and refuse to compromise it.
– that we will always be committed in private to what we profess in public.
– that we will not discredit the gospel in the eyes of the young by our own lack of credibility.

Catechism of the Catholic Church

1336 The first announcement of the Eucharist divided the disciples, just as the announcement of the Passion scandalised them: 'This is a hard saying; who can listen to it?' The Eucharist and the cross are stumbling blocks. It is the same mystery and it never ceases to be an occasion of division. 'Will you also go away?': the Lord's question echoes through the ages, as a loving invitation to discover that only he has 'the words of eternal life' and that to receive in faith the gift of his Eucharist is to receive the Lord himself.

Twenty-Second Sunday

Readings: Deut 4:1-2, 6-8. Jas 1:17-18, 21-22, 27.
Mk 7:1-8, 14-15, 21-23.

Introduction
Nothing better epitomises the Christian life than the little word, 'Help'. Coming to the help of people in need, James describes in today's reading as 'pure unspoilt religion'.

Widows and Orphans (Help)
Some years ago I was travelling on a plane from Paris to Dublin. I was seated beside an eighty-year-old man, who was none other than Seán MacBride, winner of both the Nobel and Lenin Peace Prizes. While we were talking, we were approached by a Pakistani girl in her late teens or early twenties. She was crying and seemed desperately in need of help. French immigration officials had put her on the plane to Dublin from where she had been expelled some hours earlier by Irish Immigration who judged her papers inadequate. Now she was returning to Dublin to face the same ordeal once more. Bureaucracy had turned her into a human yo-yo. MacBride gently questioned her, eliciting all he needed to know and assured her that he would accompany her to the immigration department. He asked me to come along as well. We were shown into a small waiting-room where we were left unattended for at least an hour. Eventually, a young staffer came to inform us that none of the senior people were available and he had no idea when they might be. He asked us to leave the girl with him promising that her case would be dealt with according to the regulations. MacBride refused, stating that he was now her legal counsel. He was a distinguished international lawyer. The young man left us again, presumably to consult with his unavailable seniors. When he re-

turned his attitude had become noticeably more conciliatory. He promised that overnight hotel accommodation would be provided for the girl while a decision was being reached. But MacBride would not be fobbed off by such assurances. He refused to leave the airport unless the girl was officially released into his custody. After much to-ing and fro-ing his demand was finally conceded. At this stage we had been detained almost three hours. The last I saw of them was a little old man, clutching his duty-free, leaving the airport with a tall sari-clad Pakistani girl whom he was taking to his own home.

James would have relished the incident. 'Pure unspoilt religion, in the eyes of God our Father is this,' he declared. 'Coming to the help of orphans and widows when they need it, and keeping oneself uncontaminated by the world.'

Suggested additional Bidding Prayers

We pray

– that we may always come to the help of those in need in our community.

– that officials will be sensitive to the needs of those they encounter and try to solve their problems.

– for widows and orphans and immigrants everywhere, that they may find a Christian welcome in their community.

Catechism of the Catholic Church

2208 The family should live in such a way that its members learn to care and take responsibility for the young, the old, the sick, the handicapped, and the poor. There are many families who are at times incapable of providing this help. It devolves then on other persons, other families and, in a subsidiary way, society to provide for their needs: 'Religion that is pure and undefiled before God and the Father is this: to visit orphans and widows in their affliction, and to keep oneself unstained from the world.'

Twenty-Third Sunday

Readings: Is 35:4-7. Jas 2:1-5. Mk 7:31-37.

Introduction

Nothing is more anathema to the gospel than discrimination. We cannot combine, as James tells us, faith in Jesus Christ with making distinctions between classes of people. We all have blind spots when it comes to our own local community. We should pray that Christ will open our eyes and our minds.

Making distinctions (Discrimination)

Some years ago I was invited to meet an old friend who had returned home after spending some years in South Africa. She was a girl who had been my tennis partner during our teenage years. Since then she had got married and she and her husband went to live in Johannesburg. As with friends who meet again after a lapse of years we spent that evening in her parents' home reminiscing about old times. The conversation eventually turned to South Africa and I asked her what was the situation regarding apartheid in that country. Instantly she froze up and what had been a cosy drawing-room atmosphere became noticeably tense. Her voice hardened as she informed me that people in Europe did not understand the real situation in South Africa and, in particular, that they did not realise that blacks were not 'fully human'. I was taken completely aback by this sudden outburst. The girl I used to know was generous, outgoing, uncomplicated. She came from exactly the same background as I did. She was even convent educated. And now, after a mere five years in South Africa she had become a white racist. Her parents were obviously embarrassed and I, as much for their sakes as for mine, tried to salvage what was meant to be a pleasant homecoming party by switching the conversation to more innocuous matters.

St James, if he were in my place, would not have put a tooth in it. 'My brothers, do not try to combine faith in Jesus Christ, our glorified Lord, with the making of distinctions between classes of people.' James was far too direct to make a good party-goer.

My silence also stands condemned by today's gospel. 'Ephphatha!' Christ said when he unloosed the tongue of the dumb man and gave him back his speech. 'Ephphatha!' the priest said to me when he touched my lips at baptism so that I would open my mouth to proclaim the gospel of Jesus Christ. On this occasion, as on so many others, I had failed to live up to that promise. And if that odious system of apartheid is now to be dismantled in South Africa, it is largely because a Nelson Mandela had the courage, not only to speak out, but to endure twenty-eight long years in prison rather than be silent.

Apartheid in South Africa makes headlines round the world.

Anti-semitism, when it occasionally rears its ugly head in France or Germany, sends shivers through the body politic. But our own homegrown, backyard variety of discrimination rarely achieves even local notoriety. It is all the more insidious for that. It is the type James had in mind when he wrote his letter. The teapot looking down on the saucepan. Local communities are riddled with it. And if it thrives, as thrive it does, it is because we condone it by our silence. 'Ephphatha! Be opened!' is the shortest prayer Christ used – one Hebrew or two English words. In the world we live in, there is no other prayer which so badly needs an answer.

Suggested additional Bidding Prayers
We pray
– for the victims of discrimination everywhere, that their civil rights and human dignity may be restored.
– that we will rid our own community of all vestiges of discrimination.
– that we will always have the moral courage to speak out against discrimination in our society.

Catechism of the Catholic Church
1935 The equality of men rests essentially on their dignity as persons and the rights that flow from it. Every form of social or cultural discriminations in fundamental personal rights on the grounds of sex, race, colour, social conditions, language or religion, must be curbed and eradicated as incompatible with God's design.

Twenty-Fourth Sunday

Readings: Is 50:5-9. Jas 2:14-18. Mk 8:27-35.

Introduction
Goodness can and does thrive outside religion. Tragically, it may sometimes be lacking in those who profess to be religious. For the gospel to flourish, we must match our profession of faith with good works.

Measuring up (Good Works)
Mary MacCarthy, the distinguished American novelist, wrote a book called *Memories of a Catholic Girlhood*. She had a very trau-

matic childhood. Both her parents died when she was very young, victims of the infamous influenza epidemic of 1918. Mary and her little brothers and sisters were parcelled out among uncles and aunts willing, though by no means eager, to rear them. Family duty was a much admired virtue of the period. As her name indicates, her father's family belonged to the Irish Catholic tradition while her mother's people came from a conventional WASP milieu. Circumstances were to insure that Mary's youth was fairly evenly divided between both sides. She describes her experiences dispassionately, distributing praise and blame even-handedly, though her life with her Catholic relatives was harsh to say the least. With regard to religion she makes an observation seldom enunciated but too often validated by experience: Religion is good only for good people.

If you reach back into your early life and apply that dictum to those who peopled your world then, you will find it provides most often the best explanation of their behaviour. At least, it is so in my case. I can remember some people who played a role in my childhood and teenage years who were good and religious. I can, regrettably, remember many more who were religious but were not good. Those of us over the age of forty, had, like Mary MacCarthy, a surfeit of religion during our formative years. Women, who later abandoned their religion, will continue to cherish from their convent schooldays the memory of one nun whom they loved and admired. Mary MacCarthy did so too. The others were religious, some even scrupulously so but flawed by more than their fair share of human failings. In some cases, it may well have been their concern to be religious that obviated their goodness.

Goodness can and does thrive outside religion. Religion can never thrive without it. James, as usual, hits the nail on the head. 'If one of the brothers or one of the sisters is in need of clothes and has not enough food to live on, and one of you says to them, "I wish you well; keep your self warm, and eat plenty," without giving them these bare necessities of life, then what good is that?' Faith is like that: if good works do not go with it, it is quite dead.

Sometimes, all too rarely, religion finds its match in goodness and the world momentarily rediscovers the grandeur of the gospel. Such was the impact of a Francis of Assisi. Fortunately, our own age has been graced by Abbé Pierre in France and Mother Teresa of Calcutta. Too often in life, as in history, religion shows its heartlessness. It can breed a fanaticism whose cruelty has few equals, like the Spanish Inquisition or the Beirut hostage taking. If some would suggest the world might be better rid of it in all its forms, it is because, as James insists, we do not measure up in our good works.

Suggested additional Bidding Prayers
We pray
– that we will always measure up in our good works to what we profess is our faith.
– that those in the service of the gospel will always bear authentic witness to it in their lives.
- that the church will raise up saints in every age to personify the gospel.

Catechism of the Catholic Church
2447 The works of mercy are charitable actions by which we come to the aid of our neighbour in his spiritual and bodily necessities. Instructing, advising, consoling, comforting, are spiritual works of mercy, as are forgiving and bearing wrongs patiently. The corporal works of mercy consist especially in feeding the hungry, sheltering the homeless, clothing the naked, visiting the sick and imprisoned, and burying the dead. Among all these, giving alms to the poor is one of the chief witnesses to fraternal charity: it is also a work of justice pleasing to God.

Twenty-Fifth Sunday

Readings: Wis 2:12, 17-20. Jas 3:16-4:3. Mk 9:30-37.

Introduction
'Peace be with you,' was Christ's usual greeting. We exchange the sign of peace with our neighbours at each Sunday Mass. We should strive to make it a reality in our homes, in our work-places, in our neighbourhoods.

The front line (Peace)
The World Cup has highlighted a phenomenon which is strangely out of tune with our time. In an age where pacifism has made enormous progress, at least in the western world, soc-

cer hooliganism seems a throw-back to the time of our warring ancestors. Governments are embarrassed, sportsmen horrified, and all right-thinking people aghast, at the scenes of carnage associated with major soccer matches. Sociologists can do little more than express their puzzlement. Far from being spontaneous riots triggered off by a closely disputed game, as once we innocently thought, police have now amassed evidence to show that these bloody encounters are the fruit of careful planning months in advance by rival factions in different cities and countries. A breakdown of the ring-leaders shows a surprising percentage of professionals among them. The bowler-hatted suburbanite making his way to the city, wielding nothing more lethal than his umbrella, may be returning from a weekend binge of soccer hooliganism.

Perhaps the explanation is to be found, ironically, in the very success of pacifism itself. Europe, once the deadly cockpit of international strife, has been without a war now for close on fifty years. Even the military get almost no occasion to practice their martial art. Peace-keeping is hardly an adequate substitute. Faction fights, once a constant feature of fairs and rural contest, have long since disappeared. Martial prowess has been extolled for too long in our history and culture to be quickly or completely erased from human consciousness. Society provides few opportunities for us to express our aggressions. Soccer hooliganism may be part of the price we pay for the absence of war.

Aggressiveness has deep roots in human nature and James typically comes to grips with the real issue. 'Where do these wars and battles between yourselves first start?' The governor of an English jail, devastated by prolonged and violent rioting, startled an urbane and agnostic England by suggesting that the 'explosion of evil' was 'the work of the devil'. James may well agree with the governor, but he couches it in less fundamentalist language. 'Isn't it precisely in the desires fighting inside your own selves? You want something and you haven't got it; so you are prepared to kill. You have an ambition that you cannot satisfy; so you fight to get your own way by force.' He would certainly have agreed with the governor who had proposed prayer as the answer. 'Why you don't have what you want is because you don't pray for it.'

It is significant that Christ's habitual greeting was, 'Peace be with you.' It is not surprising that the Jews, so often victimised by war, should adopt Shalom (Peace) as their greeting. But pious aspirations alone are not enough. Whatever about charity, peace certainly begins at home in our hearts, in our homes, in our work, in our neighbourhoods. Unlikely though it seem, from our domestic quarrels are spawned the world's great conflicts. The real front line is there. There the real peacemaking happens. Failure there will, someday, somewhere, exact a terrible price. Like Humpty-Dumpty, peace once shattered will tax the best efforts of 'all the king's horses and all the King's men' to put it back together again.

Suggested additional Bidding Prayers
We pray
– for peace and harmony among nations.
– for peace and unity in our families, between husbands and wives, parents and children.
– for peace in our communities, between rival factions.

Catechism of the Catholic Church
2305 Earthly peace is the image and fruit of the peace of Christ, the messianic 'Prince of Peace'. By the blood of his Cross, 'in his own person he killed the hostility', he reconciled men with God and made his church the sacrament of the unity of the human race and of its union with God. 'He is our peace.' He has declared: 'Blessed are the peacemakers.'

Twenty-Sixth Sunday

Readings: Num 11:25-29. Jas 5:1-6. Mk 9:38-43, 45, 47-48.

Introduction
The world we live in seems beset with problems, sometimes on an enormous scale. We are quick to complain and we are experts at finding scapegoats. Most of our global problems are man made and we have made our own individual contributions to them. We should accept our responsibility and make the necessary changes in our lifestyles.

Keeping something back (Responsibility)
Rural parishes may have a certain bucolic charm, but they are not always the most exciting places to live, either for the

priest or the parishioners. One such parish was inclined to wallow in its apathy. The parish priest, an elderly man, was left in no doubt about the moribund state of his parish. 'This parish is very dead, Father,' people would frequently remark to him, as he made his daily rounds of the village. The implication always seemed to be that if the bishop could only be persuaded to send them a young curate, bright-eyed and bushy-tailed, the parish could be given a new lease of life. As that species had become almost extinct, the parish priest decided to seek another solution, no less drastic. 'As it is the universal consensus here that this parish is dead,' he informed the people from the altar, 'I propose to hold a funeral for it on Sunday next.' The congregation was flabbergasted. The more charitable among them thought the old man had finally given way to senility. But when they arrived for Mass on the following Sunday, lo and behold, there was a coffin standing before the altar surrounded by six large lighted candles. There was even a large wreath placed at the foot of the coffin bearing the inscription 'From your devoted parishioners.' After the gospel, the parish priest looked at the people and said: 'As is the custom in this parish, I now invite you all to come up and pay your final respects to the mortal remains of this parish.' He then shuffled down from the sanctuary, peered into the coffin – the lid had been removed – and stood there for a few moments, his head bowed. One by one, the people left their seats and approached the coffin, some out of curiosity, others to humour their priest, all of them trying to keep a straight face. Each in their turn, peered into the coffin, winced momentarily and slunk sheepishly back to their seats, avoiding each other's glances. The mortal remains each had seen was his own smug face smirking back at him. The floor of the coffin had been lined with a crystal clear mirror.

We make up the parish, the community, the church, the people of God. 'If only the whole people of the Lord were prophets,' Moses cried out in exasperation. He would find much to exasperate him in our world. Life has become almost a spectator sport for many of us. We complain incessantly as if we were watching bad television. We see ourselves as victims of disasters over which we have no control, victims of inflation, of pollution, of drugs and crime and every other man-made aberration of our time. We invent a legion of PPs to serve as scapegoats. We sit on the fence and grumble about the constant erosion of the 'quality of life', conveniently forgetting that the quality of life is determined by the quality of our lives. You will get no sympathy from James. 'Listen to the wages that you kept back calling out.' We have all kept something back. We must all accept responsibility. If we too look into the coffin of our community we will find our own failures reflected there.

Suggested additional Bidding Prayers
We pray
– that we will accept our share of the responsibility for the problems that beset our world.
– that we will never make scapegoats of others for the shortcomings in our community.
– that we may transform our world by the quality of our lives.

Catechism of the Catholic Church
1914 Participation is achieved first of all by taking charge of the areas for which one assumes personal responsibility: by the care taken for the education of his family, by conscientious work and so forth, man participates in the good of others and of society.

Twenty-Seventh Sunday

Readings: Gen 2:18-24. Heb 2:9-11. Mk 10:2-16.

Introduction
Marriage seems to be more and more under threat in recent times. The oneness of the marriage promise gives way to the otherness of divorce. While it may well begin in love, its successful survival depends on an abiding friendship.

Best friends (Marriage)
He was a well-seasoned journalist in his early sixties when his newspaper assigned him to cover a story in Paris. I got to know him because he occupied a room across the corridor from me. Late one night he tapped on my door and asked if he could come in for a chat. We talked, or rather he talked and I listened. He missed his wife terribly on these trips abroad, he said. Every night before turning in, they had a long chat together sharing with each other the ups and downs of their day. He spoke glowingly of his wife, insisting that on my next trip to Dublin, I

would have to call out to meet her. It was a refreshing experience for me, a cynical celibate over-exposed to the problem-ridden side of marriage. He was undoubtedly one of the others, the lucky ones. His wife had become his best friend.

Falling in love has been compared to catching a cold. Infatuation and that virus do have certain features in common. We succumb to both. We lose our normal equilibrium for a time. Both are by their nature ephemeral. Infatuation has always seemed to me a very fragile foundation for the life-long and all-weather commitment of marriage. Our ancestors may have been more realistic, with their convention of arranged marriages, which might have had a better history were it not for its unscrupulous exploitation of women. Marriages now may always begin with falling in love but they survive on friendship. Infatuation is blind to the other's faults. Friends are not only aware and tolerant of them but more importantly are protective. They seek to shield their partners where they are weak. One's strengths assume the other's weaknesses. Putting up with a spouse's shortcomings is nothing but an exercise in crisis-management. The long suffering wife and the hen-pecked husband are the sad casualties of failed marriages. Both are illustrations of the absence of friendship.

Since that encounter with my journalist acquaintance I have become more observant. I have taken to watching couples in their *troisième* age strolling in Jardin du Luxembourg and often I am struck by the close physical resemblance they bear each other. I don't know whether my observations would stand up to scientific analysis but it is certainly my impression that they have 'become one body'. We come to resemble those we love. (I have also noticed in the same park that those who feed the birds, with the pigeons and robins pecking the crumbs from their palms – a feat I have notoriously failed to achieve – have always bird-like features.) It may simply be a trick played on my eyes by auto suggestion. Whatever the form it may take, marriage is about oneness. 'This is why a man leaves his father and mother and joins himself to his wife, and they become one body.'

Suggested additional Bidding Prayers
We pray
– for husbands and wives, that they may become the best of friends.

– for families, that they may grow in love and oneness.
– for broken families, that God may heal their wounds.

Catechism of the Catholic Church
2335 Each of the two sexes is an image of the power and ten-
derness of God, with equal dignity though in a different way.
The union of man and woman in marriage is a way of imitating
in the flesh the Creator's generosity and fecundity: 'Therefore a
man leaves his father and his mother and cleaves to his wife, and
they become one flesh.' All human generations proceed from
this union.

Twenty-Eighth Sunday

Readings: Wis 7:7-11. Heb 4:12-13. Mk 10:17-30.

Introduction
Wealth, especially large amounts of it, is always the product
of some form of exploitation. It also invariably corrupts. For this
reason, it is incompatible with the gospel. Those of us who dedicate our lives to making money should heed Christ's warning.

Dubious friends (Wealth)
'There was an old man from Nantuket,
Who kept all his cash in a bucket.
But his daughter, called Nan,
Ran away with a man.
And as for the bucket, Nan took it.'
There is nothing better than a limerick to drive home a point.
This particular one encapsulates a cautionary tale. It is an illust-
ration of the bible's more terse expression: 'Money is the root of
all evil.' It has a knack of coming between us and those we love.
The old man's real tragedy was not the loss of his bucket, valuable as that undoubtedly was. It was the loss of his daughter.
Had he loved his daughter as much as he loved his money, he
would probably have lost neither. The evil of wealth is that it
poisons interpersonal relationships. It makes us very dubious
friends and very certain enemies. Polonius was wise to warn his
son: 'Neither a lender nor a borrower be.' It continues to spread
its cancer even after we are gone. The tears of mourning are
scarcely dried when the long knives are out over the division of

the estate. There can hardly be a more tragic end to a lifetime spent raising and providing for a family than to have it break up over the contents of a will. It is a sad and not infrequent illustration of Shakespeare's observation: 'The evil men do lives after them; the good is oft interred with their bones.'

After the euphoria following the collapse of totalitarianism in the Russian empire, a great epidemic of unease is spreading among the inhabitants. Like animals raised in captivity they are apprehensive about life in the wild. Whatever else could be said about communist rule, it did spread its misery with a fairly even hand. Everybody was given the bare necessities. Now in the capitalistic jungle they will have to fight to survive. Life there is based on exploitation. The rich get richer and the poor poorer. The profit-motive is the engine that drives the market-economy. There is vast wealth to be made but only through exploitation.

Christ's steady and loving gaze could not detach the rich young man from his great wealth: all his other good qualities, and they were many, did not qualify him for discipleship. The problem with wealth is that you cannot love God and exploit your neighbour. No matter how cleverly it is disguised in the capitalist world by humanitarian undertakings, it remains exploitation. Christ could hardly have chosen a more telling comparison: 'It is easier for a camel to pass through the eye of a needle than for a rich man to enter the kingdom of God.'

Suggested additional Bidding Prayers
We pray
– that Christians in commercial enterprises may never exploit others.
– that the rich, people and countries, may share their wealth with the less well-off.
– for the people experiencing great changes in their societies, that they may not neglect the poor.

Catechism of the Catholic Church
1940 Solidarity is manifested in the first place by the distribution of goods and remuneration for work. It also presupposes the effort for a more just social order where tensions are better able to be reduced and conflicts more readily settled by negotiation.

Twenty-Ninth Sunday

Readings: Is 53:10-11. Heb 4:14-16. Mk 10:35-45.

Introduction

Authority is often a blatant exercise of power. For the Christian it is a service. Those who have the care of others fail them when they abdicate their authority.

The doctor's orders (Authority)

I was about eight or nine when the incident occurred. My father, who was a school-teacher, was reading the newspaper and I was doing my homework in the sitting room. A woman called to speak to my father. I left the room as she was shown in. Sometime later, I heard the sound of raised voices. The woman was shouting at my father. The angry exchange continued for a few minutes and finally the woman stormed out of the house, banging the front door behind her. I crept back into the sitting room like a frightened little mouse and tried to resume my homework. After a few moments, my father put down his newspaper. 'I suppose you are wondering what that was all about,' he said. He told me that the woman was the mother of a little boy in his school. When my father examined that class at the end of the year he found that the boy could not read or write. If he advanced to a higher class where such a skill was presumed rather than taught, there was every possibility that he would leave school as an illiterate. So my father decided against his promotion. His mother, who loved her son and shared with him the ignominy of this set back, tried to make my father reverse his decision. He refused. 'I had to deny a mother's request in the interests of her own child,' he said.

Though I did not realise it then, it was my first lesson in the exercise of authority. Authority is a service which is seldom appreciated. Parents and teachers are left in little doubt of that when they refuse children what they deem harmful for them. Only doctors enjoy the authority to administer painful medicine and be rewarded with a smile. 'On the doctor's orders' is always accompanied by 'a brave face'. The most others can expect in return for their service is a sullen acquiescence. Those who exercise authority must endure the resentment their decisions provoke. To curry favour would be an abdication of authority. Too often we succumb. 'It's no skin off my nose,' we tell ourselves blandly. Pilate washed his hands rather than face the anger of the Jews. What did one more execution matter? What does one more child gone astray matter? Just another statistic in delinquency. My father could have, to please a mother, allowed one more illiterate to join the world's ignorant masses. Had he done so, he would have been just as responsible for maiming a human life as if he had run down the boy with his motorcar.

A mother could easily have been mistaken then. From her vantage point, as the wife of a poor farm labourer, she probably never experienced authority other than as someone 'lording it over her and making their authority felt'. Authority is so often a blatant exercise of power. Rarely is it seen as a service. There are occasions when we are all called to exercise authority. We would do well to remember Christ's injunction to his disciples: 'This is not to happen among you.'

Suggested additional Bidding Prayers
We pray
– that we may never use our positions of authority to 'Lord it' over others.
– that Christians may always exercise their authority as a service to help others.
– that we will never abdicate our authority over the young and vulnerable.

Catechism of the Catholic Church
2235 Those who exercise authority should do so as a service. 'Whoever would be great among you must be your servant.' The exercise of authority is measured morally in terms of its divine origin, its reasonable nature and its specific object. No one can command or establish what is contrary to the dignity of persons and the natural law.

Thirtieth Sunday

Readings: Jer 3:7-9. Heb 5:1-6. Mk 20:46-52.

Introduction
Blindness comes in many forms. Injustice is one of them. Fanaticism is another. Often we are blind to the needs of others. We, like Bartimaeus, should pray, 'Master, let me see again.'

Opening our eyes (Injustice)

There were many things he was aware of though he had never seen them. He heard words spoken in anger. He felt the pain of them. He could sense the cruelty behind them. But he had never seen the curl of the lip, the glint in the eye, the derangement of the person consumed by hatred. Seeing adds a horror-dimension to what is merely sensed. In time he would learn to recognise with new eyes old acquaintances. He would see and identify faces of anger, hatred, prejudice, injustice, spite. He who was blind would see the blindness of rage, the blinkered eyes of injustice, the distorted vision of prejudice, the microscopic stare of fanaticism. The man in the trench coat with the parcel under his arm, 'You have three minutes to clear the hotel before the gelignite goes off,' he informs the receptionist. What does he see? He sees with a blinding lucidity the sanctity of his own cause. He sees nothing else.

Now he would see men close their eyes. He must have often wondered what kind of man used to pass him by, unseeing, as he sat there begging. He would see him now. No monster really. A fairly ordinary individual, obsessed by his own private world, shut in upon himself, blind to the needs of those around him. He would see people close their eyes to the misfortune of others. Or blindfold themselves with platitudes about idleness and the corruption of the dole. And they couldn't see that these poor wretches yearn for health, not handouts, work not welfare, a little of the light and warmth of a place in the sun out of the long cold shadow of poverty.

He would see others groping desperately to escape their misery, up blind allies of drink, drugs and sex. He would see them seek blindness because they couldn't bear to look at reality. The depths of unhappiness of those who sought temporary relief in blindness. The sad, sordid fun-places of life with the blind drunk on the pavements, the staring protruding eyes of the drug addict on his trip, the averted eyes of two strangers coupling in a brothel.

When Christ opened his eyes it was to the blindness of those who had sight. Their great misfortune and ours too is that we think we see. If only we could admit our blindness and pray that we may see. Our blindness remains only because we haven't the honesty to admit it and the humility to ask for light. 'Lord, that I may see.' It was enough from a blind man. It would be enough from us. Miracles are made from prayers like this.

Suggested additional Bidding Prayers

We pray

– that God may open our eyes to the injustices in our society.

– that God may remove the blindness of our anger, hatred and prejudice.

– for addicts to drugs, alcohol and sex, that God may rescue them from their blind allies.

Catechism of the Catholic Church

1807 Justice is the moral virtue that consists in the constant and firm will to give their due to God and neighbour. Justice toward God is called the 'virtue of religion'. Justice toward men disposes one to respect the rights of each and to establish in human relationships the harmony that promotes equity with regard to persons and to the common good.

Thirty-First Sunday

Readings: Deut 6:2-6. Heb 7:23-28. Mk 12:28-34.

Introduction

Our love of God is measured by our love of our neighbours. The world's huddled masses present no great problem. The real test for us is the less-than-lovable neighbour who lives next door.

Living next door (Neighbours)

An Australian soap opera currently running on television bears the intriguing title *Neighbours*. Tam-ratings indicate it enjoys wide popularity. It traces the life of a small rural community. Each episode seems to revolve round some row or quarrel in the neighbourhood. The same is true of all the other popular TV soap-operas like *Coronation Street, Glenroe* and *Eastenders*. The characters portrayed in these too are all neighbours. Their true-to-life quality obviously accounts for their popularity. The creators of these serials achieve this by focusing on the jealousies and feuds that dominate life in small communities. In this at least, they mirror real life so accurately. The very term 'neighbours' almost always conjures up the memory of some quarrel.

God's very remoteness from us makes him more easily lovable. He doesn't elbow his way into our lives. He isn't always sticking his nose into our business. We do not think of him as an interfering busybody. It is we who come banging on his door when we need his help. Otherwise, he keeps his distance, discreetly and lovingly. The neighbour is so often just the opposite. The old catechism used to define our neighbour as 'all mankind' but it is the one on the other side of the hedge that bothers us. We have no problem with those members of the species on the other side of the planet. If they starve of food or rights in Ethiopia or South Africa, we will show our concern and our generosity. The crux for us with this gospel commandment is the neighbour next-door. That variety comes in many forms, few of them very lovable. The Christian commandment is uncompromising. We must love him as we do ourselves.

In the Our Father, Christ taught us to pray. In it he framed a contract between us and God the Father. The bargain we strike there is no soft option. 'Forgive us our trespasses as we forgive those who trespass against us.' The great trespasser in our lives is on the other side of the fence or perhaps across the street. There is so much to forgive and the score keeps mounting. If God's judgment of us is as harsh as ours is of our neighbour, we are not giving ourselves much of a chance.

Suggested additional Bidding Prayers
We pray
– that we may respect our neighbours and show them Christian love.
– that we might find forgiveness in our hearts for those who have wronged us.
– that we will strive to preserve peace and harmony in our neighbourhoods.

Catechism of the Catholic Church
2196 In response to the question about the first of the commandments, Jesus says: 'The first is, 'Hear, O Israel: The Lord our God, the Lord is one: and you shall love the Lord your God with all your heart, and with all your soul, and with all your mind, and with all your strength.' The second is this, 'You shall love your neighbour as yourself.' There is no other commandment greater than these.

Thirty-Second Sunday

Readings: 1 Kings 17:10-16. Heb 9:24-28. Mk 12:38-44.

Introduction

Generosity was never the prerogative of the rich. The poor are often capable of acts of heroic generosity. When we are recipients of their generosity, we should accept it with humility.

The widow's mite (Generosity)

It was my first parish. Set in the west of Ireland, it comprised a narrow strip of fertile land between the Ox Mountains and the sea. My little bungalow, perched at the foot of the mountain, commanded a breathtaking view of Sligo Bay with Knocknarea crowned with Maeve's Cairn in the background. On a clear day one could see the mountains of Donegal. The parishioners consisted of rich cattle ranchers in the plain. One wife boasted to me that their monthly phone bill came to £500. The rest were poor cotters living on the mountainside. The latter had little more to live on than their spectacular view. Custom dictated that the Curate's Collection was made by a door-to-door visit by the priest to every home in the parish. Nothing in my life or the seminary had prepared me for this humiliating experience. Brought up in a salaried background where even my mother got her weekly house-keeping allowance in the form of a cheque, I was horrified at the prospect of begging my keep. The parish priest left me in no doubt about my duty. Not only was I obliged to make the collection but I was expected to raise it considerably over previous years. Reluctantly, I set out to face mad dogs and their tight-fisted owners. I fared badly in the first village. Door after door remained shut and the owners deaf to my knocking. I was almost on the point of abandoning my quest when I encountered a travelling family in a pony and trap at the crossroads. They had been about two doors ahead of me all the way. I managed to persuade them that if we carved up the day's territory between us we would both probably fare better. After that things started to improve, at least until I began to climb the mountain. Here, there was little to disguise the poverty. A section of the roof of one thatched cottage had caved in the previous winter. It was occupied by a blind man living alone. It is not easy to beg from the poor but this was the limit.

I finished my rounds, giving his hovel a wide berth. Early

next morning when I returned from saying Mass, I found the blind man huddled in my doorway sheltering from the rain. He thrust two crumpled pound notes into my hand. 'I always paid the priest,' he said. Then he turned abruptly and feeling his way with his stick he set out on the five-mile trek up the mountain to his broken-down hovel.

My refusal to knock on his door had taken from him all he had left – his pride. And all because it hurt my pride to accept an offering from a poor man. I had failed spectacularly my first biblical test. I had learned nothing from the prophet Elijah who took the last crumbs out of the mouth of the starving widow and her child. I had missed the whole point of Christ's object lesson to his disciples when he highlighted the widow's offering of a penny. Generosity was never a prerogative of the rich. The unremitting poverty of most of the modern world is proof of that. The blind man's two pounds, like the widow's two coins, were acts of heroic generosity, worthy of humble acclaim, not arrogant rejection.

Suggested additional Bidding Prayers
We pray
– that we will always respect the dignity of the poor.
– that we may come to match the poor in our generosity.
– that our alms-giving will be always humble and anonymous.

Thirty-Third Sunday

Readings: Dan 12:1-3. Heb 10:11-14, 18. Mk 13:24-32.

Introduction
As we approach the end of the church's liturgical year, we are invited to reflect on the end of the world. We are temporary residents in an ephemeral world. Christians are urged to develop a sense of detachment.

Apocalyptic warning (The End of the World)
At an international meeting of scientists in Dublin recently, one of the experts predicted that within 20-30 years Ireland can expect a tropical climate with devastating effects on its agriculture. The Earthwatch conference was told that Ireland will suffer

from increased temperatures, reduced rainfall and that sea levels will rise to cover coastal land. In the neighbouring island, plans are already being discussed to pump water from Scotland to alleviate what is predicted to be the near desert conditions in the South and East of England. All of this will be the result of global warming and what is now referred to as the Greenhouse Effect. The situation is not yet irreversible but threatens to become so unless some form of environmental control is introduced. Chernobyl has left no one in doubt as to what awaits us if we fail. The Iron Curtain lifted, only to reveal what deadly legacy communism had bequeathed to its eastern satellites. *Glasnost* has brought to light a string of Chernobyl-style nuclear plants as deadly as they are unsafe.

The itinerant preacher, predicting the end of the world on a street corner, seemed somewhat ridiculous. His apocalyptic warnings pale into insignificance compared to the dire warnings of the modern environmental expert. That the world is going to end is no longer merely the tenet of a fundamentalist faith. It is a scientific certainty. Whether it be sooner or later is open to debate. For this reason, Christianity has always encouraged its followers to live their lives *sub specie aeternitatis* (in the light of eternity). To live in the shadow of death is not sufficient for the Christian. Revelation encourages a wider-angled perspective. Death can breed a host of fanatics, from the IRA to the Hezbollah, of those seeking instant immortality in this world or in the next. Each age spawns its own crop of martyrs, our own no less than previous ages. The follower of Christ should distance himself from the world and its all-devouring causes. Detachment is the virtue best adapted to reality. The monuments raised in memory of our sacrifices will not for long outlast us. Lenin toppled from his Soviet pedestal is a salutary lesson for all. More sobering still is the near-extermination of the Aral Sea, the fourth largest inland sea in the world, through the folly of his disciples.

We need a sense of perspective, not only to cherish our threatened planet, but also to bolster our detachment from what is after all an ephemeral world. When it does finally end, we should merit Daniel's prophesy:

The learned will shine as brightly as the vault of heaven,
and those who have instructed many in virtue,
as bright as stars for all eternity.

Suggested additional Bidding Prayers
We pray
– that we will live out our lives in the shadow of eternity.
– that we will nurture in ourselves a spirit of detachment from the world and its fanaticisms.
– that we will respect and protect our environment.

Catechism of the Catholic Church
1048 'We know neither the moment of the consummation of the earth and of man, nor the way in which the universe will be transformed. The form of this world, distorted by sin, is passing away, and we are taught that God is preparing a new dwelling and a new earth in which righteousness dwells, in which happiness will fill and surpass all the desires of peace arising in the hearts of men.'

Our Lord Jesus Christ, Universal King   page 137

Year C

First Sunday in Advent C

Readings: Jer 33:14-16. 1 Thess 3:12-4:2. Lk 21:25-28, 34-36.

Introduction

Today is the beginning of Advent when we start our preparation for the coming of our Saviour. As he chose to come
amongst us in the most vulnerable state of a child in his mother's womb, it is fitting that we begin our preparation by reflecting on the most vulnerable in society, 'the least of his brethren'.

The Bruised Reed (Vulnerability)

I remember when I was a child, during the winter particularly
when there was snow, there was often a wounded bird found in
our lawn or garden. I can still recall vividly holding such a little
creature in my hands and feeling its tiny heart pounding furi-
ously against my palms as I carried it into the house. I set it
down gently beside the fire in the kitchen and my mother put a
saucer with some water and breadcrumbs under its beak. But it
stood there, eyes protruding, petrified with terror, ignoring my
mother's offering. It probably didn't help that we children stood
around gazing in fascination at our new-found feathered friend.
The usually raucous atmosphere of the kitchen took on a new
stillness with everybody talking in whispers and tiptoeing
round the fireplace lest we frighten our little visitor. I also remember that when we rushed downstairs the following morning the little bird was dead, its little body lying stiffly on the
hearth and its beak open. The content of the saucer remained untouched. I realise now that it probably died more from fright
than from its injuries.

I think there is something of a parable in this childhood
experience of mine. The world is full of wounded birds, individuals scarred by 'the slings and arrows of outrageous fortune'.
People who need to be treated with great gentleness and sensi-
tivity. All of us have scars of one kind or another. We can all be
easily upset and hurt by even relatively slight setbacks in our
lives. There is a wounded bird in each of us and in spite of our
brave faces and bragging banter, our backs are invariably
labelled 'Fragile: Handle with care'. Strong men cry like babies
when struck by even reversible setbacks like redundancy, bankruptcy or failing to get an expected promotion. Wives have cradled them in their arms and soothed their tears as their mothers

did when they were children wakened by nightmares or beaten by bullies in school playgrounds. We are all vulnerable. Our touchiness seems to grow with the years. Who hasn't been confronted at sometime or other by a friend asking 'What did you mean by that remark?' A totally innocent comment had been misinterpreted, causing pain. And occasionally we have all been victims of similar experiences, fretting for hours over unintended insinuations. We have thin skins that bleed easily.

On this first Sunday of Advent it should comfort us to remember that Christ chose the most vulnerable human state, that of a new-born baby, to begin his mission on earth. That mission has been perfectly described by St Peter: 'He went about doing good.' Those of us who wish to follow him, would do well to begin by becoming more sensitive to others. An awareness of our own vulnerability should sensitise us to the vulnerable spots in others. Above all it should make us more caring and protective of 'the least of Christ's brethren', the most vulnerable in our society.

Suggested additional Bidding Prayers

We pray
– that we may always be sensitive to the most vulnerable in society.
– that we will always defend the right to life of the unborn child.
– that we will prepare ourselves this Advent to welcome the birth of Jesus at Christmas.

Catechism of the Catholic Church

524 When the church celebrates the liturgy of Advent each year, she makes present this ancient expectancy of the Messiah, for by sharing in the long preparation for the Saviour's first coming, the faithful renew their ardent desire for his second coming. By celebrating the precursor's birth and martyrdom, the church unites herself to his desire: 'He must increase, but I must decrease.'

Second Sunday of Advent

Readings: Bar 5:1-9. Phil 1:3-6, 8-11. Lk 3:1-6.

Introduction.

John the Baptist went before Christ to prepare the way for him. He is a fitting model for us as we prepare in Advent for the coming of Christ. Those of us who have the care of children should give them a deep religious sense of the real significance of Christmas

Vox Dei (Discernment)

Probably our first awareness of this world came with the sound of our mothers' voice. We could hear before our eyes were opened. Certainly, the first awareness others had of our arrival was the sound of our crying. It is one of the great clichés of the film world. The good news is always relayed to the anxious father by the sound of a baby crying off-camera. Voices dominated our earliest years, loving, soothing, pleading voices.

Hush! little baby. Do not cry.
Mammy will sing you a lullaby.

Later came sterner voices, commanding, scolding and threatening. But we gave as good as we got with our push-button tantrums. School introduced us to a whole new world of sound, the jingles and nursery rhymes of the classroom and the high-pitched squeals of the playground. As life progressed, more and more voices competed for our attention. Soon we learned to distinguish the familiar from the strange, the friendly from the menacing. Later our antennae would be refined enough to discern voices as nuanced as those of the cynic and the sarcastic and as diverse as those of the sincere and the sycophant.

The second half of this century has experienced an enormous media explosion. The airwaves have become cluttered with myriads of voices clamouring to be heard. The Tower of Babel has come back with a vengeance. It is a far cry from the world of Millet's evocative painting *The Angelus*, depicting peasants in the fields, heads bowed in prayer. It is hard to believe now that the world depicted there is only mid-nineteenth century. God be with the days when the voice of God calling his people to prayer with the ringing of church bells had no greater competition than the occasional town-crier even in cities as large as London, Paris or Rome. But enough of this nostalgia. This brave new world of ours, loud as it may be, is just as much God's marvellous creation as those older quieter worlds, and we should cheerfully echo the words of today's psalm: 'What marvels the Lord worked for us! Indeed we are glad.' His voice sounds just as clear today as it did to Adam in the Garden of Eden or Moses on Mount Sinai. Or the voice of John the Baptist, 'crying in the wilderness', announcing the coming of Christ. The Good Shepherd himself has assured us that we will know his voice and his promise holds good even in these cacophonous times. All great religious experiences begin with hearing a voice. So it was with St Paul on the road to Damascus and St Patrick and 'the voice of the Irish' seeking conversion and Joan of Arc. Such spectacular occurrences would be more likely to guarantee insanity rather than sanctity nowadays. For us the voice of God is relayed more unobtrusively through the quiet promptings of the Holy Spirit.

One of the earliest phonographs was marketed at the beginning of this century with a picture showing a turntable with its winding handle and large trumpet-like earphone. Sitting in front of the earphone was a little dog, ears pointed, listening intently. The caption underneath read: *His Master's Voice*. In this noise-filled world of ours, our greatest concern should be to listen to and follow the voice of our Master.

Suggested additional Bidding Prayers
We pray
– that we will always hear the voice of God in our cacophonous world.
– for the gift of discernment to recognise the voice of God.
– that we will lend our voices to God to pass on his Good News.

Catechism of the Catholic Church
523 St John the Baptist is the Lord's immediate precursor or fore-runner sent to prepare his way. 'Prophet of the Most High', John surpasses all the prophets, of whom he is the last. He inaugurates the gospel, already from his mother's womb welcomes the coming of Christ, and rejoices in being 'the friend of the bridegroom', whom he points out as 'the Lamb of God, who takes away the sin of the world'. Going before Jesus 'in the spirit and power of Elijah', John bears witness to Christ in his preaching, by his baptism of conversion, and through his martyrdom.

Third Sunday of Advent

Readings: Zeph 3:14-18. Phil 4:4-7. Lk 3:10-18

Introduction.

When John the Baptist was asked by the people what they must do to prepare for the coming of the Messiah, he told them to share with those who had nothing. We must do the same if we wish Christ to be born in our lives this Christmas.

'What must we do, then?' (Solidarity)

The life of a preacher is not always easy. He sometimes plays the role of 'prophet without honour'. I have had some small experience of that. Some years ago I gave a talk on Irish television. The subject was unemployment and I took as my theme, John the Baptist's reply to the people who asked him: 'What must we do, then?' John said: 'If anyone has two coats he must share with the man who has none and the one who has something to eat must do the same.' I took the view, which I still hold, that what was true about coats then should be true about jobs now. People holding two or more jobs – and there were and are many such people in Ireland – should be encouraged to relinquish one in the interests of the unemployed. I was astonished at the outcry I caused. Letters were written to the papers and complaints were made to the broadcasting authorities.They suggested to me that I should issue a statement. The latter is called in media circles a 'damage-limitation' exercise. I didn't comply, suggesting instead that they release the full text of my talk. They didn't. It was my last appearance on the programme.

Oddly enough, it was the only time in my life I had quoted a body not generally acclaimed for their radicalism. The Irish Bishops in one of their pastorals stated: 'Men with an already adequate salary or pension, women with comfortable livelihoods and no economic need to work, have surely in present circumstances an obligation not to seek or hold on to jobs at the expense of others, especially younger people who cannot find work.' The circumstances alluded to there have greatly worsened since then. It is no secret that the bulk of work being done by people in the black economy is by people with jobs.

Job-sharing is now firmly established on every government's agenda, at least promoted in theory if not so often operated in practice. People are not so reluctant to share their work but baulk at the prospect of a diminished income. It is not the labour they resent sharing but the fruits thereof.They continue to pay lip-service to the Christian message as long as it does not hurt their pockets. Meanwhile, unemployment grows alarmingly and the gap between the 'haves' and the 'have-nots' continues to widen.

Our global record is even worse. The pittance we give in aid is a paltry restitution for what we pillaged from the Third World to create our thriving economies. 'The goods we possess are theirs, not ours,' St John Chrysostom stated bluntly about the poor, long before the era of colonial conquest. Regarding aid, St Gregory the Great was equally blunt: 'More than performing works of mercy, we are repaying a debt of justice.' About the plight of the poor in the Third World, the modern media have left us with few illusions. To our plaintiff plea, 'But when did we see you hungry?', the terse reply might well be, 'Nightly, on television.'

'What must we do, then?' The answer John the Baptist gave to those who first posed the question is even more relevant for us today. 'Share.' Solidarity with the dispossessed of our own world and the deprived of the Third World is an urgent priority for those who wish to be Christian.

Suggested additional Bidding Prayers
We pray
– that we will show greater solidarity with the poor and the dispossessed in preparation for the coming of Christ.
– that we will allot a greater share of our huge Christmas budgets to charity.
– that we will make greater efforts to create employment in our communities.

Catechism of the Catholic Church
2439 Rich nations have a grave moral responsibility towards those which are unable to ensure the means of their development by themselves or have been prevented from doing so by tragic historical events. It is a duty in solidarity and charity; it is also an obligation in justice if the prosperity of the rich nations has come from resources that have not been paid for fairly.

Fourth Sunday of Advent

Readings: Mic 5:1-4. Heb 10:5-10. Lk 1:39-44.

Introduction

Today's gospel records the Visitation, Mary's visit to her cousin, Elizabeth. It is an apt moment for us to reflect on the position of women in our society.

The Visitation (Women's Liberation)

One of the great revolutions of the modern world was the emancipation of women. Admittedly, it hasn't still achieved complete equality between the sexes. Women's rights are better recognised in the statute books than in reality. But there has been extraordinary progress in a relatively short period. Women were only given the vote in England as late as 1918. I am always somewhat taken aback when discussing this subject to find that it invariably leads to a vigorous attack on the church. It is argued that the reason women were so long deprived of their human rights was largely the fault of the church. For almost two-thousand years the church has relegated women to secondary citizenship. There are undoubtedly strong arguments in favour of that view. Very recently the Pope apologised to women for the church's attitude towards them in the past. But there is still no place for women in the hierarchical structure of the church. Its structures are male and look like remaining that way. Its laws were designed by males, and celibates at that. Its theology has been at least until very recently an exclusively male domaine. Women were consigned to the home or, in the case of the chosen few, the convent.

Yet if one takes a more global view of women, it is remarkable that the liberation movement has only taken off in what used to be termed 'the Christian West', i.e. in Europe and North America, whose philosophy and values are largely derived from Christianity. Their sisters in the Muslim world, if recent reports be true, are almost going in reverse with the reimposition of the *chaddor*, veiling all but their eyes and this even in countries as westernised as Algeria. Things are little better in Buddhist and Hindu countries where women are still assigned inferior roles in society. Probing a little deeper into why women's emancipation is confined almost exclusively to the Christian world, I would argue – though sometimes I seem to be in a minority of one –

that it is due to the remarkable position Mary holds in the Catholic tradition. Admittedly, nowadays, she doesn't often get a good press. She has been grossly caricatured by nineteenth century Italian artists with their willowy plastercasts of a miraculous madonna, stripped of all the physical attributes of her sex. They were the religious images of her on which my generation was raised and they still dominate the popular commercial *bondieuserie* market. Witness Lourdes or Knock. What the artists depicted in paper or plastercast, a sex-obsessed church reinforced theologically and devotionally. Mary was cast as the model of sex-less womanhood.

But this is all a recent aberration. Look at the great Renaissance artists which Italy also produced and their depictions of Mary in all the glory of her womanhood. You can easily recognise here the person who was the subject of that marvellous compliment paid to Christ in the gospel: 'Blessed is the womb that bore thee and the paps that gave thee suck.' And I suspect that this more authentic view of Mary has made a deeper impact on the popular imagination.

It harmonises with today's gospel account of the Visitation. Mary, by all accounts a girl in her mid to late teens, had just learnt that she was pregnant. Joseph had not yet committed himself. And it would be strange indeed if her situation, as happens in every age, including our own, did not occasion some adverse comments among wagging tongues. Yet her immediate concern was an older cousin whose pregnancy, though late, was conventional. 'Mary set out at that time and went as quickly as she could to a town in the hill country of Judah.' That simple gospel sentence belies the reality. Travelling at that time was neither easy or safe for anyone, least of all for a young pregnant girl. From the beginning Mary emerges as a 'christian' as that adjective has come to denote, somebody who places others before self. And the few biographical details the gospels provide reinforce that image. She was the guest at a wedding of a couple whose family couldn't afford the necessary wine and persuaded her son to do the needful. As a middle-aged mother she was present at the execution of her son in the most barbaric manner imaginable. This authentic gospel image of Mary has exercised an enormous influence on the religious imagination of Christians for almost two-thousand years. And it still continues. Recent research on young Catholics in America shows Mary to be their most powerful religious image. It would be strange indeed, if she, whose very first recorded concern was for another woman, had not contributed to the emancipation of her sex.

Suggested additional Bidding Prayers

We pray

– that women will be given their rightful place in society.
– for women everywhere who are victims of oppression and discrimination.
– that Mary will always intercede for us with her son.

Catechism of the Catholic Church

495 Called in the gospels 'the mother of Jesus', Mary is acclaimed by Elizabeth, at the prompting of the Spirit and even before the birth of her son, as 'the mother of my Lord'. In fact, the One whom she conceived as man by the Holy Spirit, who truly became her Son according to the flesh, was none other than the Father's eternal Son, the second person of the Holy Trinity. Hence the church confesses that Mary is truly *'Mother of God'*.

The Season of Christmas

First Sunday of Lent

Readings: Deut 26-4-10. Rom 10:8-13. Lk 4:1-13.

Introduction.

Fasting, prayer and almsgiving are the three traditional forms of expressing our conversion. Lent is the penitential season *par excellence,* which is recalled for us in today's gospel account of Christ's forty days in the desert.

Giving up for Lent (Fasting)

I read or heard somewhere, though I find it incredible, that 'somewhere on this planet earth, every twenty-four hours, a new McDonalds opens'. At last count, there were 9, 400 of them scattered throughout 46 countries. Even in Paris, the temple of *haute cuisine,* they are spreading almost like a rash. In the battle for the bellies of the next generation, the hamburger and chips seem certain winners. The Big Mac sign, like the blue jeans of an earlier period, is fast becoming the symbol of our times. One thing is certain, Big Mac is not proliferating in the Third World and certainly not in famine-stricken countries, such as Sudan and Ethiopia.

The extraordinary thing about our world and what is now referred to as the 'North-South divide', is that while two-thirds of the population are dying from hunger and malnutrition, the other third is dying from over-consumption and related ailments. And the two problems are inextricably linked. An American expert at the recent Cairo conference on world population, pointed out that the popular understanding of the problem of over-population is exactly the opposite of the reality. The world's resources are strained to the limit, not because of over-population in the Third World, but because of increasing consumption in the West and particularly in the United States. The reason being that Americans consume by far the largest percentage of the world's resources and each extra American mouth to feed condemns dozens of their less fortunate brothers to starvation. The imbalance has also historical origins. The wealth of many European countries, such as France, Spain and England, derives to a greater or lesser extent from the fact that for centuries they plundered the natural resources of Africa, India and South America. And the United States owes some of its economic growth to the cheap labour provided by the African slave-trade.

Fasting, like prayer, is one of the core notions in Christianity, as indeed in all great religions. It requires no justification. It is a traditional religious way, since the dawn of civilisation, of acknowledging one's God. The historical and economic arguments only serve to reinforce its validity. They would have been largely superfluous in other times. But moderns seem to want Christianity without the cross, the carnival but not Lent. And in this we are out of step not only with the gospel but with two-thousand years of tradition. In the Irish language, three of the seven days of the week were named by reference to fasting. Wednesday was called *Céadaoin*, the first fast, Friday, *Aoine*, fast-day, and Thursday, *Diardaoin*, a corruption of *idir dhá aoine*, between two fasts. And in those days the normal fare would now be considered subsistence rations. The virtual disappearance of fasting among Catholics is of very recent origin. I can remember very vividly my seminary days, where the normal diet was frugal to say the least, observing the strict Lenten fast of one meal and two collations a day. The latter consisted of a half slice of bread with a suggestion of butter and a cup of tea. It must be admitted, we didn't always do it cheerfully. But at least we had the comfort of knowing that we were making some little effort at imitating Christ. We could say with some sincerity the opening prayer in today's Mass:

Father,
through our observance of Lent,
help us to understand the meaning
of your Son's death and resurrection,
and teach us to reflect it in our lives.

Suggested additional Bidding Prayers
We pray
– that we will practise some form of penance, such as fasting, this Lent to express our conversion in relation to ourselves, to God and to others.
– that by our voluntary self-denial we will show solidarity with the deprived of the Third World.
– that we will alter our life-styles to conform better with the gospel.

Catechism of the Catholic Church
1438 The seasons and days of penance in the course of the liturgical year (Lent and each Friday in memory of the death of the

Lord) are intense moments of the church's penitential practice. These time are particularly appropriate for spiritual exercises, penitential liturgies, pilgrimages as signs of penance, voluntary self-denial such as fasting and almsgiving, and fraternal sharing (charitable and missionary works).

Second Sunday of Lent

Readings: Gen 15:5-12, 17-18. Phil 3:17-4:1. Lk 9:28-36.

Introduction
Today we celebrate Christ's transfiguration on the mountain. Only through prayer will we encounter the transfigured Christ and thus transfigure our lives.

Transfiguration (Prayer)
My formative years were all spent in the good-old bad-old days before Vatican II. I've always felt privileged and grateful that my religious life straddled two worlds, before and after the Second Vatican Council. It allows me now to rummage about in the store-house of my mind and pull out ideas sometimes old and sometimes new but all in their own way treasures. I can remember well how important private prayer was in that pre-Conciliar world. People were very devotional then. In the little town where I grew up, many of the teenagers, boys and girls, went to the church every evening for a visit. Of course, all that happened before television came and changed all our lives. Perhaps, we weren't any more virtuous than teenagers today. It may be that we had nothing else to do in the evenings and like all teenagers we wanted to get out of the house and meet our friends. Many a great romantic relationship began outside the church door. Many adults also went to the church every evening. There was always a steady trickle of people winding its way up and down Chapel St, from early evening until the church closed at 9.30. One of these was my mother who made a 'holy hour' there every evening. It was on occasions like these I first had my own peculiar experience of the 'power of prayer'. The only other social outlet for young people was the local cinema. But that cost money and money was scarce then. I wasn't above using religion for ulterior purposes. I would slip into the

seat where my mother was deep in prayer, and ask her in a whisper for 'the money for the pictures'. She invariably answered: 'If it's in my purse, you can take it, love.' I suspect now that on evenings such as those, St Anthony or one of the other saints who filled the niches in our church, went without their usual offering.

All that world of private prayer disappeared dramatically after the Council, though I suspect television and a host of other modern developments had much to do with it also. Because the local cinema disappeared too and Vatican II cannot be blamed for that. Change always demands some price or other and the great liturgical changes introduced then seem to have edged out private prayer. There are faint signs now that it is making a comeback. It is inevitable that it should. Inside every one of us there is a little hermit trying to break out. We have all felt that need to get away from it all, to be by ourselves for a while and try to make sense of our lives. What else is that but an urge to pray.

Today's gospel gives us a remarkable insight into the nature of prayer. 'Jesus took with him Peter and John and James and went up the mountain to pray.' We too have to climb a mountain to pray. We must find the high ground, remote enough to give us an overall view of our petty world with all its preoccupations. A mountain would give us that perspective, as indeed a lake or a desert, places where Jesus also liked to pray. Each of us has to find his own equivalent. We have to create a hermitage somewhere in our lives where we can go and pray regularly. Only by prayer can we transfigure our world. By reflecting deep down inside ourselves we will transfigure our many and often complicated relationships. Prayer will transfigure our marriages, our homes, our work and our communities. We will experience what Peter felt when he saw Jesus transfigured and exclaimed: 'Master, it is wonderful for us to be here.' And we will hear the voice he heard, telling us: 'This is my Son, the Chosen One. Listen to him.'

The famous American writer, Thurber, at the end of one of his fables, penned these two lines:

All men should learn before they die,

Where they are going to, from where and why.

Only in prayer will we find the answer to these questions.

Suggested additional Bidding Prayers

We pray

– that we may find a time and a place for prayer in our stress-filled world.

– that our lives may be transfigured by prayer.

– that through prayer we will encounter the transfigured Lord.

Catechism of the Catholic Church

554 From the day Peter confessed that Jesus is the Christ, the Son of the living God, the Master 'began to show his disciples that he must go to Jerusalem and suffer many things ... and be killed, and on the third day be raised.' Peter scorns this prediction, nor do the others understand it any better than he. In this context the mysterious episode of Jesus' transfiguration takes place on a high mountain, before three witnesses chosen by himself: Peter, James and John. Jesus' face and clothing become dazzling with light, and Moses and Elijah appear, speaking 'of his departure, which he was to accomplish in Jerusalem'. A cloud covers him and a voice from heaven says: 'This is my Son, my Chosen; listen to him!'

Third Sunday of Lent

Readings: Ex 3:1-8, 13-15. 1 Cor 10:1-6, 10-12. Lk 13:1-9.

Introduction

Today's gospel warns us of the consequences of our failure to live up to our Christian commitment. Like the barren fig tree, we will be cut down. The Lord of the vineyard offers us yet another chance to bear fruit.

Taking up ground (Dispensability)

The great German statesman, Otto von Bismarck, is reputed to have said about the Irish vis-a-vis the Dutch: 'If Ireland had been inhabited by the Dutch, it would be the bread-basket of Europe, while if Holland had been occupied by the Irish, it would long ago have been overrun by the sea.' It might be argued – though it probably would not have impressed Bismarck – that the Irish possess other gifts which enhance the quality of life, like sociability and humour, notably lacking among the industrious Dutch, and indeed, among Bismarck's own rather dour compatriots. But when it comes to industriousness, even the most fervent Irishman is forced to admit that Ireland leaves a lot to be desired. When I first travelled in Europe, I was instantly struck by the extensive cultivation of the land. There did not seem to be an inch of ground left fallow between Le Havre and Paris. Nothing but huge expanses of land growing maize, wheat, corn and other crops I could not even identify. I later saw the same in Germany in places like the Ruhr valley, where factory smoke-towers stood out in large fields of corn, like ships in the ocean. Returning home, I encountered again what we euphemistically call the wild Irish countryside, large tracts of which seem to have been untouched by human hand. It seems ironic that a people who fought so long and so passionately for the land, should have neglected it so much.

All of which brings me to the parable of the barren fig-tree. It is a parable of our own lives. All of us have been given a patch of ground in the Lord's vineyard, where we are expected to produce fruit. And for that it has to be cultivated. Each one's patch is different, often yielding different fruit. Many chose to rear families. Some also run businesses or contribute to the running of them or work at different levels in institutions. Nowadays a large percentage is engaged in what are called the 'caring' industry, working in education, medicine, the social services, religion, as teachers, doctors, nurses, social workers, priests and in similar fields. And if we are to bear fruit in our lives, the crop has to come largely from those fields.

It is a salutary thing, particularly in a time like Lent, to take stock of our little holdings and see what our returns are like. A farmer likes to take a stroll on a summer's evening, after the day's work is done, through his land. And there, leaning up against a farmyard gate and pulling on his pipe, he casts his eye over the growing crops and the grazing animals, thinking about what he has done and what remains to be done to insure a good harvest. So it should be with us. We could take stock of the quality of our family life, of our involvement or lack of it in our community, of our commitment to our jobs and our colleagues, over and above the statutory requirement. We all find a niche for ourselves in this world where we become entrenched. We feel we've earned our place. But we have to go on earning our place. Otherwise, like the barren fig-tree, we are only 'taking up the ground'. There are very few of us, if we are humble enough, who would not admit that maybe someone else could do a better job than us. None of us is indispensable. Not even Bismarck, with his enormous contribution to the creation of Germany. Modern Germany would have come into being without him and possibly without such horrendous consequences to the Germans and the rest of the world.

Like the barren fig-tree, we are all given many chances to bear fruit. Let today's gospel be one of them.

Suggested additional Bidding Prayers
We pray
– that we may earnestly cultivate that corner of the Lord's vineyard assigned to us.
– that we may keep our lives in perspective by realising that we are all dispensable.
– that our Christian lives may bear fruit.

Catechism of the Catholic Church
755 'The church is a cultivated field, the tillage of God. On that land the ancient olive tree grows whose holy roots were the prophets and in which the reconciliation of Jews and Gentiles has been brought about and will be brought about again. That land, like a choice vineyard, has been planted by the heavenly cultivator. Yet the true vine is Christ who gives life and fruitfulness to the branches, that is to us, who through the church remain in Christ, without whom we can do nothing.'

Fourth Sunday of Lent

Readings: Jos 5:9-12. 2 Cor 5:17-21. Lk 15: 1-3, 11-32.

Introduction
We celebrate in this Mass the joy of forgiveness and the Lord who welcomes sinners. We too 'have sinned against heaven and against you Father' and are in need of forgiveness as others are in need of our forgiveness.

The Prodigal (Forgiveness) See also 24th Sunday A
No matter how often I read this parable of the Prodigal Son I am always left with a vague feeling of dissatisfaction. Rather than coming away with the overpowering sense of the mercy of

God as shown to the Prodigal, I'm somewhat irked by his partiality, which is suggested by his exchange with the elder son.
Fathers do have favourite sons. I've seen them listening to complaints about the apple of their eyes and shaking their heads in
disbelief. 'You don't know him. He's not like that at all. He
couldn't do a thing like that. It's just not in him.' And you the
teacher, the priest, the guard, the neighbour, are a nosey busybody, a crank. He might even feel sorry for you. And it is not so
with all his sons. 'I don't know what to do with him, Father. He
has my heart broken. I can't understand him. He's driving me
crazy.' Could it be that the Prodigal was the favourite?

Or is it that we know too many elder sons too well? Lads who
have stayed at home to care for ageing parents. And by the time
they have buried their parents, they have buried with them the
best years of their lives. Theirs was a hard life and if they had
grudges it was hard to blame them. There is a photo on the
mantlepiece in many a country home, which shows him standing outside the old place, surrounded by his brother and his
family back on a trip from the States. It's a telling picture. There
he is in his peaked cap and collarless shirt, lean, lined, weather-
beaten face, looking more like the father than the brother of the
returned Yank.

Besides most of us probably identify with the elder son. The
monotony of our lives make us resentful of the Prodigal's
swinging escapade. We grudge the sinner his good times. It is
probably why we accept the doctrine of retribution so unquestioningly. What makes our lives a little more tolerable is the
thought that our good times are all before us and part of them,
which we can savour now, is that the playboys of this world will
pay in full for their pleasures. So in this story the elder son is carrying the standard of all the solid citizens, all the responsible
members of the community, 'the salt of the earth', while behind
the banner of the Prodigal huddle all that tattered mob of misfits, drop-outs, lame-ducks and the rest of the world's rejects.

The really puzzling thing about this parable is, why did
Christ bother with this epilogue on the elder son at all? Surely if
the message of the parable is the boundless mercy of God towards the sinner, then by the time the festivities for the returned
Prodigal are in full swing, we've got the message. The remain-
der adds nothing except to divert some of our sympathy towards the resentful elder son. Of one thing we can be sure,
knowing the story-teller, it must have a point. He was a master

of his craft. Look again at it, but this time if you can, through the eyes of one of the world's rejects, a drop-out , a misfit, or one of the many physically, mentally or socially handicapped. Perhaps this is Christ's answer to their agonised cry: 'Why me? Why was I singled out for a life of frustration? Why should I have been a faulty creation?' What the grudging elder son failed to see was that the world's prodigals are victims more often than not and have more claims on God's love and forgiveness.

Suggested additional Bidding Prayers
We pray
– that we may show our Father's forgiveness for the world's prodigals.
– for bitterly divided families that they may be reconciled.
– for ourselves that no matter how far we stray from God's grace we will always have the courage to return to our Father for forgiveness.

Catechism of the Catholic Church
545 Jesus invites sinners to the table of the kingdom: 'I came not to call the righteous, but sinners.' He invites them to that conversion without which one cannot enter the kingdom, but shows them in word and deed his Father's boundless mercy for them and the 'vast joy in heaven over one sinner who repents'. The supreme proof of his love will be the sacrifice of his own life 'for the forgiveness of sins'.

Fifth Sunday of Lent

Readings: Is 43:16-21. Phil 3:8-14. Jn 8:1-11

Introduction
Today's gospel records Christ's attitude towards the adulterous woman and the object lesson he impressed on his followers. We need to examine our conscience on how we indulge in gossip and innuendoes about our neighbour.

Throwing stones (Judging)
When the Ayatollah Khomeini called for the execution of the British writer Salman Rushdie, whose novel, *The Satanic Verses*,

he denounced as blasphemous, it sent shock-waves round the world. There was an immediate outcry everywhere at the barbaric fulmination of a religious fanatic. Even though some people thought that Rushdie's book was in bad taste, that it deliberately offended many Muslims, that it derided one of the great world religions and violated the Koran, they were horrified at the Ayatollah's decree. There were vehement protests and much righteous indignation expressed. Now, the Ayatollah is long since dead, but Salman Rushdie is still in hiding, with twenty-four hour police protection.

It struck me at the time that much of the indignation was self-righteous, or at least, that many of the loudest protesters were hardly in a position to throw stones. A few months earlier, a short distance away from where I was then living in Paris, an attempt was made by some self-professed Christians to burn down a cinema which was showing Scorsese's film *The Last Temptation of Christ*. Fortunately, no lives were lost on that occasion. A few of my friends were present. Incidents like that cannot be simply dismissed as the work of a few fanatics. As in Iran, fanaticism needs a certain climate to thrive in. Rome had previously condemned Scorsese's film as blasphemous. More recently still, abortion clinics in the United States were attacked with bombs and doctors who worked in them shot dead. The perpetrators claimed to be acting in the name of religion.There are periods of the church's history we would dearly like to forget, such as the Roman Inquisition and the burning of heretics at the stake. But their memory lives on, if only as a stick to beat Rome with. As late as a hundred years ago, an imposing statue was erected in Campo de Fiori in Rome, a mere stone's throw from the Vatican, to Bruno, an Italian friar who suffered such a fate. Quite recently, I noticed that somebody had laid a fresh bouquet of flowers at its base. Prominent in the fresco depicting the scene of Bruno's burning, were two fat friars, smirking contentedly.

The world today can be divided in two, between those who believe in God – whether it be the Christian God or the Muslim God or a myriad of Hindu Gods and Goddesses – and those who don't. And when incidents like those occur, we all get tarred with the same brush. They hurt all believers, and even those non-believers who are well-disposed to us are confirmed in their view that the world would be a better place without religion. The Rushdie's or the Scorsese's are not the real blasphemers.

The incident recorded in today's gospel shows how Christ

reacted to such situations. The scribes and Pharisees were the religious gurus of their time. They were the officially accredited experts in the interpretation and application of God's word. They thought they would embarrass Jesus by confronting him with this adulterous woman. The reverse happened. They, rather than she, received the severer judgement. Closer scrutiny of the text reveals some surprising detail. The woman was 'caught committing adultery'. The sexual act, either licit or illicit, is never committed in public, either now or then. And people who commit adultery, then as now, were extremely discreet about it. That her accusers should have caught her in the act speaks volumes about them rather than her. It takes two to commit adultery, yet only the woman is subject to the terrible penalty of stoning proscribed by their law. People have always been intrigued by what Christ may have written on the ground with his finger. Commentators have speculated about what he may have written in clay in letters big enough for each to read. Perhaps the sins of each of her accusers. We shall never know. He may simply have doodled in the sand simply to give them enough time to reflect on the magnitude of the crime they were about to commit. 'If there is one of you who has not sinned, let him be the first to throw a stone at her.' And again the doodling. Then they began to shuffle off, ' beginning with the eldest', presumably because he had the longest record and knew it. And soon there was nobody left but the woman herself, probably surrounded by little abandoned heaps of stones. 'Neither do I condemn you,' said Jesus. We, his followers, would do well to be as sparing in our condemnations as our Master.

Suggested additional Bidding Prayers
We pray
– that we will be sparing in our condemnations of others.
– that we will never be guilty of rash judgement, calumny or detraction of others.
– that we will always seek to interpret the behaviour of others in a favourable light.

Catechism of the Catholic Church
2478 To avoid rash judgement, everyone should be careful to interpret insofar as is possible his neighbour's thoughts, words and deeds in a favourable way.

Third Sunday of Easter

Readings: Acts 5:27-32, 40-41. Apoc 5:11-14. Jn 21:1-19.

Introduction

Peter and the other apostles were commissioned by Christ to be 'fishers of men'. The miraculous draught of fish recorded in today's gospel reminds us that we ourselves are those other fish they were sent out to catch.

The Big Catch (Salvation)

Fish are funny creatures. They are always so busy and yet so pointlessly busy. Ever on the move, they flit about, dashing and darting hither and thither, full of agitation and enthusiasm. How easily they are alarmed by every ripple, every shadow on the water! Always keyed-up, on the alert, so ready for the unexpected, and yet so easily duped. So quick to react to the first rumours of danger and yet so easily caught.

There is a certain 'fishiness' about us to. We are after all the fish Christ sent Peter out to catch. Like fish, we are immersed in a sea of troubles and distractions, easily alarmed and agitated by every ripple of excitement, every shadow of doubt that crosses our paths. We expend so much energy on trivialities. We dally so dangerously with temptations, and allow ourselves to be hooked to so many creature comforts from cigarettes to status symbols. It is little wonder that Christ showed a marked preference for fishermen when he chose his first apostles.

Today's miracle is also the miracle of our lives. Christ, through his church, has thrown his net over us, a net of grace. Christ says: 'The kingdom of heaven is like a net that was thrown into the sea and caught fish of every kind.' And like a fisherman's net it remains unseen beneath the surface. And we are drawn into it, in spite of life's storms and currents and baits with their cunningly concealed hooks. And even in spite of our own struggling.

The miraculous catch of fish recorded today recalls that other big catch to which Christ compared the kingdom of heaven. We may be keen judges of the world and its ways. We might well be accurate in our judgement of individuals. We may be keen assessors of those whose behaviour falls short of the demands of the gospel. But we cannot have but a miser's notion of the sufficiency of God's grace. There is no telling what size the catch will be until the net is finally drawn in at the end. Like this miraculous draught, it may well astonish even the most seasoned of fishermen. Who knows what queer fish will be caught there sputtering and gasping at the size of God's mercy? The 'big catch' is Christ's answer to those prophets of gloom who would put so many outside his reach.

Suggested additional Bidding Prayers
We pray
– that we may be caught in the net of God's grace.
– that those the world deems 'queer fish' may experience God's mercy.
– that our greed will stop threatening those many species of sea creatures that God so generously gave us.

Catechism of the Catholic Church
645 By means of touch and the sharing of a meal, the risen Jesus establishes direct contact with his disciples. He invites them in this way to recognise that he is not a ghost and above all to verify that the risen body in which he appears to them is the same body that had been tortured and crucified, for it still bears the traces of his Passion.

Fourth Sunday of Easter

Readings: Acts 13:14, 45-52. Apoc 7:9, 14-17. Jn 10:27-30.

Introduction
Today we celebrate Christ our Shepherd. We hear his voice in the proclamation of the gospel. We follow him by living the gospel.

Shepherding the flock (Leadership)

Some years ago I was making a television documentary in Spain. Ours was a small company with very little resources. Time was money, so we had pack lunches rather than sit-down restaurant meals. Once on the road from Madrid to Salamanca we stopped somewhere in the high sierras to escape the midday sun and eat our sandwiches in the shade by the side of the road. The landscape was mountainous and bleak, bereft of all signs of human life, with scarcely any vegetation. Lizards scuttered under rocks beneath our feet. While we munched our sandwiches, contemplating this scene of desolation, a shepherd with a flock of sheep appeared in the distance coming in our direction. Soon, a second shepherd appeared on the opposite horizon, also approaching us. Eventually, their paths crossed in front of us, a short distance from where we sat. The two shepherds stopped to exchange some pleasantries or more probably information as to where the best grazing might be found. It was a truly biblical sight. We could have travelled all the way back to Palestine in the first century. While the two shepherds chatted, their two flocks mingled. There must have been several hundred sheep in each flock. I remember thinking to myself, 'There's going to be one helluva problem separating that lot when the time comes to move!' That was a few minutes later. The shepherds shook hands and parted, each going in the opposite direction, without as much as glancing over their shoulders. Each strode ahead purposely, carrying his staff, like a Moses in search of the Promised Land. I heard them whistle and call out in Spanish something I did not understand and all without even breaking their stride. The great mass of sheep disentangled itself in minutes, each following its own shepherd, and I was left gazing once more at a desolate panorama.

I think I learnt more scripture in those few minutes than in all my seminary courses. Nobody told me then that sheep were led from the front, not driven from behind. The only sheep I ever saw in the west of Ireland where I grew up, were the flocks driven into town to the fair. And they were always followed by loudly cursing farmers wielding sticks and barking dogs snapping at their heels. Woe betide the unfortunate sheep who strayed from the straight and narrow. He was shown no mercy by farmer or dog. It was a style of behaviour, mirrored by those other pastors in my childhood, who bullied and brow-beat their flocks for the glory of God and their eternal salvation. They too wielded the big stick, beating the bushes to drive out courting couples and frighten the recalcitrant sinner into submission. But then, they too, might never have learned that sheep are led, not driven. Their scripture studies seemed to have ended with the Old Testament. In school, too, the big stick was the primary educational tool. The past so often dissolves into idyllic rosiness. Memory is highly selective. How easily we forget the little boy who feigned sickness at home to escape punishment at school or wet his pants on the way there in anticipation of the wrath to come, because he hadn't done his homework or got his sums right.

'Sure it did us no harm' they say now. In a world awash with drugs and crime, the temptation to 'bring back the big stick' is enormous. Politicians are woo'd by the growing constituency of the old and the frightened, who believe their security can only be assured by more police on the street and stiffer penalties in the court. Right-wing parties have made spectacular advances in recent times. The death penalty has been re-enacted in all but two states in the United States. Yet the explosion in the prison population everywhere continues to be out-run only by the galloping crime statistics. Some people never get their sums right. It did not work in the past. It doesn't work now. There are countries, even in the twentieth century, where thieves are punished by having their hands cut off. Yet there is no evidence to show that the crime of robbery is diminishing in these countries. Some of the biggest thieves of all are politicians and top business executives as the recent *mani puliti* (clean hands) investigation in Italy and the spate of sackings, resignations and imprisonments of government ministers in England and France have shown.

If there is an answer to corruption in our time, I think it is the one which has never been tried, the one proposed in today's gospel:

The sheep that belong to me listen to my voice;
I know them and they follow me.
I give them eternal life; they will never be lost
and no one will ever steal them from me.

Suggested additional Bidding Prayers
We pray
– that pastors may lead their flocks by word and example.
– that we will hear and recognise the voice of the Good Shepherd and follow him.
– that we will resist the temptation to condemn those who differ from us.

Fifth Sunday of Easter

Readings: Acts 14:21-27. Apoc 21:1-5. Jn 13:31-35.

Introduction

Today's gospel records Christ's last message to his disciples to love one another. Two-thousand years later there is little evidence to show that the message was ever received. Only love will make 'the whole of creation new'.

Never been tried (Charity) See also 6th Easter B and 4th Sunday C

I was following a course in communications some time ago. As now seems customary in these courses, we were divided into small working groups, with about half a dozen people in each group. There was a young man assigned to my group, who was handicapped and confined to a wheelchair. I was the only priest in the group. After lunch on the first day, he asked me would I assist him to the toilet. Somewhat chuffed that he had asked me, I cheerfully grabbed the handles of his wheelchair and steered it along the corridor towards the toilet. When I got there, I opened the door and carefully wedged the wheelchair in. I was about to turn away and wait for him outside when he motioned me to stay. To my horror, I discovered that my services were required for the whole operation. I was almost overcome by an attack of nausea. It had never occurred to me that handicapped people cannot accomplish such basic and intimate chores as 'calls of nature' without the assistance of others. For the rest of that week I was to remain his chosen assistant. On the final night, we all went out to celebrate in the local pub. You can imagine how much my services were in demand by the time my friend had reached his third pint. I don't think I learned much about communications that week but I did get a new insight into the expression 'intimate friendship'.

The gospel denotes a totally different phenomenon. The more traditional word 'charity' is probably a better description of it. It is the greatest of the three great Christian virtues and unquestionably the hardest to practise. Above all, making heroic sacrifices for people for whom you have not the slightest tinge of affection. Or even, perhaps, for whom you feel a deep revulsion. Like Damian of Molokai, who spent his life among the lepers, caring for them, and contracted leprosy himself. A more modern example would be looking after some one who is dying from AIDS.

Opinion polls the world over place Mother Teresa of Calcutta at the top of the list of those whom people most admire. Imagine what it would do for Christianity if she represented the rule rather than the exception.

By this love you have for one another,
  every one will know that you are my disciples.
The opposite, unfortunately, is more likely to be the case. For the last twenty-five years, Belfast, in the world's press, has become almost a synonym for hate among Christians. Yet it is reputed to have the highest practising rate in the world, both for Protestants and Catholics. Someone once said: 'The tragedy about Christianity is not that it has failed, but that it has never really been tried.' For that, you and I have much to answer.

Suggested additional Bidding Prayers
We pray
– that we may be recognised as Christians by our love.
– that warring Christians may be reconciled.
– for AIDS victims that they may receive the loving care they need.

Catechism of the Catholic Church
1823 Jesus makes charity the new commandment. By loving his own 'to the end', he makes manifest the Father's love which he receives. By loving one another, the disciples imitate the love of Jesus which they themselves receive. Whence Jesus says: 'As the Father has loved me, so have I loved you; abide in my love.' And again: 'This is my commandment, that you love one another as I have loved you.'

Sixth Sunday of Easter

Readings: Acts 15:1-7, 22-29. Apoc 21:10-14, 22-23. Jn 14:23-29.

Introduction
We celebrate today Christ's ascension to his eternal glory in heaven and express our hope that where he has gone before us, we will one day follow to live forever in the kingdom of our Father.

Saying goodbye (Adieu)

To speak a foreign language well, one needs to think in that language. Most beginners tend to translate from their mother-tongue. I remember when I first started speaking French and I squirm now at the thought of what the unfortunate natives were subjected to. I was spending the summer working in a parish in the suburbs of Bordeaux. On one occasion I was invited out to dinner by a family in the parish. At one point during the meal, Madame offered me a second helping, which I declined. I should have said, *Merci, non. J'ai bien mangé.* (No thank you. I have eaten well.) Instead, I used an expression which was commonly used in Ireland on such occasions and translated it literally into French. 'No thanks. I'm full,' I said. There was a sudden burst of laughter from the younger members of the family which earned them a stern rebuke from *Maman*. Later I discovered the reason for their amusement. Their priest-guest had just informed them that he was pregnant. 'To be full' was a local expression to describe the state of pregnancy.

French is a more precise language than English. It often has two words, where English has only one. 'Goodbye' is a case in point. The French use *Au revoir* for those everyday temporary separations, while *Adieu* is reserved strictly for final definitive departures. There is no English translation but it means roughly 'until we meet in heaven'. Life is a succession of *Adieus*. The number grows with the passing years. Our past is peopled with faces that once were dear to us. Some, like our parents, died. Others moved away out of our lives never to reappear again. Sometimes their names crop up in conversation and we say, 'I wonder what became of so-and-so'. They probably make the same remark about us occasionally. Life is a series of little deaths until our own death which for us will be the last great *Adieu*. Paris must be the capital of goodbyes. People live there for a while and then move on and settle down elsewhere. With all its charm, it doesn't seem the kind of city where people strike roots. More a temporary haven for nomads. The modern world is becoming more and more like Paris. It is said that Americans change home on average every four years. More often than you and I change our cars. And in this, as in so many other facets of life, we are all becoming more and more Americanised. Our 'goodbyes' are growing at an ever accelerating rate.

We are, as never before, a pilgrim people. We need faithful friends who travel with us. In today's gospel, Jesus is alerting his disciples to his imminent departure, his ascension into heaven. He doesn't say *Adieu* but *Au revoir*. 'I am going away and shall return'. We never say goodbye to God: He always goes with us. It is striking to note how immigrants who leave their families, friends, language and cultures and settle, often penniless and in a hostile environment, on the other side of the globe, begin by building houses of worship. Such was the case with the Irish in the second half of the nineteenth century in America or Australia. Such is the case today with Muslims from North Africa and elsewhere building mosques in France. God is all they have left to cling on to. It is a striking proof that God has kept his promise to be with us always. He will always keep his side of the bargain. It is up to us to keep ours. And when we come to the end of our pilgrimage here and have to make our last goodbye, it will be literally *Adieu*, i.e. 'to God'.

Suggested additional Bidding Prayers
We pray
– that one day, we too may follow Christ into the kingdom of our Father.
– that we will be reunited with our departed friends in heaven.
– that the faithful departed may be reunited with the ascended Christ.

Catechism of the Catholic Church
659 'So then the Lord Jesus, after he had spoken to them, was taken up into heaven, and sat down at the right hand of God.' ... Jesus' final apparition ends with the irreversible entry of his humanity into divine glory, symbolised by the cloud and by heaven, where he is seated from that time forward at God's right hand.

Seventh Sunday of Easter

Readings: Acts 7:55-60. Apoc 22:12-14, 16-17, 20. Jn 17:20-26.

Introduction

We pray today for the unity of all Christians, as Christ prayed in today's gospel. We need to examine frankly and honestly our attitudes towards the scandal of Christian unity.

'May they all be one' (Unity) See also 3rd Sunday A

A few years ago, France and indeed the rest of the world, celebrated the bicentenary of the French Revolution. That happening, just over two-hundred years ago, was probably one of the greatest milestones in history. It is probably true to say that it gave birth to the modern democratic world. But the French Revolution included many events which even the French would like to forget and certainly contributed nothing to the advance of civilisation, such as the execution of the king or the Reign of Terror. When you look at two neigbouring countries, Britain and France, with approximately the same population, which were in fact traditionally what the French call *'frères-enemies'*, both are equally democratic today, while England retains her monarchy and some aristocratic institutions, such as the House of Lords. And even though it was bitterly opposed to the French Revolution, it has, like everywhere else, been transformed by it.

The precise event itself which opened a new chapter in our history took place between the 20-26 August 1789. It was in fact 'The Declaration of the Rights of Man and of the Citizen' to give it its full title. It was the charter of a new age. It is a short document, with not many articles, which can be summed up in that marvellous slogan which became the catch-cry of the Revolution, 'Liberty, Equality and Fraternity'. Had the Revolution produced nothing else but that slogan, it was guaranteed to win the minds and hearts of future generations. Liberty was defined as the right of the individual to act freely, provided he did not harm another.

Since then, what we now call civil rights have had a long and difficult birth. The American blacks only achieved theirs in the sixties, under the leadership of Martin Luther King, who paid for them with his life. Those of their colour in South Africa had to wait another thirty years before apartheid was dismantled and Nelson Mandela had paid a ransom of twenty-eight years in prison. There were other martyrs, too numerous to mention in the Gulag Archipelago, who did not survive to see the Berlin Wall collapse and the establishment of civil liberties in the Soviet Bloc. There are many places still in the world where the message of the French Revolution has not yet penetrated. But at least now civil rights are firmly on the agenda. If they too wish to join the club, and there are now compelling economic reasons for doing so, they must first improve their record in human rights.

In today's gospel, Christ makes his farewell. It takes the form of a prayer for his disciples:

Holy Father,
I pray not only for these,
but for those also
who through their words will believe in me.
May they all be one.
Father, may they be one in us,
as you are in me and I am in you,
so that the world may believe it was you who sent me.

He could see the history of his followers as clearly as we can see it today, with all the bickerings, dissensions, schisms and religious wars, leading eventually to the break-up of Christianity. Hence his final prayer for unity. Tragically, his followers wanted to impose uniformity instead.

At the time of the Revolution, Irish bishops were warning their flocks not to be contaminated by what they called the 'French disease'. They were wasting their breath. It was contagious. It was only at Vatican II that the church finally took the revolutionary creed on board, with its decree on religious freedom. At the opening of that Council, the great Pope John XXIII quoted an ancient maxim which had long since, unfortunately, fallen into disuse:

In what is doubtful, freedom.
In what is essential, unity.
In all things, charity.

In her eagerness for uniformity rather than unity, the church, like so many secular regimes, had sacrificed both freedom and charity.

Suggested additional Bidding Prayers

We pray

– for unity among all those who profess to be followers of Christ.

– for forgiveness for the wrongs committed against others in the name of religion.

– for tolerance and respect for those who differ from us.

Catechism of the Catholic Church

820 Christ always gives his church the gift of unity, but the church must always pray and work to maintain, reinforce and perfect the unity that Christ wills for her. That is why Jesus himself prayed at the hour of his Passion, and does not cease praying to his Father, for the unity of his disciples: 'That they may be one. As you Father are in me and I am in you, may they also be one in us ... so that the world may know that you have sent me.' The desire to recover the unity of all Christians is a gift of Christ and a call of the Holy Spirit.

Second Sunday of the Year

Readings: Is 62:1-5. 1 Cor 12:4-11. Jn 2:1-12.

Introduction
Mary's discreet intervention at the marriage at Cana to save
a young couple from embarrassment is a model of how we
should help those in our community who have problems. We
should help without being asked and do so without their awareness of being helped.

'They have no wine' (Helping)
In the Middle Ages, there was an organised group of Irish
Benedictines, called the *Schottenkloster*, who established monasteries in Europe, extending from Germany to Kiev in the Ukraine.
Some traces of their foundation still survive, particularly in
Germany. There is a memorial plaque to one of them, St
Makarius, in the Mariankirche in Würzburg. He was the founder
of the Irish monastery in that city. It is recorded that on the day
that his monastery was officially dedicated, he performed a miracle. Lest his young Irish novices be overcome by the grandeur
of that occasion, he turned the wine into water. A most un-Irish
miracle and, arguably, an unChristian one too. It was the reverse
of the Cana miracle in more senses than one. He devalued the
wine and diminished the festivities.

The miracle at Cana as recorded by St John in today's gospel,
has some surprising details, worth reflecting on. Mary seemed
to be the first to notice that the wine had run out. Certainly, the
person in charge, the steward, was not aware of it, nor it seems
was the bride and groom. That it should happen at all indicates
that the newly-weds were not very well-off. It was the sort of
happening that could have caused them enormous embarrassment, and ruined what should have been the happiest day of
their lives. Weddings, then as now, were events of enormous
social importance. It is one of those rare occasions when families
put themselves in the public arena to be judged by their peers.
Even families who can ill-afford it will splash out for a daughter's wedding. Failure to measure up here might mean that they
could never hold their heads high again among their neighbours. Cana was a small, close community. 'Remember the day
the wine ran out at so-and-so's wedding', would be duly entered in the annals. Mary was well aware how much was at

stake. She approached the only one present whom she knew could do something about it, her son, Jesus. Yet, Jesus had never performed a miracle and there must have been umpteen times when that little family in Nazareth could have done with one. Whenever one was needed there, it was Mary who had performed it. Now, when a neighbour's child was in need, it was up to him. 'They have no wine,' she said. No fuss. No histrionics. What followed largely explains why Catholics have always had this extraordinary devotion to Mary. How many husbands have said to their wives, how many sons have said to their mothers, what Jesus said to Mary? 'Why ask me? What can I do?' Mary knew, as countless wives and mothers know, they will not be refused. 'Do whatever he tells you,' she instructed the servants. If the story was leaked, and it must have been leaked – otherwise it would not be read today – it was not Mary who leaked it. Probably it was the servants. 'Only the servants who had drawn the water knew.' Nobody else knew, not the steward, and mercifully not the bride and groom and their families. And that above all accounts for the charm of this miracle.

It is a marvellous model as to how we should act, when helping others. We should be sensitive enough to anticipate their needs. We should help them without their ever knowing, being scrupulously careful to avoid putting them under obligation to us. And whatever we do, we should never mention it to anyone. Most people who need help don't want other people's charity, and those who most need it are the least likely to ask for it.

Suggested additional Bidding Prayers
We pray
– that we will be sensitive to the needs of others and help them without their knowing.
– that we will always ask Mary to intercede for us with her son.
– for all those who are getting married that God will help them to remain faithful to each other.

Catechism of the Catholic Church
1613 On the threshold of his public life Jesus performs his first sign – at his mother's request – during a wedding feast. The church attaches great importance to Jesus' presence at the wedding at Cana. She sees in it the confirmation of the goodness of marriage and the proclamation that thenceforth marriage will be an efficacious sign of Christ's presence.

Third Sunday

Readings: Neh 8:2-6, 8-10. 1 Cor 12:12-30. Lk 1:1-4, 4:14-21.

Introduction
Today we celebrate Christ's Mystical Body of which we all, laity as well as clergy, form a part. We should use creatively that vast reservoir of talent that God bestowed on his church.

The same but different (The Mystical Body)
A little over fifty years ago, a young teacher rented a house in my home town and started a secondary school for boys. There had long been one for girls run by the nuns in the local convent. The bulk of the population in this area were very small farmers, who migrated seasonally to England to boost their meagre incomes to raise and educate their children. The only secondary school then available for boys was the diocesan college which was situated in another town. Only shopkeepers, teachers and other professionals could afford boarding-school fees. So there was great joy and support for this enterprising young teacher. It was short-lived. The Sunday after the 'Academy', as it was grandly called, opened, the parish priest handed down an interdict from the pulpit, threatening to excommunicate all those who sent their children to this school. The reasons given were that it was a threat to the diocesan college and, more importantly, that it usurped the church's prerogative in the field of education. There was consternation. A protest was started, spearheaded mostly by women. It didn't help that the most vociferous of these were, like my mother, themselves the wives of teachers whose school manager was the same parish priest. Deputations were sent to the bishop. The upshot of the affair was that the bishop instructed the local curate to start another school under the aegis of the church, which, in fact, opened just in time for me to begin my secondary education. As for the enterprising lay-teacher, he found a post in a neighbouring diocesan college, where he spent the rest of his life until retirement. If he was embittered by his earlier treatment, he has left no record of it.

Looking at recent newspaper reports of teachers' congresses and parents' associations, and the green papers and white papers issuing from the department of education, it is a far cry from those heady days when the church claimed to be the sole arbiter in educational matters. What is sad to observe is that here and elsewhere, every concession, from communion in the hand to girl altar-servers, had to be wrenched from a reluctant church. Now in full retreat, she continues to fight a rear-guard action, to preserve zones of interest she has neither the mandate nor the manpower to maintain. If the present crisis of vocations continues, she may not even be able to assure her sacramental mission in the future. And all this with a vast reserve of talent and goodwill in her pews only waiting to be tapped. One might be forgiven the untheological thought that there must be one very frustrated Holy Spirit somewhere out there.

I have often wondered why St Paul's vision of the church as the body of Christ, with its different parts, each exercising different functions, never really caught on. Was it because its more egalitarian overtones clashed with the more enduring vertical vision of a hierarchical church? 'In the one Spirit we were all baptised,' he wrote to the Corinthians, 'Jews as well as Greeks, slaves as well as citizens, and one Spirit was given to us all to drink. Nor is the body to be identified with any one of its many parts. Now you together are Christ's body; but each of you is a different part of it.' It doesn't sit well with the more familiar chain-of-command version we are accustomed to.

Thirty years ago, when last the Holy Spirit officially intervened in church affairs at Vatican II, Pope John XXIII spoke of a 'new Pentecost'. The Council Fathers spoke enthusiastically of collegiality and the active participation of the laity. It seemed the dawn of a new age. The church as the Body of Christ was about to become a reality. Since then the old regime seems to have reasserted itself, at least temporarily. The Body of Christ continues to bleed. If we do not share its responsibilities, we share its ills. Recent disclosures of clerical scandals have brought home to us St Paul's observation: 'If one part is hurt, all parts are hurt with it.' Perhaps, it is the Holy Spirit's way of teaching us that, like it or not, we clergy and laity alike are all part of the church, the Body of Christ.

That school of dubious origin I mentioned at the beginning has long since passed away. There may be a moral there somewhere.

Suggested additional Bidding Prayers
We pray
– that the church will use that vast reservoir of lay talent that Christ provides her with.

– that the clergy will yield gracefully to their lay brothers and sisters some of their authority and responsibility.

– for the grace of humility for the church humiliated by recent clerical scandals.

Catechism of the Catholic Church

791 The body's unity does not do away with the diversity of its members: 'In the building of Christ's Body there is engaged a diversity of members and functions. There is only one Spirit who, according to his own richness and the needs of the ministries, gives his different gifts for the welfare of the church.' The unity of the Mystical Body produces and stimulates charity among the faithful: 'From this it follows that if one member suffers anything, all the members suffer with him, and if one member is honoured, all the members together rejoice.' Finally, the unity of the Mystical Body triumphs over all human divisions: 'For as many of you as were baptised into Christ have put on Christ. There is neither Jew nor Greek, there is neither slave nor free, there is neither male nor female; for you are all one in Christ Jesus.'

Fourth Sunday

Readings: Jer 1:4-5, 17-19. 1 Cor 12:31-13:13. Lk 4:21-30.

Introduction

We read in St Paul's letter to the Corinthians his famous description of Christian charity. It consists of the little gestures in our lives that express our kindness, patience, politeness and above all forbearance and joy in the success of others.

'Love is. ... (Charity) See also 5th Easter C and 6th Easter B

There was, and for all I know, still is, a cartoon which is featured in the daily newspapers. It is entitled 'Love is ...' and depicts a scene where a spouse, usually the husband, shows his love for his wife by some thoughtful little gesture. 'Love is ... remembering her birthday or bringing her flowers occasionally or breakfast in bed at weekends.' The list of such expressions of love is endless. It is a nice idea and a reminder to those who have committed themselves to each other for life, that nothing should be taken for granted and every little gesture helps to preserve their relationship. There is probably no more abused word in the English language than the word 'love', with the possible exception of that other four-letter word, which dictionaries strangely like to define as 'making love' or 'the act of love'. Nowadays, the word 'love' is used almost exclusively to express romantic attachment.

Almost every adult has had some experience of romantic love or has been, at least, brushed by passion, however fleetingly. They are among the strongest feelings they will ever know in their lives. Girls, in particular, are fed a diet of romance from their first fairytale encounter with 'Sleeping Beauty'. Their adolescence is filled with dreams of a Prince Charming and his awakening kiss. Such love stories provide the themes for every film churned out from that greatest of all dream factories, Hollywood. Commenting on the British Royal Family, which has so captivated the world's press, one journalist (incidentally, a woman herself) had this to say: 'The love for which disco-songs and advertisements and soap operas and magazines preach a gospel is the most irrational ideology ever to hold a civilisation in thrall.' It is ironic that the House of Windsor whose survival had been insured for centuries by carefully arranged marriage treaties, seems now about to founder on the romantic vagaries of the heir to the throne.

St Paul preaches a very different gospel. His love-letter to the Corinthians has another theme altogether. These same named qualities are not even distant cousins. His is an heroic virtue, not an obsessive infatuation. Like other scripture writers, Paul prefers to define it negatively. What it is, is more often better communicated by what it is not. As in the case of Christ's parables, commentary here seems not only superfluous but even diminishing. His words speak for themselves:

> Love is always patient and kind; it is never jealous; love is never boastful or conceited; it is never rude or selfish: it does not take offence, and is not resentful. Love takes no pleasure in other people's sins but delights in the truth; it is always ready to excuse, to trust, to hope, and to endure whatever comes.

Suggested additional Bidding Prayers
We pray
– that we will always show our love for others by our patience and kindness.

– that we will always show our love by never taking offence or being resentful.

– that we will show our love by being always ready to excuse, to trust, to hope and to endure whatever comes.

Catechism of the Catholic Church

1822 Charity is the theological virtue by which we love God above all things for his own sake, and our neighbour as ourselves for the love of God.

Fifth Sunday

Readings: Is 6:1-8. I Cor 15:1-11. Lk 5:1-11.

Introduction

Hope is the virtue *par excellence* of not only fishermen but of Christians. When Christ told Peter to 'put out into the deep' he was encouraging him to have hope. In our world, where so many young people resort to death-dealing drugs, our Christian hope has much to contribute.

'Put out into the deep' (Hope)

The first time I caught a fish, I nearly fell out of the boat, I was so astonished. I'm not a fully-fledged fisherman by any calculation. In fact most fishermen would regard me with disdain. I practise what is called trolling. I row a boat up and down a lake, trailing a line in the water behind me. Even now, I always get a tremor in my spine when I feel a bite at the end of the line. I never cease to be amazed. The odds against catching a fish seem enormous. There I am in a boat, in the middle of a lake, surrounded by a huge expanse of water, into which I drop a tiny little hook. Fish have so much space and depth in which to swim and feed. That it should find and bite my little hook seems incredible. It is not as if you could see them, track them down into a narrow inlet and drop your hook within inches of your prey.

I've always been fascinated by the number of references to fish in the gospel. In Matthew's gospel, Christ says: 'The kingdom of heaven is like a net that was thrown into the sea and caught fish of every kind.' When he miraculously fed the multitude he used fish as well as bread. He even found the money to pay his taxes in the mouth of a fish. Fish figured so prominently in the gospel that the early Christians in Rome, chose the symbol of a fish to designate their tombs in the catacombs. The letters which make up the Greek word for fish, 'ichthus' came to signify 'Jesus Christ, Son of God, Saviour.'

There were a lot of other people in Palestine in the time of Our Lord, besides fisherman. Yet when it came to picking his apostles, he showed a marked preference for them. He made 'the big fisherman', Simon Peter, their head. And he reserved his special miracles, such as the transfiguration and the raising to life of the little girl, only for him and his two fishing partners, James and John.

'Put out into deep water', he told Peter. Peter knew, as every fisherman knows, that fish only feed in shallow waters. Jesus was testing him. After a whole night covering the best feeding-grounds on the lake, it was asking a lot. But Peter complied, almost as if to humour Jesus. His compliance was amply rewarded. More importantly, he had passed the test. 'From now on,' Christ told him, 'it is men you will catch.' (Or as Mark phrased it: 'Follow me and I will make you fish for people.')

The one virtue, above all others, that fishermen need, is the virtue of hope. To cast a small hook into a large expanse of water in the expectation of catching a fish, is an act of hope. And to do it time after time, hour after hour without catching anything, without even the tiniest bite, is to hope beyond hope. It was the one virtue Christ needed in the person he chose to lead his followers. He was, as history has shown, launching Peter into very deep waters indeed. But he knew what Teilhard de Chardin expressed almost two thousand years later, that 'the world belongs to him who will give it its greatest hope'.

Suggested additional Bidding Prayers
We pray
– that come what may we will never lose hope in the goodness of God.
– that all those, and particularly the young, who are tempted to commit suicide may be given the gift of hope.
– for all those, particularly the Samaritans, who work with those who are depressed and desperate, that God will bless their efforts.

Catechism of the Catholic Church
1818 The virtue of hope responds to the aspiration to happiness

which God has placed in the heart of every man; it takes up the hopes that inspire men's activities and purifies them so as to order them to the kingdom of heaven; it keeps man from discouragement; it sustains him during times of abandonment; it opens up his heart in expectation of eternal beatitude. Buoyed up by hope, he is preserved from selfishness and led to the happiness that flows from charity.

The Sixth Sunday

Readings: Jer 17:5-8. 1 Cor 15:12, 16-20. Lk 6:17, 20-26.

Introduction

The beatitudes are a charter of the Christian life. They are not a moral code or a set of minimal precepts to avoid God's punishment. They are ideals to raise our perspective above the constraints of worldly interest.

Identikit of a Christian (Beatitudes) See also 4th Sunday A

In the old cowboy films set in the Wild West, it was the sheriff's job to catch the outlaw. Posters were printed depicting the wanted man and hung in saloons, usually with the caption: 'Wanted dead or alive' and offering a reward. Modern police departments have developed a more sophisticated version of this. Where the criminal is unknown, they create what is called an identikit picture, from descriptions they get from interviewing eye-witnesses. A likeness is built up from the size and shape of the mouth, nose and chin, the height of the forehead, the spacing between the eyes etc. The resulting portrait, surprisingly often, leads to the apprehension of the criminal.

It would be interesting to attempt to produce an identikit, not of the physical traits but of the personality make-up (or moral traits) of certain types. Let's pick the obvious one, the one we are most familiar with, the pop-idol, media-mogul, star-athlete, leading politician, TV personality, the one everybody is talking about. Mr Success himself. The one we all yearn to be, model ourselves on, and encourage our children to be. The new secular saint.

He/she must be highly motivated. Money is the great driving force. Money means power. As Cardinal Newman put it: 'All bow down before wealth. Wealth is that to which the multitude of men pay an instinctive homage.' To get it and the 'good life' that comes with it, he/she must be aggressive, rough-riding subordinates, trampling on underlings, ruthless with incompetents, unscrupulous with competitors. Needless to say, an ambivalence towards the law and an indifference to morality are prerequisites. The rash of corruption scandals presently making the headlines, not only in Italy but right across the globe, leave little doubt about that. Worldly success is rarely achieved with 'clean hands'. Throw in a few other features, such as pride, avarice, covetousness, anger, and lust, and our portrait is complete.

No modern image-maker or star creator would look twice at someone whose outstanding qualities were humility, compassion, poverty, self-denial and selfless dedication to the service of others. Yet, these, as the Sermon on the Mount outlines for us today, form the identikit of a Christian.

Suggested additional Bidding Prayers
We pray
– for the courage to make the moral choices outlined for us in the Sermon on the Mount.
– that we will find the true happiness promised in the beatitudes.
– that we may seek the love of God above all human achievement.

The Catechism of the Catholic Church
1723 The beatitude we are promised confronts us with decisive moral choices. It invites us to purify our hearts of bad instincts and to seek the love of God above all else. It teaches us that true happiness is not found in riches or well-being, in human fame or power, or in any human achievement – however beneficial it may be – such as science, technology or art, or indeed in any creature, but in God alone, the source of every good and of all love.'

Seventh Sunday

Readings: 1 Sam 26:2, 7-9, 12-13, 22-23. 1 Cor 15:45-49. Lk 6:27-38.

Introduction
In today's Eucharist we celebrate Christ the Lord of compassion and love. If we bear grudges against others, we cannot approach his altar. We ask him to rid us of our petty vengefulness.

Settling old scores (Revenge) See also 7th Sunday A

All America is watching it. And much of the rest of the world as well. The major TV networks are paying astronomic sums for the exclusive rights. The trial of a football star who is alleged to have murdered his former wife and her boy-friend. So what's new? Nothing. It's the oldest crime in history, dating all the way back to Cain and Abel. Shakespeare based his finest play – *Hamlet* – on the same theme, revenge.

Life is full of people with chips on their shoulders, real or imaginary, all waiting for a chance to get their own back. They carry their scars through life, refusing to let them heal until they have settled accounts. Feuds, vendettas and grudges are nurtured in parishes, in streets and even in families. Some are even passed down from one generation to the next. A colossal amount of human energy is expended on settling old scores and exacting vengeance. The *lex talionis* – 'an eye for an eye and a tooth for a tooth' – is alive and well and thriving in every human environment. In the corridors of power, in the velvet setting of plush boardrooms, the knives are long and sharp and when the opportunity arises are slipped between pin-striped shoulder-blades without a pang of remorse.

It is strange that honour is always at stake when the God of vengeance is invoked. So are loved ones. We owe it to our wives and children. 'Getting even' is raised to the level of a virtue. The world has nothing but contempt for the one who turns the other cheek.

What is refreshing about today's gospel is that it recognises us as we are, full of pettiness, exacting hurt for hurt, trading blow for blow. No mushy sentimentality here.

Christ takes for granted what we prefer to ignore. 'Who me? Enemies?' And those who hate us and curse us and treat us badly. Loving them is a call to perfection and the reward is great. 'You will be sons of the Most High, for he himself is kind to the ungrateful and the wicked.'

Suggested additional Bidding Prayers

We pray

– that God will rid us of the grudges we bear others.
– that love will distil the poison of vengeance in our hearts.
– that God will break the cycle of violence in Bosnia.

Catechism of the Catholic Church

2262 In the Sermon on the Mount, the Lord recalls the commandment, 'You shall not kill', and adds to it the proscription of anger, hatred and vengeance. Going further, Christ asks his disciples to turn the other cheek, to love their enemies. He did not defend himself and told Peter to leave his sword in its sheath.

Eighth Sunday

Readings: Eccles 27:4-7. 1 Cor 15:54-58. Lk 6:39-45

Introduction

Today's gospel invites us 'to take the plank' out of our own eyes before we try to take the splinter out of others' eyes. We are asked to take a hard look at ourselves and our own shortcomings.

Blind man's buff (Self-Awareness)

Blindness, for children, seems to hold no terror at all. They love even to fake blindness in many of their games like *Blind man's buff*. Maybe it's because they're so terribly afraid of the dark that they always make a game out of blindness. If only blindness could always remain a game children play!

But it's not so. Of all the forms blindness takes among adults, physical blindness is the most uncommon and the least terrible. Look at Algiers, where a few weeks ago a car-bomb went off killing thirty-five innocent bystanders and maiming three times as many. Or Bosnia where every day brings a new horror or Rwanda with its genocidal massacres. You don't have to look any further than your TV screen to see people who are blinded by hate and ignorance, fear and prejudice. The terrorist who sees only the sacredness of his own cause and nothing else. He certainly doesn't see his brother in other men or God in all men. Few countries in the world can claim to be immune from terrorism.

There are those in high places and in places not so high, who cast a blind eye on all the corruption, fiddling and dishonesty that surrounds them. The 'clean hands' investigation in Italy represents only the tip of an ice-berg. Scandals and cover-ups are confined within no frontiers. The kick-back, the back-hand, the pay-offs are convertible currency world-wide.

Other blindnesses are more pitiable. Those unhappy creatures whose lives are locked up in blind alleys, from which they can see no way out. Addicts of all kinds but above all those addicted to hard drugs like heroin or cocaine. And the cartels who feed their addictions give a new horror dimension to the expression 'the blind leading the blind'.

As for the rest of us, who pride ourselves on our sharp eye, our balanced view, our long-term perspective, how blind we are to our own shortcomings. How often we close our eyes to the crying needs of those even in our own immediate circle, not to mention the poor, the old, the handicapped. How often we try to take the speck out of our neighbour's eye, while neglecting the beam in our own. Such is the *Blind man's buff* we grown-ups play. And the sad thing is that, unlike children, we think we can see.

Of all those who followed Christ, looking for this, that and the other thing, there was only one, a blind beggar called Tim in the city of Jericho, who asked simply: 'Lord, that I may see!' Like Tim, we are all blind beggars and his is a little prayer we could all say and often.

Suggested additional Bidding Prayers
We pray
– 'Lord, that we may see.'
– Lord, open our eyes and our hearts to the crying needs of the poor.
– Lord, free our minds from prejudice and hatred.

Ninth Sunday

Readings: 1 Kings 8: 41-43. Gal 1:1-2, 6-10. Lk 7:1-10.

Introduction
Christ praises the faith of the Roman centurion. The church has preserved the centurion's words in the Mass just before Communion. We are invited to practise our Master's tolerance in our attitudes to people of other faiths.

Unconsecrated ground (Tolerance)
A large crack appeared suddenly in the steeple of our church.

It occurred to no one at the time that it might be an omen of tur-
bulent times ahead. Our church seemed then, like the community
it housed, as solid as the Rock of Gibraltar. Our parish priest's
immediate concern was to find some competent steeple-jacks to
repair the damage. Scotland, apparently, was the nearest place
which could provide such expertise. So one fine day, there arrived in our town a couple of Scottish steeple-jacks. As it was
deemed a job of long duration, they brought with them their
wives and children and found rented accommodation in the
town. They were Scots Presbyterians, or as we described them in
those pre-ecumenical days, people 'who kicked with the other
foot.' As there wasn't a single Protestant in the entire parish,
they were immediately lionised by all and sundry. Then, one
day, tragedy struck. One of their little boys was electrocuted in
his bath. The town was shattered. The whole population turned
out massively to pay their final respects. It was the biggest funeral ever held in our parish. The schools were closed and I lined
up with the rest of my classmates to form a guard of honour for
the little white coffin that bore Norman's remains to the local
graveyard. Somewhere, a Presbyterian minister was found to
conduct the service. Norman was buried in a plot of unconsecrated ground in a corner of the graveyard, far removed from the
sacred ground where all the Catholics were laid to rest.

I was reminded recently of that sad occasion. When re-read-
ing Shakespeare's *Hamlet*, I came across the passage describing
Ophelia's burial. Ophelia, in a bout of insanity, had committed
suicide. She, like Norman, was buried in unconsecrated ground,
in the briefest of ceremonies, permitted by the church on such
occasions. Her brother, Laertes, appalled by the brevity of the
priest's prayers, burst out in anger:

Lay her in the earth;
and from her fair and unpolluted flesh
may violets spring ! I tell thee,
churlish priest, a ministering angel
shall my sister be, when thou liest burning.

I think he spoke for everyone at Norman's grave or, at least, for
this ten-year old mourner.

I am reminded again of that sad incident in my childhood,
when I read in today's gospel about Christ curing the servant of
the centurion. They have curious details in common. Both
Norman's father and the centurion were foreigners. One was a
Scottish steeple-jack, the other a Roman soldier. Neither shared

the religion of the majority population with whom they lived. Yet one built the Jewish synagogue in Capernaum and the other restored the Catholic church steeple in Swinford. Both deserved well of Christ's favour, as the local communities readily agreed. And I am sure that just as Christ cured the servant of the centurion, he received little Norman into his kingdom. A short time later, no doubt inspired by the overwhelming sympathy shown them in their terrible grief, his family were received into the church. That church has not always shown the tolerance so conspicuous in its Master nor recognised the outstanding qualities of those who do not share its faith. 'Not even in Israel, have I found faith like this,' Christ exclaimed in admiration of the centurion. 'Lord, I am not worthy to have you under my roof,' the centurion had told him, 'but give the word and let my servant be cured.' His words remain, forever enshrined in the Mass, when we are invited to look up a the consecrated host just before we receive communion.

On a recent visit home, I went to the graveyard to look for Norman's grave. There were no violets blooming there. In fact, it was overgrown with weeds. But that unconsecrated plot was no longer isolated from the rest. Most of those, like my mother and father who mourned at Norman's grave, have since joined him in the cemetery. And their graves enclose his with a garland of crosses.

'God's kindly earth, is kindlier than men know,' as Oscar Wilde wrote about the grave of another outsider.

Suggested additional Bidding Prayers
We pray
– that we will recognise the truth and goodness in other religions.
– that we may never be dismissive of what is sacred to others.
– that we may be given the grace of tolerance.

Catechism of the Catholic Church
843 The Catholic Church recognises in other religions that search, among shadows and images, for the God who is unknown yet near since he gives life and breath and all things, and wants all men to be saved. Thus, the church considers all goodness and truth found in these religions as 'a preparation for the gospel, and given by him who enlightens all men that they may at length have life.'

Tenth Sunday

Readings: 1 Kings 17:17-24. Gal 1:11-19. Lk 7:11-17.

Introduction

Christ in his compassion restored to life the widow's son. It recalls for us our hope in the resurrection when Christ will raise us up on the last day.

A mother's tears (Compassion)

There is a story attributed to Oscar Wilde, which takes up where today's gospel ends. It runs something like this:

One year later, Jesus came once more to this town called Nain, accompanied by his disciples and a great number of people. When he was near the gate of the town it happened that there was a woman sitting on the roadside weeping bitterly.

When the Lord saw her he felt sorry for her. 'Do not cry,' he said. Looking up, the woman saw Jesus standing there and began to weep even more loudly. 'Why do you weep so?' Jesus asked the woman. 'Because of you,' the woman answered. 'I curse the day I met you when I was burying my only son and you brought him back to life. Now I wish he was dead.' 'Why do you speak so?' Jesus asked the woman. The woman answered, 'When my son came back to life, his fame spread throughout Judaea and all over the countryside. Many people came to do him homage. Before, he had been a dutiful son to me, his widowed mother. Now, his head was turned and he squandered all my savings on wastrels and harlots who fawned upon him, abandoning me on the wayside with neither son or home.' When Jesus heard these words he was astonished and, turning round, said to the crowd following him, 'I tell you, not even in Israel have I found ingratitude like this.'

The moral of this story, according to Wilde, was that nobody, not even God, should interfere in other peoples' lives.

Wilde's theology fell very far short of his undoubted literary skills. In the gospels there is no miracle which is futile, trivial or unwholesome. Nor are there miracles which inflict punishment on anybody. Christ's miraculous intervention in our lives, albeit extremely rare, is always benign. In the case of the bereaved widow, the gospel expressly mentions that 'he felt sorry for her'.

His motive was to heal her pain, not to replace it with another. The motive of this miracle was compassion: its message was God's victory over death. All the miracles of Jesus are the prelude to his own resurrection, which was the decisive triumph of the power of God.

Suffering was to bring Oscar Wilde deeper insights into the compassion of God. Falling from grace, the once literary lion of glittering London society became a social outcast, committed to Reading gaol. In his prison cell, he began to wonder:

For who can say by what strange way
Christ brings his will to light.

Lodged there among the dregs of human society and after a long and painful odyssey, he came like the broken-hearted widow of Nain, to experience the compassion of God:

Ah! happy they whose hearts can break
And peace of pardon win.
How else may man make straight his plan
And cleanse his soul from sin?
How else but through a broken heart
May Lord Christ enter in?

Suggested additional Bidding Prayers
We pray
– that Christ will restore us to the life of his grace.
– that we may always show concern for those who are bereaved.
– that the Lord will raise us up to new life on the last day.

Catechism of the Catholic Church
994 Jesus links faith in the resurrection to his own person: 'I am the resurrection and the life.' It is Jesus himself who on the last day will raise up those who have believed in him, who have eaten his body and drunk his blood. Already now in this present life he gives a sign and pledge of this by restoring some of the dead to life, announcing thereby his own resurrection, though it was to be of another order.

Eleventh Sunday

Readings: 2 Sam 12:7-10, 13. Gal 2:16, 19-21. Lk 7:36-8:3.

Introduction

David and Mary of Magdala acknowledged their sins and were forgiven. In our world, where the very notion of sin is almost extinct, we are invited by today's readings to accept personal responsibility for our wrong doing and seek God's forgiveness.

Shifting responsibility (Sin)

Nowadays, television frequently re-runs old Hollywood films, often in black and white. And strangely enough, there seems to be to be a fairly sizeable audience for them among the young. Whenever Hollywood chose a Catholic theme, and that was not often, it seemed to be particularly fascinated by the practice of confession. The relationship between the penitent in confession and the priest has always intrigued non-Catholics, and nothing more so than what is called the 'seal of confession'. A priest may never 'break the seal of confession', that is, he may never reveal what he has been told in confession, even to save his own life. This was the stuff that thrillers were made from. Murderers were believed to have revealed their crimes to a priest in confession, who had to carry this terrible secret, forbidden ever to reveal it. Even Catholics believed when I was a young priest, that all priests were bearers of such secrets. I think it largely accounted for the mystique attached to priests then. Now I wonder what the young, Catholic or not, make of such films. Most young Catholics who are not very familiar with confession, have never heard of the seal of confession.

When I was young, in what I now tend to think of as 'the age of sin', confession loomed very large in our lives. Every Saturday, at least up to my early teens, I was ordered to go to confession, and was often asked that evening, usually by my mother, 'was I at confession?' We all knew then about the seal of confession. Priests then were distinguished between those who were approachable and those who seemed to take personal offence at our little peccadillos. We didn't know which to fear most, the wrath of God or of the priest. Sin, mortal and venial, dominated religion. Occasions of sin abounded. For some, confession itself was one. When the change came, it came none to soon and I for one shed no tears for the demise of those sin-full times.

But there is a profit and loss in all change. Nobody today, who reads a newspaper or watches a television news, can be unaware that sin is alive and well, and thriving as never before. They chronicle day after day 'man's inhumanity to man', ranging from atrocities in Bosnia to massacres in Rwanda. But sin is never mentioned. They speak of 'crimes against humanity' or 'human rights violations'. The sense of sin is dead or well on the way towards extinction.

We have become observers rather than participants in the human tragedies of our times. We tut-tut from the comfort of our armchairs as the problems of our world are relayed into our homes. We have shifted responsibility from the first to the third person. It is 'they' and 'it' rather than 'I' who must accept the blame. We have institutionalised sin. It is the fault of governments, totalitarian regimes, big business etc, etc, etc. We are the victims of the system and we wallow in our inability to do anything about it. But just as 'i' is the middle letter of 'sin', 'I' is the centre of sin. And that is the message of today's readings. David had taken Bethseba, Uriah's wife and what was much worse had placed Uriah in the front line of his army where certain death awaited him. Confronted by the prophet Nathan, David accepted responsibility for his crime: '*I* have sinned against the Lord.' The tears of Mary Magdalen, moved Christ to say: 'Her sins, her many sins must have been forgiven her, or she would not have shown such great love.' David and Mary Magdalen accepted their guilt. Today's Psalm says it all:

But now *I* have acknowledged my sins;
My guilt I did not hide.
I said: '*I* will confess
my offence to the Lord.'
And you, Lord, have forgiven
the guilt of *my* sin.

God and sin, good and evil, are reverse sides of the same coin. One does not exist without the other. Those who have lost their sense of sin may be well on the way to losing their sense of God as well. The very first step we take towards God is a step away from sin. Like the Prodigal we begin our return to the Father with a recognition of our sinfulness: 'Father, *I* have sinned against heaven and against you.'

Suggested additional Bidding Prayers
We pray
– that we may recognise and acknowledge our sins.
– for the grace of repentance for our sins.
– for God's forgiveness for the sins we have committed.

Catechism of the Catholic Church
387 Only the light of divine revelation clarifies the reality of sin and particularly of the sin committed at mankind's origins. Without the knowledge revelation gives of God we cannot recognise sin clearly and are tempted to explain it as merely a developmental flaw, a psychological weakness, a mistake, or the necessary consequence of an inadequate social structure, etc. Only in the knowledge of God's plan for man can we grasp that sin is an abuse of the freedom that God gives to created persons so that they are capable of loving him and loving one another.

Twelfth Sunday

Readings: Zech 12:10-11. Gal 3:26-29. Lk 9:18-24.

Introduction
Jesus warns his disciples about his suffering and death. Only by taking up the cross can they follow him. We too become followers of Christ by accepting the crosses that come our way.

The Cross (Suffering) See also 22nd Sunday A and 5th Sunday B
Nowhere has change been so remarkable in recent times than in the field of medicine and all our lives have been radically transformed by it. As little as forty years ago, the life of a priest was dominated by what were then called 'sick calls'. Day or night he could be called, and often was, to administer the last sacraments to the dying. He daren't leave his house without leaving explicit instructions as to where he could be found and if for some reason he had to leave his parish, he would always contact a neighbouring priest, to cover his parish in his absence. No priest today feels this awesome responsibility. Most people now die in hospitals, where they are cared for by chaplains. Most people then died in their homes. Everybody, including children, would have seen death at close quarters. They would have watched over a dying member of the family, for days and

weeks and months, as life slowly ebbed away until at last it flickered out. Sooner or later, 'the Great Reaper', so luridly depicted as a skeleton wielding a scythe, was a visitor in every home. Almost the only use made of the 'parlour' in country houses was to lay out the dead and hold the wake.

Sickness and death were always accompanied by suffering. There were no pain-killing drugs then. People turned to what they called 'the consolations of religion'.

They had an instinctive empathy for the suffering and death of Christ, which we can barely comprehend now. The Stations of the Cross had an enormous appeal for them. It helped them make sense of their own lives. They were encouraged to unite their sufferings to the sufferings of Christ. Suffering was seen as 'the will of God', and 'resignation' in the face of suffering was the great virtue. They were taught 'to offer it up' in reparation for their own sins and those of others. It explains the enormous popularity of somebody like St Thérèse of Lisieux, the Little Flower, who was canonised in the first decades of this century. She died from tuberculosis in her early twenties and her diary 'The Little Way' had enormous appeal in Ireland, where there was scarcely a home that had not lost a young boy or girl prematurely as a result of TB.

Now TB has been eradicated, only to be replaced by cancer, which in turn seems about to be conquered by medical science. But a new epidemic, AIDS, is sweeping the world, for which medicine so far has no answer. Suffering may not now occupy the centre-stage in our lives, as it did formerly, but it will remain, like death, a permanent part of the human condition. Just as the cross will remain forever at the core of Christianity. For the first time in history, in this post-Christian era, it is probably more worn as an ornament rather than as a religious symbol. A pretty thing we wear around our necks, rather than a cruel burden that we carry on our shoulders. It is what makes us Christian. What Christ said in today's gospel, he says to all: 'If anyone wants to be a follower of mine, let him renounce himself and take up his cross every day and follow me.'

Suggested additional Bidding Prayers
We pray
– that God will give us the strength to carry the crosses which come our way in the course of our lives.
– for all those who are sick at this time.
– for doctors and nurses and all those who care for the sick.

Catechism of the Catholic Church
1501 Illness can lead to anguish, self-absorbtion, sometimes
even despair and revolt against God. It can also make a person
more mature, helping him discern in his life what is not essential
so that he can turn toward that which is. Very often illness provokes a search for God and a return to him.

Thirteenth Sunday

Readings: 1 Kings 19:16, 19-21. Gal 5:1, 13-18. Lk 9:51-62.

Introduction
St Paul reminds the Galatians that they were called to liberty
and warns them not to abuse their freedom by self-indulgence.
We should reflect today on the freedom we have and on those
who are still denied it.

The price of freedom (Liberty)
On 14 July, a little over two-hundred years ago, an event took
place in Paris, the Fall of the Bastille, which shook the world.
The recent fall of the Berlin Wall pales into insignificance in
comparison to it. In fact, future historians may well link, the dramatic collapse of the Soviet Bloc with the revival of interest in
the French Revolution on the occasion of its bicentenary. In any
case, the timing of that recent event seems more than coinciden-
tal. The fall of the Bastille had enormous symbolic appeal to oppressed peoples everywhere and nowhere more than in Ireland
where its anniversary was celebrated with large parades and
demonstrations in Dublin and Belfast. The Bastille was an imposing fortress-prison in the centre of Paris, which for many
Parisians had come to symbolise tyranny. It was widely thought
that its numerous dungeons were crammed with prisoners, the
unjust victims of an oppressive system. In fact, there were only
seven inmates, three of whom were insane and had been committed there by their families. The other four were professional
swindlers. They were carried shoulder-high through the streets
of Paris and later melted into the crowd with the practised ease of
professionals, the first beneficiaries of the revolutionary *liberté*.
    It could have been St Paul that day who had fired up the
mob to attack the Bastille instead of the Revolutionary orator,
Camilles Desmoulins. His message to the Galatians, related in

today's epistle, would have raised rousing cheers from that Parisian crowd. 'My brothers, you were called to liberty. Stand firm, therefore, and do not submit again to the yoke of slavery.' This is the stuff revolutions are made of.

Had Paul been its leader, the Revolution might have unfolded very differently. The terrible blood-lust, culminating in the Reign of Terror, might never have happened. 'Be careful,' he warned the Galatians, 'or this liberty will provide an opening for self-indulgence.' It is a warning the French could have done with. But Madame La Guillotine was destined to have her way and the French indulged in an orgy of self-destruction. 'O liberty, what crimes have been committed in thy name,' Danton, himself a victim of the guillotine, is reputed to have exclaimed.

It seems to have set a standard for all subsequent revolutions. Ireland began its era of independence with a civil war. So did most African States. Now, we have the spectacle of the Balkans, just freed from dictatorship, locked in fratricidal combat. No sooner has freedom been gained than power-hungry factions enter the fray to carve out their own niches in the vacuum left. Paul had foreseen it all: 'If you go snapping at each other and tearing each other to pieces, you had better watch or you will destroy the whole community.'

Somebody once said: 'The price of freedom is eternal vigilance.' It re-echoes St Paul's warning to the Galatians: 'Be careful or this liberty will provide an opening for self-indulgence.' One of the first targets of the French Revolution was the Catholic Church, so far had it departed from its evangelical origins. It is a warning to us all. Our record in the past leaves a lot to be desired. We subscribe to a gospel which above all proclaims: 'The truth will make you free.'

Suggested additional Bidding Prayers
We pray
– for oppressed peoples everywhere.
– for all those who are imprisoned for daring to speak out against those in power.
– that we may always be vigilant in protecting our freedom.

Catechism of the Catholic Church.
1738 Freedom is exercised in relationships between human beings. Every human person, created in the image of God, has the natural right to be recognised as a free and responsible

being. All owe to each other this duty of respect. The right to the exercise of freedom, especially in moral and religious matters, is an inalienable requirement of the dignity of the human person. This right must be recognised and protected by civil authority within the limits of the common good and public order.

Fourteenth Sunday

Readings: Is 66:10-14. Gal 6:14-18. Lk 10:1-12, 17-20.

Introduction
The peace of Christ which we celebrate today should leave its mark on us so that we become messengers of peace to all around us.

'Peace to this house' (Peace)
Almost eighty years ago the First World War was optimistically described as 'the war to end all wars'. A lot of water has flowed under the bridge since then and much of it has been rivers of blood. The macabre sight of bloated corpses, victims of the tribal massacre in Rwanda, floating eerily in the waters of Lake Victoria, flashed across the world's TV screens, confirmed the pessimism of many who see no sign of the 'end-of-all-wars' epoch in sight. The collapse of the Soviet Empire may have heralded the end of the Cold War but it brought in its wake a spate of bloody conflicts in countries we did not even know existed before.The birth-pangs of a new world order, the experts tell us. Sure, some progress has been made recently in resolving age-old conflicts, such as the dismantlement of apartheid in South Africa and tentative steps towards peace in Northern Ireland. Even in Christ's native land some peace accords have been established between Israel and a few of her Arab neighbours, notably the Palestinians and Jordan. However welcome such peace is, it scarcely merits Isaiah's promise:

>   Now towards her I send flowing
>   peace, like a river,
>   and like a stream in spate
>   the glory of the nations.

Rivers of blood rather than rivers of peace continue to irrigate our world.

Far from being a benign influence, religion so often seems not only to ignite but even to prolong and embitter conflicts between peoples. Bosnia, in the heart of Europe, whose cruel war continues to defy the best efforts of peacemakers to resolve, is a lethal cocktail of Catholics, Orthodox and Muslims. An alphabetical tour of the planet, from Algiers to Zagreb, presents a similar picture. A modern atheist observer might be forgiven his assumption that such epithets describe not religions but warring factions. At least those of them who make our daily headlines seem more often to be fanatical followers of a God of vengeance rather than quiet devotees of the God of love. But the modern media is biased towards the sensational and its headlines chronicle the world's disasters. Ordinary lives make no news. The great masses of humanity live their day-to-day lives in peace and harmony with their neighbours. Many of them live heroic lives dedicated to the service of others. Occasionally, even the media cannot avoid them. A TV documentary on the horrors of a refugee camp in Rwanda may briefly feature a young Irish girl volunteer or a French *medecin san frontière* holding a sick child in their arms. 'A single picture is worth a thousand words.'

Lest we become discouraged, two things about the modern world are worth remembering. Modern technology has created weapons of mass destruction which enable relatively few to cause widespread death and destruction. Secondly, the modern media instantly relays worldwide the resulting horror. As a result it is easy for us to overlook the enormous progress peace has made over much of the world in our time. For most of history war was endemic everywhere. Now it has been isolated to relatively few flash-points. It only takes an single incident to start a war. Establishing peace is a long and painful process. But Christ the Prince of Peace is on our side and the outcome is assured. And our reward will be great. 'Blessed are the peacemakers, for they shall see God.'

Suggested additional Bidding Prayers
We pray
– that conflicts everywhere may be resolved by peaceful means.
– for peace in our homes and communities.
– for peacemakers that their work may bear fruit.

Catechism of the Catholic Church
2305 Earthly peace is the image and fruit of the peace of Christ, the messianic 'Prince of Peace'. By the blood of his cross, 'in his own person he killed hostility', he reconciled men with

God and made his church the sacrament of the unity of the human race and of its union with God. 'He is our peace.' He has declared: 'Blessed are the peacemakers.'

Fifteenth Sunday

Readings: Deut 30:10-14. Col 1:15-20. Lk 10:25-37.

Introduction

The parable of the Good Samaritan is Christ's answer to the question 'Who is my neighbour. It should inspire us to 'go and do the same ourselves'.

The Good Samaritan (Fraternity)

'Liberty, Equality, Fraternity' was a brilliant piece of propaganda. But it was an odd threesome as a programme for revolution. Laws can be and were enacted to guarantee liberty and equality but no government can make a law to enforce fraternity. There is little evidence of fraternity during revolutions and in this the French Revolution was no exception. But there was one notable example and that on the side of those who were described as the 'enemies of the revolution'. When the king was condemned to death by the National Assembly, he asked to have a priest attend him at the end. His request was granted and he wrote the name and address of a priest, stipulating that if the priest did not wish to risk his life on such a dangerous mission, the king would understand. The man he chose was an Irish priest, the Abbé Edgeworth. Most French priests had by then fled or gone into hiding for fear of the revolutionaries. The Abbé Edgeworth immediately accepted. He presented himself at the prison where the king was lodged, spent the last night with him, offered Mass in the morning and accompanied the king to the guillotine. When the king was beheaded, the priest, spattered with his blood, turned to descend the scaffold. Confronting him were more than fifty-thousand armed soldiers, drawn up in serried rows round the scaffold together with a huge mob of rabid revolutionaries, who had come to cheer at the king's execution. He approached the front row of armed guards, expecting to be seized, but it parted to let him pass, as did the second and third and so on to the end, until he was out of danger. In a strange way, it was almost as if they were forming a guard of honour for the departing priest. The French revolutionaries, like others, re-spected bravery, even in their enemies.

This story, though known to few in Ireland, is widely known in France, if for no other reason than the countless illustrations of the execution of Louis XVI which appeared shortly after-wards and are frequently re-produced since. In these Abbé Edgeworth is depicted standing beside the king and holding aloft a crucifix.

What is not well-known, either there nor here, is the subse-quent history of the priest. Shortly afterwards, he was forced to flee France. The king's brother, already in exile in Northern Prussia, invited the Abbé to join him and the royal family as their chaplain. In spite of his delicate health, he agreed and spent the rest of his days he what he described as 'the land of ice'. In the winter of 1806, the French Revolutionary army under Napoleon had advanced as far as Warsaw. Many of the French soldiers contracted fever and some were left to die near where the Abbé was in exile. When he heard of their plight, he went immediately to minister to them despite warnings from his friends. He caught the fever and died shortly afterwards. He died nursing the soldiers of the Revolution which had beheaded his king.

We read in today's gospel: 'Now a priest happened to be travelling down the same road, but when he saw the man, he passed by on the other side.' It is heartwarming for us to know that there was at least one priest, a product of that decadent church of the *ancien régime* who did not 'pass by on the other side'. Not once, but at least twice in his life, he played the Good Samaritan. But more importantly, Abbé Edgeworth's story, like that of the Good Samaritan, should inspire us to take up Christ's challenge: 'Go and do the same yourself.'

Suggested additional Bidding Prayers
We pray
– for ourselves that we may show our love for God by showing charity to our neighbour in need.
– for the Samaritans, the St Vincent de Paul Society and other charitable organisations that God will bless their work in help-ing the needy.
– for those in need that our generosity will alleviate their plight.

Catechism of the Catholic Church

2447 The works of mercy are charitable actions by which we come to the aid of our neighbour in his spiritual and bodily necessities .... The corporal works of mercy consist especially in feeding the hungry, sheltering the homeless, clothing the naked, visiting the sick and imprisoned, and burying the dead. Among all these, giving alms to the poor is one of the chief witnesses to fraternal charity: it is also a work of justice pleasing to God.

Sixteenth Sunday

Readings: Gen 18:1-10. Col 1:24-28. Lk 10:38-42.

Introduction

Christ's advised Martha that she should not be preoccupied by the everyday chores. It is these worldly preoccupations that give us all our worries and anxieties. Like Mary we should sit at the feet of Our Lord and listen to him.

The better part (Other-worldliness)

The world is made up of Martha's and Mary's – the doers and the dreamers – and it would seem the former are far more numerous than the latter. The industrial and commercial society of today places a huge premium on achievement. It is results that count. Targets are set for production and sales and only those who achieve or surpass them are rewarded. Captains of industry everywhere are pushing hard to have pay related to production. Their message is 'shape up or ship out'. And those who can't or won't are made redundant. It is all about 'turnover' in a profit-and-loss society. We live in Martha's world.

Yet history shows that the greatest contributions to our civilisation were made by dreamers. By those, who in that memorable phrase of President Kennedy, 'saw things that never were and asked why not'. From Plato to Albert Einstein our world has been shaped by a long line of visionaries who could see a world other than the one they were born into. In their time they were mostly ignored, often reviled and sometimes, like Galileo, condemned. It is ironic that Christ's followers so seldom show his marked preference for the Marys of this world. They toiled away in their garrets, often in poverty, elaborating their dreams and bringing to birth a better world for future generations. Recognition, if it came, always came posthumously. We at least are in no doubt now that they 'chose the better part'. They have left us forever in their debt.

The achievers, who largely dominate the pages of our history books, have left us an altogether more dubious legacy. From Alexander the Great to Stalin, their rampaging armies have re-drawn the world's map in blood, imposed alien languages and laws in the name of conquest and left behind a tangled web of feuds and hatreds that centuries later peoples still struggle to unravel. Their successors in our century, the giant international corporations, in their quest to conquer the world, are now threatening its very survival. In the name of production, they are polluting the atmosphere, pillaging the seas and de-foresting the land. Whole species have become extinct or are threatened with extinction. They have condemned us to live in the shadow of a Chernobyl waiting to happen.

But, mercifully, we still have our dreamers. 'I have a dream.' Who can forget those words of Martin Luther King? 'I have climbed the mountain and seen the Promised Land.' He was gunned down by an assassin but his people were emancipated. Recently, another great prophet of our time, Aleksandr Solz-henitsyn, returned to his homeland, Russia, after years of exile in the West. He travelled the length and breath of the mother-land, listening to the voices of the simple Russian peasants. Then, looking and sounding like an Old Testament prophet, he delivered a scathing condemnation of Russia's new achievers to the parliament in Moscow. Those, like him, who chose to be the conscience of a people, may seem to be ignored, but their mes-sage lives on.

The message of today's gospel, is that we, like our Master, should cherish such dreamers. It is the poets and prophets, writ-ers and thinkers, philosophers and mystics, who like Mary, have chosen the better part.

Suggested additional Bidding Prayers
We pray
– that we will always cherish our intellectuals, our poets and writers.
– that by listening to Jesus we will shed our worries and anxi-eties.
– that God will bless our lives with good and lasting friendships.

Seventeenth Sunday

Readings: Gen 18:20-32. Col 2:12-24. Lk 11:1-13.

Introduction
Christ taught his disciples to call God 'Our Father'. We are his children and like all children if we need anything we ask our Father for it and it will be given to us.

'Give us this day ' (Petition)
Shortly after I was ordained I went to Lourdes for the first time. I was spending the summer working in a parish in Bordeaux. Just before I was due to leave, I took the train down to Lourdes. By this time my money was running out. The French church with its evangelical contempt for Mammon, had not acquired the habit of remunerating its visiting priests. By the time I reached Lourdes, which was before midday, I had not the wherewithal even to buy a sandwich and my return train did not leave until 10pm. I set out for the Grotto where I intended to say Mass. I enquired there for the direction to the chapel and was told to stand in one of the many queues. 'When they see you are a priest you will be called in.' I was told. Sure enough, minutes later a steward spotted me and beckoned me to follow him. I could hear water being sloshed around. 'A strange place to have the chapel,' I thought to myself. But it was not the chapel. It was the baths. Too late to back out, I stripped as I was told and after a perfunctory prayer, I was duly immersed. Groping for a towel, I was informed that the custom was to dress without drying. Back outside, I sat on a wall in the sunshine, feeling water dripping down my back and into my shoes. Soon after, I began to sneeze. By the time I had reached Ireland, twenty-four hours later, I was quite feverish and was confined to bed for a week. I had been granted the Lourdes-miracle in reverse. I had arrived there in the whole of my health and returned home sick.

It was twenty-five years later before I was persuaded to return. A group of young Irish in Paris invited me to accompany them on weekend pilgrimage. Being their chaplain, I could hardly refuse. This time was different. A lot of water had passed under the bridge. I was no longer the young priest with the world at his feet. I may not have been crippled, like so many of those I saw there waiting outside the baths, but life had left me my share of scars. And I had had one slight brush with death in the form of cancer. I found it much easier now to identify with the sick and handicapped there, knocking at heaven's doors, looking for an answer to their prayers. Lourdes had not changed in these twenty-five years, but I had. I knew how to ask now, because I had things to ask for. Only those who have reasons to ask, know how to pray. Maybe my sickness on that first trip was a little miracle after all. Perhaps God was warning me that I too had need of his help.

There was nothing wrong, as far as we know, with the disciple who asked Jesus how to pray. His answer is for all:

Ask, and it will be given to you; search and you will find; knock, and the door will be opened to you. For the one who asks always receives; the one who searches always finds; the one who knocks will always have the door opened to him.

Suggested additional Bidding Prayers
We pray
– that God our Father will help us to use wisely the blessings he has given us.
– that God our Father will give us each day our daily bread.
– that God our Father will forgive our sins against him as we forgive others who have wronged us.

Catechism of the Catholic Church.
2765 The traditional expression 'the Lord's Prayer' – *oratio Dominica* – means that the prayer to our Father is taught and given to us by the Lord Jesus. The prayer that comes to us from Jesus is truly unique: it is 'of the Lord'. On the one hand, in the words of this prayer the only Son gives us the words the Father gave him: he is the master of our prayer. On the other, as Word incarnate, he knows in his human heart the needs of his human brothers and sisters and reveals them to us: he is the model of our prayer.

Eighteenth Sunday

Readings: Eccl 1:2, 2:21-23. Col: 3:1-5, 9-11. Lk 12:13-21.

Introduction
The parable of the rich Man is particularly relevant for us

who live in what is termed 'the rich man's club'. Our greed condemns those in the Third World to die of hunger and poverty.

Vanity of vanities (Avarice)

Poverty breeds its own virtues. 'Necessity is the mother of in-
vention.' For the generation who grew up after the great depression of the thirties and the rationing of the Second World War,
the great virtue was 'waste not, want not'. Life then seemed to
be one great salvage operation. There was a Jacobs biscuit tin on
every mantlepiece, where all sorts of bits and pieces were stored,
like buttons and safety-pins and pieces of string. It was a hold-
all wherein was stored the wherewithal to repair the wear and
tear of daily life. Hoarding then was a virtuous necessity rather
than a vice. Garbage disposal was no problem then. Most things
had disintegrated long before they got that far. Even the ashes
from the fire were used in the garden to kill slugs and worms in
the rhubarb patch. Clothes were patched and woollen socks
were darned out of recognition and when they could no longer
be worn they began life anew as dusters and mops. Toilet paper
had not been invented then; yesterday's newspaper served the
purpose more than adequately. For those who came in the middle of families, most of their clothes were hand-me-downs. Sizes
tended to be approximate rather than exact. Hems alternated between being 'let down' or 'turned up'.

After all this rigid training in economising we were plunged
into the consumer society and the era of the disposable. Cities
and governments spend millions on the collection and disposal
of waste. Plastic garbage bags figure on every shopping list.
Television shows us harrowing pictures of children and families, foraging for survival in the public dumps of Rio de Janeiro
and Manila. Whole shanty-towns have grown up round them. It
is a vivid illustration of the ever-widening gap between the
'haves' and the 'have-nots', between our avarice and their desti-
tution.

Governments and businesses vie with each other in promot-
ing avarice in their citizens and customers. It is one of the great
civic virtues. The good of the economy depends upon it. The
Lotto has become a national craze. And lest we might suffer
from tweaks of conscience occasionally, we are re-assured by
the list of hospitals and other charitable institutions who benefit
from our avariciousness. But avarice is one of the seven deadly
sins, 'deadly' because it spawns a host of other sins. No one who

reads a newspaper can doubt that. The litany of political scandals make daily headlines. Government ministers in Italy, France and England have recently resigned or been sacked and even arrested for taking bribes. The Mafia and drug-barons are laughing all the way to the bank.

St Paul puts it bluntly in today's epistle: 'That is why you must kill everything in you that belongs to the earthly life ... and especially greed, which is the same thing as worshipping a false god.' 'You can't take it with you' was a common expression one time in Ireland about money. Which proves, if it proves nothing else, that the Irish knew their gospel. 'Fool, this night do I require thy soul of thee.' For those who seek God, the church has always recommended poverty, chastity and obedience – and in that order. The hand that reaches out for God must be empty.

Suggested additional Bidding Prayers
We pray
– that we may never blight our lives and our loves by our greed.
– that the pursuit of money may never dominate our lives.
– that we may share our surplus with the needy.

Catechism of the Catholic Church
2547 The Lord grieves over the rich, because they find their consolation in the abundance of goods. 'Let the proud seek and love earthly kingdoms, but blessed are the poor in spirit for theirs is the kingdom of heaven.' Abandonment to the providence of the Father in heaven frees us from anxiety about tomorrow. Trust in God is a preparation for the blessedness of the poor. They shall see God.

Nineteenth Sunday

Readings: Wis 18:6-9. Heb 11:1-2, 8-19. Lk 12:32-48.

Introduction
Today we celebrate Abraham, 'our father in faith'. We aspire to his faith which 'is the assurance of things hoped for, the conviction of things unseen'.

The adventurous patriarch (Faith)

The bishop had invited me to preach at confirmation. It was one of those clerical chores masquerading as an honour. I was a soft target, being the youngest priest in the diocese and these extra assignments were usually dumped on the newly arrived. It was a rural diocese in the west of Ireland, not my own, and I was unfamiliar with its geography. On my way there I got lost. When, at last, I found the little village, I was informed that the parish church was situated a few miles outside it. Finally, I got there only to find that the ceremony had already begun. But I was still just in time to give my homily. I quickly donned my surplice and soutane and almost sprinted to the pulpit. It's a daunting experience for a young priest to preach on such occasions in the presence of the bishop and a large contingent of clergy who turn up, I suspect, more for the sumptuous clerical dinner that followed than for the ceremony itself. It's more like a public oral examination than a pastoral exercise. I cannot remember now what I said, but I doubt very much it was anything very radical, given the times and the circumstances. But my late arrival condemned me from the start, confirming the reputation I had already acquired of being something of a maverick. At the end we all processed out led by the altar-servers, then the clergy, with myself and the bishop bringing up the rear. The choir had struck up *Faith of our fathers*. I always thought the music of that rousing anthem more suited to a football stadium than a church. The clergy joined in the refrain, raising their voices noticeably for the last line, which a clerical jester had changed ever so slightly:

We will be true to thee til death
in spite of dungeon, fire and Swords.

The enigmatic smile on the face of the bishop, registered approval.

Faith, in the sense of rigid adherence to the church's teaching, was paramount then. There was almost never a dissenting voice among the clergy. The people had no opinions, as was expected of them. Their role was simply to 'pray, obey and pay.' Every issue from creation to the end of the world was dealt with magisterially and majestically by the church. From the cradle to the grave we were kept in tow, if not in line, by her teaching. The catechism in the classroom and the catechetical instruction from the pulpit, left us in no doubt where she stood and where we were expected to follow. Doubts, like scruples, were kindly but firmly treated as neurotic disorders. Scripture was a dubious extra, still suspect from its Protestant past. It was a safe, comfortable, if unexciting world, and there are still some who regret its passing. But pass it did when a twinkling Sputnik encircling our planet raised our eyes and removed our certainties.

Our notion of faith then was a far cry from that which inspired Abraham, 'our father in faith.' The *Letter to the Hebrews* gives us today its best definition: 'Faith is the assurance of things hoped for, the conviction of things not seen.' The models we had then were rigid guardians, minding their deposit of faith like keepers of a bank-vault, far removed from that adventurous patriarch who invested his in a risky future.

'It was by faith that Abraham obeyed the call to set out for a country that was the inheritance given to him and his descendants, and that he set out without knowing where he was going. By faith he arrived, as a foreigner, in the Promised Land, and lived there as if in a strange country.' His octogenarian wife, Sarah, was weaving a cradle when she should have been making a death-shroud. But their courageous faith was rewarded. Their descendants today are as promised, as numerous 'as the stars in the sky and the sands on the seashore.' Though it might be added that those children of Abraham, the Jews, the Arabs and the Christians, have become ever more querulous with the passage of time.

We now, like Abraham and his, are wanderers in a world of uncertainties. We are 'only strangers and nomads on earth.' Like them, we 'live in tents while we look forward to a city founded, designed and built by God.' And as the *Letter to the Hebrews* observes: 'People who use these terms about themselves make it quite plain that they are in search of their real homeland.' We too are searching for the Promised Land and, like Abraham, our faith should help us to realise, in the words of another great adventurer, Robert Louis Stevenson, that 'to travel hopefully is a better thing than to arrive.'

Suggested additional Bidding Prayers
We pray
– for faith to live in this world as 'strangers and nomads'.
– for faith to live in this world as in a strange land.
– for faith to continue our journey in search of the Promised Land.

Catechism of the Catholic Church

145 The *Letter to the Hebrews,* in its great eulogy of the faith of
Israel's ancestors, lays special emphasis on Abraham's faith: 'By
faith, Abraham obeyed when he was called to go out to a place
which he was to receive as an inheritance; and he went out not
knowing where he was to go.' By faith, he lived as a stranger
and pilgrim in the promised land. By faith, Sarah was given to
conceive the son of the promise. And by faith Abraham offered
his only son in sacrifice.

Twentieth Sunday

Readings: Jer 38:4-6, 8-10. Heb 12:1-4. Lk 12:49-53.

Introduction

The theme of today's readings is moral courage, a virtue in
very short supply in our world. It is fashionable nowadays to
keep our heads down and go with the herd. It is not acceptable
behaviour for Christians. Victims everywhere cry out to us to
speak out on their behalf.

For evil to triumph (Courage)

There is a little cemetery in the seminary of Maynooth. There
rest the remains of the students and professors who died there in
the course of its two-hundred year history. It is not a much visited spot. During my seminary days, I liked to sneak there occasionally if only to escape briefly the enforced camaraderie of
student life. The graves are marked by headstones of varying
heights, all bearing effusive Latin tributes to the virtues and
scholarship of the deceased. Nothing here recalls Job's famous
dictum: 'Naked I came into the world and naked I leave it.' The
occupants of these tombs went to meet their Maker, heavily
draped in the eulogies of their contemporaries. Only one grave
has no headstone at all. Instead, there is a small diamond-
shaped flag laid horizontally over the centre of the plot. It bears
the name Walter MacDonald. Apparently, he had died under a
cloud. What he had published to earn the disapproval of his fellow professors and the opprobrium of the hierarchy, I don't really
know. I suspect it wouldn't raise many eyebrows now. The
anonymous admirer who arranged his burial, added one short
line in Latin on the small memorial plaque. It read simply: *Obiit*

in festo Sancti Athanasii. ('Died on the feast of St Athanasius.') In that one little phrase, he paid his departed friend a greater tribute than all the other eulogies put together. St Athanasius was a fourth-century Bishop of Alexandria, much maligned by his contemporaries. Persecuted by emperors and people alike because he opposed their erroneous views, he was exiled no less than five times from his diocese. His outstanding courage earned him immortality with the Latin dictum *Athanasius contra mundum* ('Athanasius versus the world'). Walter MacDonald, like the saint whose feast he shares, also achieved some posthumous recognition. The great Irish playwright, Sean O'Casey, dedicated a volume of his autobiography to him. An extraordinary tribute to a Maynooth professor from such a distinguished anti-cleric.

Moral courage is a virtue in short supply in today's world and it has been for much of this century. It is just fifty years now since the true horror of the Nazis concentration camps was first exposed to the world. Few can now doubt that butchery on such a massive scale could have been carried out without the compliance or connivance of a large section of the population. The Nuremburg Trials condemned a few of the ringleaders; another court will judge their numberless accomplices. Nor could the now dismantled system of apartheid in South Africa have been maintained so rigorously for so long without a conspiracy of silence on the part of the majority of the white population. It took far more than the numerous informers, apparatchiks and jail-keepers to fill and maintain the Siberian gulags of Stalinist Russia. The totalitarian regime there, like those in Nazi Germany or Fascist Italy or Mao Tze-tung's China, could only have come to power and stayed in power, with the tacit approval of an enormous number of people. 'For evil to triumph, it is enough that good people do nothing.'

But all was not black. Those terrorist regimes of our notorious century produced their little crop of heroes. Some, like Aleksandr Solzhenitsyn, have lived to tell their terrible tale. Others, like Andrei Sakharov, died within sight of the promised land. A few, like Nelson Mandela, survived long years in prison and achieved their hard-earned recognition. The Polish priest, Maximilian Kolbe, gave his life for another inmate of Dachau and has since been canonised. 'But there are others, of whom there is no record, whose godly deeds have not failed.' Many went to their graves unknown and unsung.

We are the heirs of these horrendous events, the first to learn their terrible lesson. It may well be that 'the price of freedom is eternal vigilance', but it requires a lot of moral courage of ordinary citizens to make it thrive. Our world too is awash with victims whose cries for help so often go unheeded and unheard. The battered child in our neighbourhood that goes unreported. The drug-pusher in the inner city who plies his deadly trade in broad daylight. The sexually-harrassed employee in our company whose plight we watch in silent disapproval. Uninvolvement is the easy option. Nobody wants to tempt a neighbour's wrath or lose his job or risk assault. But such are the demands of the gospel for the followers of Christ. 'Think of the way he stood such opposition from sinners and then you will not give up for want of courage' the *Letter to the Hebrews* tells us. And Christ leaves little doubt as to what our courage will entail: 'I am not here to bring peace, but rather division.'

Suggested additional Bidding Prayers
We pray
– for moral courage to speak out against evil in our society.
– for moral courage to risk our peace, our jobs and our security to defend the victims in our society.
– we pray for martyrs everywhere who give their freedom and lives in the cause of justice.

Catechism of the Catholic Church
1808 Fortitude is the moral virtue that ensures firmness in difficulties and constancy in the pursuit of the good. It strengthens the resolve to resist temptations and to overcome obstacles in the moral life. The virtue of fortitude enables one to conquer fear, even fear of death, and to face trials and persecutions. It disposes one even to renounce and sacrifice one's life in defence of a just cause. 'The Lord is my strength and my song.' 'In the world you have tribulations; but be of good cheer, I have overcome the world.'

Twenty-First Sunday

Readings: 66:18-21. Heb 12:5-7, 11-13. Lk 13:22-30.

Introduction
The theme of the *Letter to the Hebrews* today is punishment, a

subject that has become almost taboo in our society. We are invited to reflect on this theme in the light of today's reading.

The stick and the carrot (Punishment)

The little four-year-old boy was sulking under the table. He had been refused a second helping of ice-cream. His mother ordered him out, but the boy wouldn't budge. She tried coaxing. Nothing doing. Finally, she promised him the ice-cream, and he trotted out triumphantly and they both went out to get the ice-cream from the fridge. I was left alone with the other witness of this little domestic scene, the little boy's grandmother. While mother and son were being re-united over a dish of ice-cream in the kitchen, the old lady said to me, 'She isn't fair to the little boy; he doesn't know any better. She should have punished him.' I'd never heard it put that way before. Punishment as a service due to a child. It also underlined the change in attitude towards punishment between the two generations.

This change was confirmed by a survey carried out in 1987-88 on the religious attitudes of Irish university students. The little boy might well have been one of those questioned then. While 56% said they believed in heaven, only half that number, 28%, believed in hell. The ice-cream approach to wrong-doing won handsomely. Reward as an incentive rather than punishment as a deterrent, was easily the more acceptable answer to wrong-doers. Incidently, 58% of those interviewed believed in wrong-doing, i.e. sin. Rather than pointlessly arguing the merits of each of them, I cannot see why both rewards and punishments should not be both acceptable. Such was the received wisdom, where the 'stick and the carrot' both had an honourable role in the formation of the people of God. While our first parents were expelled from the Garden of Eden as punishment for eating the forbidden fruit, the complaining followers of Moses were rewarded with manna to encourage them on their difficult way through the desert.

I suspect that the present rejection of punishment is largely due to the media. Popular journalism dislikes subtleties. Bald, bold statements make strong headlines. The rarer the happening, the more newsworthy the story. 'Man bites dog' gets disproportionate coverage. The battered child report can make parents shy away from inflicting even the mildest punishments on their erring children. It hasn't helped either that whenever punishment is discussed, it is always prefixed by either 'corporal' or 'capital'. These two adjectives alone have assured a very bad press for punishment in our time. 'Spare the rod and spoil the child' may no longer be acceptable in our time, more because of our perception of the harm it may do to the perpetrator than the hurt it inflicts on the victim. Victims may suffer more long-term damage from the withering verbal abuse that so often now replaces that much-spared rod.

The spate of political scandals now rocking European governments, involving corruption and bribery which we were led to believe was endemic only in the Third World, should give us all reason to reflect. In Italy, one former prime-minister has fled the country while another is awaiting trial on charges of accepting bribes and sinister Mafia connections. Italy may be more spectacular, but similar scandals are being reported in Spain and England, France and Belgium, all involving highly-placed public figures. It is tempting to speculate that they may have been the little boys who picked their mother's purse or robbed the family till, secure in the belief that they would get away with it or, at least, if caught, that they would go unpunished. Those of them attending Sunday Mass today in their prison chapel, will get small consolation from the second reading. The *Letter to the Hebrews* has no reservations about punishment which it places firmly in the context of parental love. It is worth repeating at length:

> For the Lord trains the ones he loves and punishes all those that he acknowledges as his sons. Suffering is part of your training; God is treating you as his sons. Has there ever been any son whose father did not train him? Of course, any punishment is most painful at the time, and far from pleasant; but later, in those on whom it has been used, it bears fruit in peace and goodness.

Suggested additional Bidding Prayers
We pray
– that the punishment life inflicts on us for our wrong-doing will bear fruit in peace and goodness.
– for all those who are punished unjustly in our society.
– for victims of physical abuse, especially battered wives and children.

Catechism of the Catholic Church
2266 The primary effect of punishment is to redress the dis-

order caused by the offence. When his punishment is voluntarily accepted by the offender, it takes on the value of expiation. Moreover, punishment has the effect of preserving public order and the safety of persons. Finally punishment has a medicinal value; as far as possible it should contribute to the correction of the offender.

Twenty-Second Sunday

Readings: Eccl 3:17-20, 28-29. Heb 12:18-19, 22-24. Lk 14:1, 7-14.

Introduction

The Eucharist we celebrate today is a banquet to which all are invited. It is the only table we share with the poor in our society. Christ would have us invite the poor to our parties for which 'repayment will be made to us when the virtuous rise again.'

Having a party (Almsgiving)

Someone had given me a turkey for Christmas. I didn't know what to do with it. I mentioned it to a few friends in the parish and somebody came up with the idea of putting on a meal for the travelling people. A number of poor families were camped on the roadside on the outskirts of the town. One woman offered to cook the turkey with her own on Christmas Day. The plan was that we would all have our Christmas dinner with our families. Afterwards we would meet at a selected venue, prepare the meal for the travellers and when everything was ready, a number of cars would collect them from the camps. I was deputed to call to the camps in advance and let them know. The idea was taken up with great enthusiasm. Originally, it was intended to keep the organisational side to about a half-a-dozen of us, but inevitably, the word leaked out. We were showered with presents of all kinds, toys for the children, Xmas crackers, plum-pudding, sweets and ice-cream. A local publican gave us a crate of beer and stout. I found an empty cupboard in the presbytery kitchen where I stored everything. I planned to hold the party in the presbytery as all the priests were going away on Christmas Day. I thought it better not to say anything in case objections might be raised. The day came and my friends and I arrived to begin preparations. The cupboard was completely empty. I was flabbergasted. I managed to contact one of the priests as he was sitting down to his Christmas dinner with his family. 'Oh! I gave it all away to the travellers,' he said, 'I thought the housekeeper had bought all that stuff under the mistaken assumption that we were all staying for Christmas.' 'Well, Father certainly spiked your guns,' one of my friends commented. I rushed out to the camps to try and get it all back again. I remember standing in one camp begging the old woman in the bed to give me back the bottle of stout she was cradling in her lap. As I emerged with it, a parishioner who was taking a pre-prandial stroll and had witnessed the whole scene, was shaking his head in disbelief and dismay. I don't think I ever explained it to him.

I was a young priest then and probably something of a prig. Looking back after more than twenty-five years, the whole incident now smacks of a 'holier-than-thou' exercise. There was too much trumpet-playing and banner-waving. There was more 'do-goodism' than Christian charity about it. It had probably more to do with making me look good than with feeding the poor. If a younger colleague attempted a similar venture now, I might well be tempted now to sabotage it myself. It certainly did not quite comply with Jesus' advise to his host in today's gospel:

When you give a lunch or a dinner, do not ask your friends, brothers, relations or rich neighbours, for fear they repay your courtesy by inviting you in return. No; when you have a party, invite the poor, the crippled, the lame, the blind; that they cannot pay you back means that you are fortunate, because repayment will be made to you when the virtuous rise again.

Suggested additional Bidding Prayers
We pray
– for the grace of kindness to give generously and anonymously to the poor.
– that the needy will always find a place in our hearts and homes.
– that our government will give priority to those in greatest need.

Catechism of the Catholic Church
2447 The corporal works of mercy consist especially in feeding the hungry, sheltering the homeless, clothing the naked, visiting the sick and imprisoned, and burying the dead. Among all these, giving alms to the poor is one of the chief witnesses to fraternal charity: it is also a work of justice pleasing to God.

Twenty-Third Sunday

Readings: Wis 9:13-18. Phil 9-10, 12-17. Lk 14:25-33.

Introduction

Jesus warned the crowds who accompanied him that they could not be his disciples 'unless they gave up all their possessions.' Without the spirit of detachment we cannot become true disciples of Christ.

Last will and testament (Detachment)

Every so often, I think of making a will. For much of my life I seem to have been living out of a suitcase, a situation that does not lend itself to amassing vast possessions. Living for so long in a bed-sitter I didn't have much space for luxuries but no doubt all that will change when I finally take up residency in an Irish parochial house. In the course of my historical researches, I have come across numerous wills of Irish exiles in France in the seventeenth and eighteenth centuries and I've been invariably edified by what I have found there. Some were priests, others were laypeople but all had been deeply imbued by the spirit of the gospel. They all began by invoking God's mercy and the intercession of Our Lady and the saints. Next they stipulated that they should be buried without any pomp or ceremony in the parish where they die and left some money for Masses for the repose of their souls. But, more importantly, a sum of money was set aside to be distributed among the poor of the parish. Servants came next. Everybody had servants then in that 'upstairs-downstairs' world. Faithful servants were treasured and their loyalty amply rewarded. They were often more life-long companions than hired hands. Besides much of the furniture, all of the linen and the wardrobe of the deceased and of course their wages, they were often left a little annuity as well. The settlement of debts came next. Friends were usually left a ring or piece of silverware as a token to be remembered by. Finally came the family, which for celibate priests or bachelor soldiers consisted of nephews and nieces in Ireland. What remained was left to them to provide them with education or sometimes in the case of nieces, with dowries. With very few exceptions, most of the Irish exiles in France left very little with which to endow their heirs. One of them, in fact, began his will by stating that he 'owned nothing, not even the bed on which he was lying'. It was a fitting 'last will and

testament' from the author of the celebrated catechism. His name
was Andrew Donlevy and he had spent his whole life in the Irish
College, Paris, educating priests for the Irish mission.

Unlike him, most of us accumulate at least a modest amount
of possessions in the course of a lifetime. Most of us need a
house and all that goes with it, a car, a couple of luxuries and
may be a little nest-egg in the bank as insurance against the
'rainy day'. There is no great harm in that. It is not the things we
possess that harm us, it is the things that possess us. These are
the sort of things that poison our relationships; that can come between us and our friends and, tragically, sometimes between us
and our families. They are to be found more often among the
poor than the rich.These are the things that occasionally people
are willing to kill for. There is a powerful play by the Irish
dramatist, John B. Keane, which has since been made into a film.
It is called 'The Field'. A poor farmer is induced to commit murder to acquire a miserable piece of land. The success of the play
and the film is due to the universality of the theme. We all have a
'field' for which we are capable of committing murder. These
are the possessions which separate us from God.

There is a story told about an early Celtic hermit who gave
up everything to find God. Living alone in his hermitage deep in
the forest, he befriended a fly, a mouse and a cock. The cock
would wake him up every morning at dawn, to say Matins. The
fly would move along each line of his Breviary as he read. And
the mouse would nibble his ear to wake him up every time he
dozed off. One day the fly stopped and moved no more. It was
dead. Soon death claimed the mouse and the cock also. The hermit was devastated by his loss. In his grief, he wrote to his
Abbot, St Columba, in Iona. Columba showed no sympathy.
'What else can you expect but grief,' he replied, 'when you put
your trust in possessions?'

It is good to make a will. Everyone should do so. But the best
will of all is goodwill. Mothers and fathers who leave children
behind them who love them and love each other, have made the
best wills. The possessions they had in life they converted into
goodwill. We should pray like the Psalmist today:

Make us know the shortness of our life
  that we may gain wisdom of heart.

Suggested additional Bidding Prayers
We pray
– for the spirit of detachment which will make us true disciples of Christ.
– for those who have consecrated their lives to God that he will give them the grace to remain true to their vows.
– for the rich that they may use their wealth to earn God's mercy.

Catechism of the Catholic Church
2544 Jesus enjoins his disciples to prefer him to everything and everyone, and bids them 'renounce all that (they have)' for his sake and that of the gospel. Shortly before his Passion he gave them the example of the poor widow of Jerusalem who, out of her poverty, gave all she had to live on. The precept of detachment from riches is obligatory for entrance into the kingdom of heaven.

Twenty-Fourth Sunday

Readings: Ex 32:7-11, 13-14. 1 Tim 1:12-17. Lk 15:1-32.

Missing, presumed dead (Repentance) See Fourth Sunday of Lent C
Hundreds of people go missing every year. At any given moment, worldwide there are hundreds of thousands of missing persons. Their families try everything to find them. Descriptions of them are circulated by the police, broadcast by radio and television; their photos are posted at the entrances to supermarkets and other public places. Even recently one popular breakfast cereal agreed to carry such pictures on their boxes.

Missing people comprise all sorts, children, adults, husbands and wives, singles of both sexes and they come from all types of backgrounds, rich and poor alike. A husband pecks his wife's cheek as he rushes out to work in the morning, but he never gets there or home again. A wife takes her dog for a walk in the park in the afternoon. Only the dog is found, and his secret can never be discovered. The most pathetic are children. A little girl is sent by her mother down the street to do a message and never comes back. A little boy runs out of school with his school bag on his back, and runs into oblivion. A teenager says good-bye to friends after a disco and is never seen again. It is almost as if they had vanished into thin air. Most of them are never found.

Of all the tragedies that beset the family, none causes greater pain than this. It was always said of hell, that the greatest suffering there was the eternal pain of loss. It is what a mother suffers whose child has gone missing. If it had died or been killed she could have mourned it and come to terms with her grief. But there is no relieving this loss. Every time the door-bell sounds or the telephone rings, she thinks her child is returning. She clings on to every reported sighting, no matter how distant or unlikely. She wakes up at night, hearing her child call out. She feels that it is somewhere out there crying out for help and for her, and she can do nothing. And that great healer, time, can offer nothing to kill her pain. 'Missing, presumed dead' is not enough to let the healing start. No presumption will release her from her purgatory. Only such a parent can fathom the joy of the father in today's parable at the return of his son who 'was dead and has come back to life, was lost and is found.'

Churches keep no files on their missing members but by all accounts they are numerous, particularly in recent times. There is a steady trickle of people who walk away from God's house and never come back. Their problem, it appears, is not with God, but more often with the company he keeps. Too many scribes and pharisees there who complain that Jesus 'welcomes sinners and eats with them'. 'Church-atheists' is the new term coined to describe them. Some of them return to the church, but probably far less than is generally claimed. Mercifully, most return to God in heaven where we are told 'there is more rejoicing over one repentant sinner than over ninety-nine virtuous men who have no need of repentance'.

Suggested additional Bidding Prayers
We pray
– for all those who have strayed away from the church that they may find their way home to God.
– for the grace of repentance for the sins we have committed against God and against others.
– for missing people everywhere that they may be re-united with their grieving families.

Catechism of the Catholic Church
1439 The process of conversion and repentance was described by Jesus in the parable of the prodigal son, the centre of which is the merciful father: the fascination of illusory freedom; the aban-

donment of the father's house; the extreme misery in which the son finds himself after squandering his fortune; his deep humiliation at finding himself obliged to feed swine, and worse still, at wanting to feed on the husks the pigs ate; his reflection on all he has lost; his repentance and decision to declare himself guilty before his father; the journey back; the father's generous welcome; the father's joy – all these are characteristic of the process of conversion. The beautiful robe, the ring and the festive banquet are symbols of that new life – pure, worthy and joyful – of anyone who returns to God and to the bosom of his family, which is the church. Only the heart of Christ who knows the depth of his Father's love could reveal to us the abyss of his mercy in so simple and beautiful a way.

Twenty-Fifth Sunday

Readings: Amos 8:4-7. 1 Tim 2:1-8. Lk 16:1-13.

Introduction
We live in a world where many are manipulated for the economic gain of the few. Exploitation is rampant everywhere. Christ reminds us that though money is tainted, it is only our misuse of it that separates us from God. We 'cannot be the slaves both of God and of money.'

Filthy lucre (Money)
I never knew what the expression 'filthy lucre' really meant until recently. I always thought it was only a metaphor for money. When I was a curate in a Dublin parish, one of my jobs was to supervise Bingo on a Friday night. Bingo provided half the parish revenue. It fell to me and a few loyal helpers to count the takings at the end of each session. When the count was completed our fingers were black with grime. It always amazes me, in this hygiene-conscious age, how eagerly we grab hold of whatever money we are offered, without the slightest fear of contamination. Yet we have not the faintest idea where it has come from. It doesn't seem to bother us what contagious disease its previous owner had. Yet, more often than not, it shares the same pocket with some very dirty handkerchiefs.

When I was at school, there was an essay in my English reader entitled, 'The adventures of a shilling.' God be with the days when a shilling was a lot of money! I've always thought since what an interesting series of short stories or TV episodes could be made tracing the history of a ten-pound note or a ten-dollar bill. I think the average banknote has a life-span of about twelve months. After that they are recalled and incinerated. It would be fascinating to follow its history from the moment the fresh crisp note comes off the mint to its extermination in the incinerator, some twelve months later. Every well-worn crease on it, every stain on it, has its own story to tell. God only knows where it has been and what it has done, for good or for bad. It has its joyful mysteries and its sorrowful mysteries. It may even have had its glorious mysteries. Its last owner could have used it to buy a fix of heroin or cocaine, or bribe a government minister to secure a contract, or buy an official's silence. It could have been picked from a poor pensioner's pocket. It may have paid a prostitute for her favours. It may even be blood-stained. It may have been a contribution towards the bomb that blasted a casual group of shoppers into eternity and blighted the lives of the widows and orphans left to pick up the pieces. And if it feels crisper and cleaner than usual, it may well be that it has just been 'laundered' by drug-barons and arms-traffickers. Such are the sorrowful mysteries of a ten-pound note.

It could also have bought medicine for a sick child or education for a gifted one from a deprived background. And all the countless presents it might have bought to bring a little joy into otherwise bleak lives. It could have been an anonymous donation to any of our world's countless worthy causes. It could have been a poor person's contribution to someone more needy than themselves. It could have been to the Third World and back. It could have fed a whole family there for a week.

There is a lot of talk in modern times about devaluation. People complain all the time about the shrinking purchasing power of the money in their pockets and they reminisce ruefully about what their ten-pound note could have bought, even as little as five years ago. But in a real sense money is only devalued by the use we make of it. 'Use money, tainted as it is, to win you friends,' Christ told his disciples, 'and thus make sure that when it fails you, they will welcome you into the tents of eternity.' We may well be depressed at how little it can buy on High Street, but in the poor back-streets of this world, its value never fluctuates.

Oscar Wilde once described a cynic as 'one who knows the price of everything and the value of nothing'. A Christian should be the reverse. One who has no interest in the price of anything but knows the value of everything.

Suggested additional Bidding Prayers
We pray
– that we may use money, 'tainted as it is', to gain eternal life.
– that we may never corrupt others with money or be corrupted by it.
– that we may always be given the grace to choose God before money.

Catechism of the Catholic Church
952. '… Everything the true Christian has is to be regarded as a good possessed in common with everyone else. All Christians should be ready and eager to come to the help of the needy … and of their neighbours in want.' A Christian is the steward of the Lord's goods.

Twenty-Sixth Sunday

Readings: Amos 6:1, 4-7. 1 Tim 6:11-16. Lk 16:19-31.

Introduction
The parable of Lazarus and the rich man has a particular relevance for us who are 'ensconced so snugly' in the First World. Our indifference towards the poor in the Third World makes a mockery of our profession of the gospel. We should heed the warning of Amos: 'the sprawlers' revelry is over.'

Sprawlers' revelry (Riches)
It is fascinating to observe, how, as de-christianisation advances in our time, the secular calendar grows. We are all aware now of Father's Day and Mother's Day and all the other days that are designated on certain dates. I suppose we shouldn't really complain, as most of our religious festivals were originally pagan festivals that we christianised. Now, it would seem, the process is being reversed. The latest addition to our secular calendar is Animal Day on the first Sunday in October. I don't begrudge our fur and feathered friends a little bit of special atten-

tion as they now occupy an important place in our lives, at least in the West. The statistics for France are revealing and I imagine they are closely matched elsewhere in Europe. There are thirty-four million domestic animals in that country, of which ten million are dogs, nine million caged birds, seven million cats, and six million fish in bowls. The other two million include hamsters, white mice, rabbits etc. It is a veritable Noah's Ark. The annual expenditure on these animals comes to 28 billion francs, or fifteen per cent of the total annual expenditure in France. It would seem that dogs and other household pets are no longer fed on the scraps that fall from our tables, as they were in former times. TV ads for dog-food and cat-food, so often at peak-viewing times, give an indication of how dramatically our pets' eating habits have changed.

With what we spend on them alone, we could maintain the two-thirds of humanity who are dying of starvation.

It is ironic that when we listen to today's gospel about Lazarus and the rich man, we tend automatically to identify with Lazarus. We miss the whole point of the story. We, in fact, collectively are the rich man. Apart from spending twenty-eight billion francs on our pets, we have a mountain of beef, a mountain of cereals, a mountain of butter, a lake of wine and a lake of milk, that cost us a fortune to maintain. These are only the crumbs that fall from our table. Amos' warning is aimed directly at us: 'Woe to those ensconced so snugly in Zion.' The problem about being collectively responsible for the world's starving masses is that we can so easily shrug off our personal responsibility. You may be living in a bed-sitter with few comforts or struggling to meet the mortgage repayments on your home. Yet all the services we benefit from, our public transport system, our education, our health services etc, etc, etc, derive from the rich man's club to which we belong. We dine at the rich man's table. And much of our wealth derives from the natural resources our forefathers looted from the Third World. We still take their primary resources for a pittance, like the coffee we drink every morning, and sell it back to them at exorbitant prices. And now, adding insult to injury, our ships are plying the seas in search of a Third World country willing to accept our toxic waste. Having robbed them of their riches we are now returning them our rubbish.

Now, at last, we are beginning to wake up to the magnitude of our greed. And not because our conscience has finally got to us. But because we realise that we are fouling our own nest. Our wantonness is coming home to roost. In that memorable phrase of Amos, 'the sprawlers' revelry is over'. Our world is too small to bear such inequalities. Unless we share our table with the world's hungry, we will all end up in a hell of our own creation.

Suggested additional Bidding Prayers

We pray
– for generosity to share our teeming table with the world's hungry.
– that we will make greater efforts to persuade our government to increase its aid to the Third World.
– that we will accept a more frugal lifestyle in solidarity with the Third World.

Catechism of the Catholic Church

2831 But the presence of those who hunger because they lack bread opens up another profound meaning of this petition. ('Give us this day our daily bread.') The drama of hunger in the world calls Christians who pray sincerely to exercise responsibility towards their brethren, both in their personal behaviour and in their solidarity with the human family. This petition of the Lord's Prayer cannot be isolated from the parables of the poor man Lazarus and of the Last Judgement.

Twenty-Seventh Sunday

Readings: Hab 1:2-3, 2:2-4. 2 Tim 1:6-8, 13-14. Lk 17:5-10.

Introduction

The apostles asked Christ to 'increase their faith.' St Paul described faith to Timothy as 'sound teaching'. In a world fascinated by the bizarre and the sensational, we should not be easily duped by the 'miraculous'.

Something precious (Faith)

Civitavecchia is an Italian seaport. Recently, it was the scene of a strange phenomenon widely reported by the media. It was claimed that a little statuette of the Madonna had shed tears of blood. The story began some months earlier, when the local parish priest returned from a visit to Medjugorje, bringing with him as a souvenir a little plaster ikon of Our Lady, such as can be found in vast numbers at any of the Marian shrines. He presented it to a young couple in his parish who built a miniscule grotto for it in their garden. One day their little five-year old daughter came running in from the garden saying that 'the Madonna was crying'. She brought her father out to see. He saw what appeared to be tears of blood streaming from the eyes of the statue. Word spread rapidly and soon people were flocking in their hundreds to get a glimpse of the 'bleeding Madonna'. The mayor, a former communist, in a scenario so reminiscent of *The Little World of Don Camillo*, began to devise grandiose schemes for the construction of hotels, car-parks etc to cater for the anticipated huge influx of pilgrims. The more sceptical parish priest decided to repossess the statue which he consigned to his bishop. He in turn alerted the Vatican who advised him to send the statue to a medical institute for expert analysis. It duly issued a report stating that the red blotches were indeed blood – albeit male. At this point, the procurator of the Republic intervened claiming that the statue was an 'incitement to incredulity' and had it confined under seals in a cupboard in the bishop's residence. By this time, following the now-accepted pattern in such circumstances, a number of similar phenomena were being reported from other places in Italy, some involving Madonnas and others the stigmatist, Padre Pio, leading *Newsweek* to quipp, 'It's a wonder there's a dry ikon in the country'.

Without prejudice to the final outcome of the Church's investigation of this phenomenon, it is important to place it in the context of faith which is the subject of today's readings. 'The signs worked by Jesus attest that the Father has sent him. They invite belief in him … they bear witness that he is the Son of God.' So states the *Catechism of the Catholic Church* which goes on to warn that 'they are not intended to satisfy people's curiosity or desire for magic'. The great enemy of faith is superstition, which so often masquerades itself as true faith. Its casualties include not only the gullible, who accept too readily whatever 'signs and wonders' are presented, but they also, in this media age, bring true religion into disrepute and reinforce the scepticism of millions.

In today's second reading, St Paul has a timely word on the subject:

Keep as your pattern the sound teaching you have heard from me, in the faith and love that are in Christ Jesus. You have been trusted to look after something precious; guard it with the help of the Holy Spirit who lives in us.

Suggested additional Bidding Prayers
We pray
– for the grace to preserve our faith from superstitious practices and beliefs.
– for the grace to guard our faith from ignorance.
– for the enlightenment of the Holy Spirit to strengthen our faith.

Catechism of the Catholic Church
548 The signs worked by Jesus attest that the Father has sent him. They invite belief in him. To those who turn to him in faith, he grants what they ask. So miracles strengthen faith in the One who does his Father's works; they bear witness that he is the Son of God. But his miracles can also be occasions for 'offence'; they are not intended to satisfy people's curiosity or desire for magic.

Twenty-Eighth Sunday

Readings: 2 Kings 5:14-17. 2 Tim 2:8-13. Lk 17:11-19.

Introduction
Today's gospel records the curing of the Ten Lepers by Christ of whom only one returned to thank him. We have come here to celebrate the Eucharist which means literally 'giving thanks'. We all have much to thank God for. Going to Mass best expresses our gratitude.

Going to Mass (Gratitude)
I imagine most priests have had the experience. They call to a friend's house on a social visit and out of the blue they are asked to perform a delicate pastoral mission on some member of the family. It has happened to me.

'Would you ever have a word with Eileen?' her mother whispered to me, taking me aside by the arm.

'What's wrong with Eileen?'

'She doesn't go to Mass anymore.'

Eileen was going on nineteen. I had baptised her, like her brothers and sister. They were almost family to me. I was very fond of her and, as far as I knew, the feeling was reciprocated. Which was why I didn't feel at all keen on playing the priest with her. Besides, why should I succeed in five minutes where her parents had failed after nineteen years? However, I had no option but to try. A year or two earlier, Eileen had been in the guitar-group at the folk-Mass and couldn't wait for Sundays to come round. Now she had out-grown that.

'What's this about Mass?' I said, when I got her alone for a few moments, trying desperately to sound casual.

'I don't get anything out of it anymore.' she said.

For hundreds of years, people have been going to Mass on Sundays and it never once occurred to them that they might 'get something out of it.' They went because they were expected to or at worse because it was a mortal sin not to go. Whatever their reasons, they went and it was not always easy for them. For centuries in this country they were persecuted for going. There were no churches. Masses were said in secret, in secluded spots, in the open-air with look-outs posted, in all sorts of weather, mostly bad. And those who travelled long distances on foot to attend such Masses ran the risk of fines or imprisonment or worse. At the very least, a good drenching. That is what our ancestors could expect 'to get out of it.' And for good measure, the Mass was mumbled in Latin by a priest you couldn't hear and would be lucky to get a sight of his back.

I didn't tell Eileen that. Or that the Mass is a thanksgiving service. The word 'eucharist' derives from the Greek verb 'to give thanks'. It got its name from the gospel description of the Last Supper, where Jesus took bread into his hands and 'giving thanks' he blessed and broke and gave to his disciples. We go to Mass for no other reason than to thank God for all he has given us. We all complain, and particularly the young, about the shortage of jobs, the crippling rate of taxation, the almost unbearable mortgage repayments, the growing crime rate or even the price of the pint. We are like the beggar with no shoes who never stopped complaining until he met another beggar with no feet. In this media age, it cannot have escaped even those who feel most deprived, that two-thirds of the world's population go to bed hungry every night. We have an awful lot to be thankful for.

I didn't tell her either about the ten lepers that Christ cured. And that only one came back to thank him. *Plus ça change!* The average percentage of those who attend Sunday Mass in what used to be called the 'Christian West' remains much the same.

Not much more than one out of ten come back regularly to say thanks. I didn't say any of these things to Eileen because it wasn't the time or the place. Like most priests, I realised that preaching to young adults can be counter-productive. The party line cuts no ice with them. Instead, I talked about myself.

'You know, Eileen,' I said, 'that for the last twenty years I say Mass at 7 o clock every morning in a convent for a few elderly nuns. What do you think I get out of it?'

'Then, why do you keep doing it?' she asked.

'Because, like you, I believe in God and I think I should let him know.'

'I never thought of it like that.' she said.

Suggested additional Bidding Prayers

We pray

– that we shall remain faithful to the Mass to thank God for all the gifts he has given us.

– that we will always show our gratitude to those who have helped us by their kindness and friendship.

– for those who no longer practise that they may know that they will always be welcome.

Catechism of the Catholic Church

1359 The Eucharist, the sacrament of our salvation accomplished by Christ on the cross, is also a sacrifice of praise in thanksgiving for the work of creation. In the Eucharistic sacrifice the whole of creation loved by God is presented to the Father through the death and the Resurrection of Christ. Through Christ the church can offer the sacrifice of praise in thanksgiving for all that God has made good, beautiful and just in creation and in humanity.

1360 The eucharist is a sacrifice of thanksgiving to the Father, a blessing by which the church expresses her gratitude to God for all his benefits, for all that he has accomplished through creation, redemption and sanctification. Eucharist means first of all 'thanksgiving'.

Twenty-Ninth Sunday

Readings: Ex 17:8-13. 2 Tim 3:14-4:2. Lk 18:1-8.

Introduction

Today Christ tells his disciples about the need to pray continually and never lose heart. God will see justice done 'to his chosen who cry to him day and night, even when he delays to help them.'

God help me! (Prayer)

A middle-aged man once came to see me and he told me the following story. He had married in his early forties. His wife was just slightly younger than him. They were very much in love and for the first year he was rapturously happy. Towards the end of that time they got the good news. She was pregnant. They were overjoyed at the prospect of a child. It was almost too good to be true at their age. In due course she gave birth to a little boy. But the mother died giving birth to the child. The man disintegrated completely. He took the little baby and left it with his own mother, the grandmother of the child, and fell apart. He went on a drinking spree that went on for a number of years. He totally neglected his home, his farm and his little boy almost as if they had never existed. Late one evening, as he was leaving town on his bicycle, after a long bout of drinking, he was caught in a squally shower of rain so typical of the west of Ireland. He was just opposite the church at the time and he sought shelter in the church-doorway until the worst of the shower was over. Standing there, he glanced into the church, looking hazily in the direction of the altar. There were, as was common in most churches at that time, two life-size statues standing on pedestals on each side of the altar, one of Our Lord and the other of Our Lady, both with their arms outstretched in greeting. He tried to focus on the one of Our Lord and in what must have been a reflex from his childhood, he muttered a prayer or an exclamation. 'God, help me!' Suddenly, he thought he saw the statue beckoning to him.

At this point in the story, I must admit, I became uneasy. Priests tend to attract a certain number of eccentrics, and this was long before the 'moving statues' phenomenon. But I was caught now and there was no escape. Mercifully, there was little left to tell.

He lurched up the aisle and before he had gone very far, he could see the statue clearly and its hands were as lifeless as the plaster they were made of. The shower had passed. He got on his bike, went to his mother's, picked up his little boy and his life, and since then, has never looked back.

Miracles, even in the most ideal conditions, are extremely hard to prove and, given the self-confessed state our friend was in, this one would surely be a non-starter. But even the most-hardened cynic would be hard put to explain the sudden and dramatic change in his life without God's intervention. It was an answer to prayer, somebody's prayer. Probably his mother's. She must have pestered heaven day and night with her prayers and her tears, like the widow in today's parable. And no doubt, by now she had taught the little lad to pray for his Daddy too. God was only waiting for a nod from himself to unleash his healing grace.

As Jesus, explaining to his disciples 'about the need to pray continually and never lose heart', said: 'Now will not God see justice done to his chosen who cry to him day and night even when he delays to help them? I promise you, he will see justice done to them and done speedily.'

Suggested additional Bidding Prayers
We pray
– that we will never lose confidence in the power of prayer.
– that we will always be faithful to the practice of prayer in our lives.
– that God 'will bend his ear and hear our prayer'.

Catechism of the Catholic Church
2613 Three principal parables on prayer are transmitted to us by St Luke:
– The first, 'the importunate friend', invites us to urgent prayer: 'Knock and it will be opened to you.' To the one who prays like this, the heavenly Father 'will give whatever he needs', above all the Holy Spirit who contains all gifts.
– The second, ' the importunate widow', is centred on one of the qualities of prayer: it is necessary to pray always without ceasing, and with the *patience* of faith ....

Thirtieth Sunday

Readings: Eccl 35:12-14, 16-19. 2 Tim 4:6-8, 16-18. Lk 18:9-14.

Introduction

In our celebration today we look forward to the day when Christ will return as our judge. The one thing we know for certain about his judgement is that it will favour the humble, and those who humble themselves will be exalted.

The great achievers (Humility)

There is a tradition in rural Ireland for men to congregate at the back of the church during Sunday Mass. In the recent past, it was customary for them to take off their caps, place them on the floor and kneel on them on one knee. Generations of peevish parish priests thundered at them from the altar, in an effort to eradicate the custom. But this was one battle the parish priests of Ireland lost. I don't know when it originated. It has been suggested, with some plausibility, that it derived from the penal times when there were no churches. The Mass-houses and cabin-chapels were small primitive buildings, providing shelter only for the priest and a handful of the faithful. The men remained outside, exposed to the elements, leaving to women and children whatever shelter was available.

My own theory is that it derives from today's gospel. Whatever about sermons, there can be no doubt that the Sunday gospel has had enormous impact on the ordinary people down through the centuries, especially parables like the Prodigal Son and today's parable about the Pharisee and the Publican (as he used to be called until lately). Incidentally, as far as the Irish are concerned, scripture scholars would have done better to have left the misnomer 'publican'. People in small rural communities could easily identify with their local friendly publican: the same cannot be said for the tax-collector. They had a great contempt for those few in every village who 'put on airs and graces'. 'The pot calling the kettle black' was their expression for it. They reserved their greatest contempt for those who paraded their religion, the 'holier-than-thou' individuals. The 'people who prided themselves on being virtuous and despised everyone else' as Jesus described them. Rural society welcomed any opportunity 'to pull them down a peg or two' and relished the odd occasions when they were 'cut down to size'. It is always nice to discover that Jesus shares our sentiments.

The virtue of humility has been very much down-graded by modern society. It describes a person, who in any other age would have been admired as humble, as having 'a very low self-esteem'. We are encouraged to be self-assertive. One could hardly do better than the Pharisee in self-assertion. He managed to use 'I' six times in his three-line prayer. There is a world of difference between self-assertion and self-confidence. Each individual is a unique creation by God. We need no other justification for our self-confidence. Such self-confidence is totally compatible with humility. Self-assertion is the original sin of Adam in the garden. It is the assertion that we no longer need God.

There is a general belief that the great achievers were people with enormous egos. History records some megalomaniacs who left their mark on our world such as Napoleon Bonaparte or Adolf Hitler. Few would claim that they made any worthwhile contribution to civilisation. Those who did were usually people of extraordinary humility. I could cite a Francis of Assisi or in our own time a Mother Teresa of Calcutta but I might be accused of religious partiality. There were other extraordinary saints too like Mahatma Ghandi or Martin Luther King or Nelson Mandela whose humility was transparent. And the great intellectual geniuses, whose contributions far surpass all others, such as Socrates, Galileo or Albert Einstein, were humbled by the enormity of their discoveries. Like Socrates they discovered that 'they knew that they knew nothing'.

Probably, nobody's contribution to the history of Ireland was more profound or more enduring than that of St Patrick. Yet he was a man of outstanding humility. Who else could have begun his autobiography with the statement: 'I, Patrick, a sinner and the least of men'. Worlds were changed by people who thought like that. It is no wonder Christ said: 'Blessed are the meek, for thy shall inherit the earth.'

Somebody summed up today's parable in verse:
Two went to pray or rather say,
one went to brag, the other to pray.
One stands up close and treads on high
where the other dares not send his eye.
One nearer to God's altar trod,
the other to the altar's God.

Suggested additional Bidding Prayers
We pray
– for the gift of humility towards God and each other.
– that we may never 'lord it over others.'
– that success will never make us proud or contemptuous of
those less fortunate.

Catechism of the Catholic Church

2559 'Prayer is the raising of one's mind and heart to God or
the requesting of good things from God.' But when we pray, do
we speak from the height of our pride and will, or 'out of the
depths' of a humble and contrite heart? He who humbles himself will be exalted; *humility* is the foundation of prayer. Only
when we humbly acknowledge that 'we do not know how to
pray as we ought' are we ready to receive freely the gift of
prayer; 'Man is a beggar before God.'

Thirty-First Sunday

Readings: Wis 11:22-12:2. Thess 1:11-2:2. Lk 19:1-10.

Introduction

Today's gospel records the incident in Jericho when the
short-sized Zacchaeus ran ahead and climbed a tree to get a
glimpse of Jesus. He was rewarded for his efforts when Jesus
chose to stay in his house. We too must make efforts if we wish
Jesus to come and stay with us.

Small boys (Making an effort)

Small boys, as everyone knows, love to climb trees. It is almost as if God created trees for little boys to climb. In the little
playgrounds reserved for children in the public parks in cities,
municipal planners install contraptions where children can indulge their craze for climbing. There is one in the Jardin du
Luxembourg in Paris. In a park like that, with such an abundance
of fine trees, it is a poor imitation of the real thing. But it is blessing for little boys whose childhood world is largely confined
within the limits of a fifth floor apartment. In the age of the cinema, Tarzan, swinging from tree to tree in the forest, was every

boy's hero. He could hardly wait to get home to climb the nearest tree. Sycamores were the best climbing trees, stretching out their broad branches as regularly as rungs on a ladder.

It is probably stretching it a bit far to suggest that our early enthusiasm for tree-climbing is a throw-back to our pre-human origins, when our four-legged hairy ancestors swung from giant trees in primeval forests. It is certainly true that of all the animals, only our ancestors succeeded in getting up on their hind legs and remaining that way. It was their urge to look up that got them eventually to stand up. Their looking up led inevitably to their discovery of God.

Zacchaeus seems to have been a little boy who never grew up. And I'm not referring to his short stature. We all know small men but we would never be foolish enough to mistake them for little boys. More often than not, they tend to make up in self-importance what they lack in inches. They would never dream of behaving in such a delightfully outrageous fashion as Zacchaeus did on that famous occasion in Jericho. Imagine a solid citizen of the social stature of Zacchaeus, who 'was one of the senior tax collectors and a wealthy man', exposing himself to ridicule by climbing a tree in a crowded street to catch a glimpse of an itinerant preacher. Small people are sensitive about their height. The last thing they would dream of is calling attention to it. He must have looked funny enough running down the street on his short legs but only a small boy would have climbed the sycamore tree. It was probably the small boy in Zacchaeus that caught Jesus' eye. He had said on another occasion: 'Unless you become little children, you will not enter the kingdom of God.' Zacchaeus was taking him literally.

We are all spiritual dwarfs. Our vision is confined to eye-level. Like Zacchaeus, we cannot see over the heads of the crowd. We see the world around us and our own reflections in shop windows. We have eyes for nothing else. We must figuratively climb a tree to see Jesus. We must make a special effort. Unless we see Jesus we cannot discover God.

Suggested additional Bidding Prayers
We pray
– that we will make an effort to catch a glimpse of Jesus in our crowded world.
– that we will work to overcome the defects in our lives which block access to God.

– for people who are handicapped by their size, that public authorities will be sensitive to their need in designing public amenities.

Catechism of the Catholic Church

2447 The works of mercy are charitable actions by which we come to the aid of our neighbour ... giving alms to the poor is one of the chief witnesses to fraternal charity: it is also a work of justice pleasing to God.

Thirty-Second Sunday

Readings: Mac 7:1-2, 9-14. 2 Thess 2:16-3:5. Lk 20:27-38.

Introduction

Today, in this November season of the dead, we celebrate Christ who is God, not of the dead but of the living; for to him all men are in fact alive. We are members of the Communion of Saints.

Immortal diamonds (Communion of Saints)

No warmth, no cheerfulness, no helpful ease,
No comfortable feel in any member,
No shade, no shine, no butterflies, no bees,
No fruit, no flowers, no leaves, no birds –
NOVEMBER

There are no leaves on the trees. But there are dead leaves everywhere on the ground. On the pavements. In the gutters. Gusts of wind heap them together in sheltered corners, like mounds of earth on a grave. November reeks of death. Another year is laid to rest.

The liturgy follows the secular season by commemorating the dead in November. When we recite the *Creed* every Sunday we declare our belief in the 'communion of saints'. It is a close community, made up of the saints in heaven, the souls in purgatory and ourselves. While living in Paris I shared a building with a little Polish seminary. All their liturgies were in Polish which meant I could not participate with them. During the week, I followed the time-honoured tradition of celebrating a private Mass in one of the little chapels specially designed for that purpose, a custom somewhat frowned upon in more recent times. The centuries-old chapel was saturated with history. Being a historian I was familiar with many of its former occupants. Because I believe in the community of saints, I was never short of a congregation. They were probably so numerous, they were hanging from the rafters!

The Preface in the Mass for the Dead, says 'life is changed, not ended'. When we die, we change from this life to eternal life. The 'forever and ever' which punctuates so many of our prayers is not a happy choice. It conveys the impression of never ending time. But time only exists in this world. It is the measurement of change. The days turn to nights and the seasons rotate. Eternity is a timeless 'now', a futureless present. The beautiful hymn *Ag Críost an síol* (Christ's is the seed), so frequently sung at funeral Masses, describes the pilgrim soul going 'from death to rebirth'. It reflects well how Jesus expressed it when he spoke about those in the other world who 'can no longer die, for they are the same as the angels'.

'Now he is the God, not of the dead, but of the living; for to him all men are in fact alive'. Thoughts about the resurrection of the body are sometimes best expressed by poets. A priest-poet, Gerald Manley Hopkins, put it like this:

In a flash,
as a trumpet crash,
I am all at once
What Christ is.
Since he is what I am.
And this jack, joke, poor potherd,
patch, match-wood, immortal diamond,
is immortal diamond.
You and I, and all of us are immortal diamonds.

Suggested additional Bidding Prayers
We pray
– for the gift of hope as we look forward to the resurrection from the dead.
– that the saints in heaven, especially those of our own kin who have gone before us, may intercede for us with the Father.
– for the souls of the faithful departed that they may rest in peace.

Catechism of the Catholic Church
954 *The three states of the Church.* 'When the Lord comes in

glory, and all his angels with him, death will be no more and all things will be subject to him. But at the present time some of his disciples are pilgrims on earth. Others have died and are being purified, while still others are in glory, contemplating "in full light, God himself triune and one, exactly as he is."'

955 'So it is that the union of the wayfarers with the brethren who sleep in the peace of Christ is in no way interrupted, but on the contrary, according to the constant faith of the church, this union is reinforced by an exchange of spiritual goods.'

Thirty-Third Sunday

Readings: Mal 3:19-20. 2 Thess 3:7-12. Lk 21:5-19.

Introduction

In those dying weeks of the church's year, the liturgy recalls for us the 'last things' and today, in particular, the end of the world. We should live our lives in the light of eternity.

No lasting city (The end of the world)

It was in this month just a few short years ago, on 9 November 1989 to be exact, that the infamous Berlin Wall came tumbling down. It was a concrete symbol of what Winston Churchill had described as the 'Iron Curtain', which for almost fifty years had divided Europe into two ideologically hostile camps. It was the era of the 'Cold War'. Most people then, or at least the more optimistic, always believed that some day Europe would be re-united again and this wall of shame would come down. But when it happened, it was so sudden that everybody in the East and West was taken completely by surprise. Some of the Communist dictators, like Honnecker in East Germany, had not even time to clear their desks and hightail it, before the day of retribution was upon them. Now, so few years later, even souvenir-hawkers cannot find 'a single stone left on another' to sell to eager tourists at the annual commemoration.

Everything in this world, sooner or later, comes to an end. And the world itself will come to an end. In these dying weeks of the year, with the winter gloom upon us, the liturgy recalls for us the 'last things'. Last Sunday, it was death and resurrection; today it is the end of the world. 'The time will come,' Jesus told his disciples, 'when not a single stone will be left upon another: everything will be destroyed.'

Scientists tell us that it all began with a 'big bang' and it's all going to end with a big bang. There can be very few now who doubt that this world of ours will come to an end some day. If modern science proves nothing else, it proves that the world is already dying. Whether its ailment is terminal or reversible is open to debate. But the signs are ominous. The thinning of the ozone-layer, the shrinking of the polar ice-caps, the pollution of the air and the oceans are symptoms of a disease that might well prove fatal. Environmentalists at least are alarmed. Species of plants and animals are disappearing constantly. They are fighting what seems to be a losing battle. Great mammals like the elephants in Africa and the deep-sea whales are now on the danger list. The Amazon Forests, the 'lungs of the world' because they produce so much oxygen, are threatened by de-forestation. The earth is dying because we are killing it. 'Increase and multiply' our Creator told our ancestors when he entrusted this world to their care. Instead, in our greed we have preferred to 'decrease and make die'. Chernobyl, it seems, was but the tip of an iceberg. There is a whole series of aging and ailing nuclear reactors waiting to explode and spread their poisonous fumes into our atmosphere.

This doomsday scenario is not intended to frighten anybody, less still to spoil the enjoyment of Sunday. The message is simply that we live our lives *sub specie aeternitatis*, in the light of eternity. Not only are we ourselves going to die, but the world itself is going to disappear. That is what is meant by 'putting everything into perspective.' Problems we all have, more or less pressing, but ultimately, as St Paul put it: 'We have here no lasting city.' Malachi expresses it more vividly: 'The day that is coming is going to burn them up, says the Lord of hosts, leaving them neither root nor stalk.'

Suggested additional Bidding Prayers
We pray
– that we may keep a balance perspective in our lives by reflecting on the end of the world.
– that we may never become too pre-occupied by material things.
– that we may never sin against our environment by polluting the air and the streams, or in any way endanger any of the species created by God.

Catechism of the Catholic Church

677 The church will enter the glory of the kingdom only through this final Passover, when she will follow her Lord in his death and resurrection. The kingdom will be fulfilled, then, not by a historic triumph of the church through a progressive ascendancy, but only by God's victory over the final unleashing of evil, which will cause his Bride to come down from heaven. God's triumph over the revolt of evil will take the form of the Last Judgement after the final cosmic upheaval of this passing world.

Our Lord Jesus Christ, Universal King

Readings: 2 Sam 5:1-3. Col 1:11-20. Lk 23:35-43.

Introduction

On the last Sunday of the church's year we honour Christ the King. In a world where faithfulness is declining, it is a timely reminder to us that we should always remain faithful to Christ and his gospel.

Christ the King (Faithfulness)

As little as eighty years ago most of the countries in Europe had kings or royal heads of one kind or another. Russia had a Czar, Germany a Kaiser and Austria-Hungary an Emperor. They were absolute monarchs who ruled their kingdoms, if not with an iron-fist, with very few constitutional restraints. Then the First World War happened. In fact, that horrendous event was caused by the assassination of Archduke Ferdinand. He was gunned down by a Bosnian Serb in Sarajevo in 1913. By the time the war ended in 1918 most of the crowns of Europe had toppled like a pack of cards. All that remained was a handful of decorative figureheads as in England, Holland and Belgium.

Today is the last Sunday of the liturgical year and we go out on a high. It is the feast of Christ the King. Most people imagine this feast dates from the early church or at least the days of the Holy Roman Empire. In fact, it was instituted only in the 1920s. The church decided to give Christ a crown, precisely when most other kings were losing theirs. Of course he was a king. The gospels leave no doubt about that. His mother and father went to Bethlehem for his birth as it was David's royal city, and Christ was 'of David's house and line.' His death is described in today's gospel, crucified between two thieves, with the inscription over his head, 'This is the King of the Jews'. In fact, it was his claim to be king that his accusers used so cleverly to convince a frightened Pilate to pass the death-sentence. 'We have no king but Caesar,' left Caesar's puppet with no alternative.

All this we and the church knew for two thousand years. Why now in the twentieth century should the church give its official recognition? I like to think it has to do with faithfulness or loyalty, that virtue, above all, which kings inspired in their subjects. People were willing to make any sacrifice, even give their lives 'for king and country'. In fact, kings personified their country. Now they are asked to fight and die 'for the flag', perhaps a tricolour as in Ireland, France or Italy, some randomly chosen colours on a piece of cloth. Even a national anthem as stirring as the *Marseillaise* might provoke a few tears from a gold-winning athlete at the Olympics, but not much more. Faithfulness is to persons not symbols.

Faithfulness seems no longer a virtue of our times. We seem to be losing the habit of remaining faithful. It shows in statistics for marriage break-downs: husbands no longer faithful to their wives or wives to their husbands, children less faithful to their parents. Too often, the elderly are institutionalised, not because they are in need of professional care, but because they are deemed a burden by their own offspring. Faithfulness within families is declining. In religion, the statistics paint a similar picture: the numbers of priests and nuns who are no longer faithful to their calling; the number of young people who are no longer faithful to the Mass.

We need a king who can inspire faithfulness in us. Our king is Christ.

As king he claims dominion over all creation,
that he may present to you, his almighty Father,
an eternal and universal kingdom:
a kingdom of truth and life,
a kingdom of holiness and grace,
a kingdom of justice, love and peace. *(Preface)*

Suggested additional Bidding Prayers
We pray
– that we may always remain faithful to Christ our king.

– that husbands and wives may always remain faithful to each other, and children to their parents.

– that we may always remain faithful to the Mass and the sacraments.

Catechism of the Catholic Church

680 Christ the Lord already reigns through the church, but all the things of this world are not yet subjected to him. The triumph of Christ's kingdom will not come about without one last assault by the powers of evil.

Immaculate Conception

Readings: Gen 3:9-15, 20. Eph 1:3-6, 11-12. Lk 1:26-38.

Introduction

Our Lady was humanity's most beautiful person. Her beauty derived from her sinlessness. She was without stain, without sin.

Transparent Beauty (Mary)

It is the age of the visual. Television forms an ever-increasing portion of our daily diet. Advertising is a multi million-dollar industry. Pretty girls seduce us from every hoarding-board, from the pages of every glossy magazine, from every TV screen. Physical beauty is a marketable product. 'Miss World' is not born, she is assembled by those whose business is to market beauty. Hence, the millions spent on cosmetics and fashion. One even gets the impression that the recent health-consciousness craze is aimed more at producing better figures than healthier bodies. Behind the modern cult of youth, too, one can detect this obsession with physical beauty. For those who can read the neon signs of the times, the message is loud and clear. War has been declared on ugliness.

And on sin too. Heirs to an age over-obsessed with sin and evil, when occasions of sin included every fleeting glimpse of female flesh and the convivial atmosphere of every local pub, our generation has reacted by a massive rejection of the very notion of sin itself. But sin will not go away by being simply dismissed, by taking away people's awareness of it.

A world so obsessed by physical beauty and so dismissive of sin, is condemned to futility. We need the saving grace of a Redeemer, not the bland inducements of an advertiser.

Real beauty is not a matter of the length of a nose or the shape of a mouth. It has to do with the quality of the person. Probably, two of the most beautiful people of recent times were John XXIII and Mother Teresa of Calcutta. Neither of them would have distinguished themselves in a beauty contest. Yet nobody would hesitate to call them beautiful people.

Undoubtedly, the most beautiful creature to grace this planet was Mary the mother of Jesus. 'Our tainted nature's solitary boast.' Sadly, she has often been badly served by her most devoted followers. They have given us so often a miraculous madonna or plaster-cast virgin instead of the marvellously beautiful person she really was.

Probably the finest compliment ever paid her came from the lips of an earthy old peasant woman who cried out to Jesus, 'Blessed is the womb that bore you and the paps that gave you suck.'

Mary's transparent beauty derived not from any physical endowments but from her sinlessness. It is a pity we are accustomed so often to think of sinlessness as a negative thing. It wasn't what she didn't do which made her sinless and beautiful but what she did. It was the marvellous harmony of her nature which made her so sensitive, so caring, so other-oriented. Her first concern, on being told she was to be the mother of God, was for her older cousin, Elizabeth, pregnant with John the Baptist. Christmas-cards, depicting the flight into Egypt and the nativity, give no idea of the sturdy virtue of the teenage girl who delivered her child in such appalling conditions. Thirty years later, at the marriage of friends in Cana her sensitive and tactful concern for the newly-weds provoked Christ's first miracle. The woman beside the cross on Calvary is an unforgettable model of love and fidelity. Mary was a beautiful person unscarred by sin. She was a woman for all seasons.

Suggested additional Bidding Prayers
We pray
– that Mary will always inspire us by her sinlessness.
– that by rejecting sin our personalities may grow in grace and harmony.
– that by following Mary's example we will become more other-oriented.

Catechism of the Catholic Church
491 Through the centuries the church has become ever more aware that Mary, 'full of grace' through God, was redeemed from the moment of her conception. That is what the dogma of the Immaculate Conception confesses, as Pope Pius IX proclaimed in 1854:

'The most Blessed Virgin Mary was, from the first moment of her conception, by a singular grace and privilege of almighty God and by virtue of the merits of Jesus Christ, Saviour of the human race, preserved immune from all stain of original sin.'

St Patrick's Day

Readings: Jer 1:4-9. Acts 1:46-69. Lk 10:1

Introduction

St Patrick today is more a national symbol than a saint. We have to dig deep beneath a mountain of patriotic sentiment to uncover the real person. He was a man of faith, of prayer and, above all, of extraordinary humility.

Symbol or Saint (St Patrick)

A master of one-upmanship. With great ease and sharp wit he demolished his English and Scottish counterpart. He wins in the witty tales what he loses in the rat-race of daily life. Perhaps the creation of an inferiority-complex, of a conquered race. He has all the qualities attributed to the Irish Paddies themselves. A sharp wit, a quick tongue, a fertile imagination, a pride in physical strength and alcoholic capacity. A rough-living, hard drinking, devil tearing, gregarious bull of a man. On his back were built the roads and railroads of half the world. A friendly son of St Patrick!

There were other builders too who carried his name. The sons and daughters of institutions. The later generations of the Irish diaspora. More respectable, more respectful but still brash and boastful. They built cathedrals and parish churches, hospitals and schools. And they called their institutions and their children after him. There was a lot of nostalgia for the 'oul sod' in them and a lot of 'look what we have achieved' in their monuments. And by their efforts St Patrick became middle class – a gentleman, no less!

But all this trafficking of Patrick at home and abroad has exacted a price. And this is not surprising in a country where religion is nationalistic and nationalism a religion. Patrick has become a national symbol and the man who, single-handed, converted the Irish has been well and truly buried beneath fifteen hundred years of national pride. 'It's a great day for the Irish,' we sing on St Patrick's day. A national holiday.

Our ambassadors present heads of State with sprigs of shamrock. Our exiles paint the traffic lines on Fifth Avenue green. And upon all this celebration we expect the saint to 'bestow a sweet smile'. It is the Irish we are honouring, not St Patrick.

Scholars argue interminably over the Patrician question. But the real Patrician question is concerned with separating the man from the myth, the saint from the symbol. Whoever it was converted the Irish virtually single-handed, from the bottom rather than from the top, in the teeth of a highly-established Druidic religion, and all that without a single drop of martyr's blood being shed, which produced such an extraordinary harvest of saintly monasticism and which survived fifteen hundred years, centuries of which were of violent and systematic persecution – whoever it was, must have been a man of outstanding human qualities, and singular sanctity. A man worth remembering, a saint worth honouring.

Courageous he must undoubtedly have been and energetic too. A man of great faith and strong feet. But in an age which prefers action to adoration and protest to prayer, it might be worth remembering that Patrick was above all a man of prayer. And that the last great non-violent revolution in this country was the work of a man who wrote of himself: 'The love of God and the fear of him increased more and more and my faith grew and my spirit was stirred up, so that in a single day I prayed as often as a hundred times and by night almost as frequently, even while I was in the woods or on the mountain.'

Suggested additional Bidding Prayers
We pray
– that we may always remain faithful to the faith brought to us by St Patrick.
– that with St Patrick as model we will cultivate the habit of prayer.
– that through his intercession the island of Ireland will be blessed with peace.

Mission Sunday

Readings: Is 49:1-6. Rom 10:14-18. Mk 16:15-20

Introduction
We are an called to be missionaries. Our mission is to journey inwards. Self-evangelisation always entails the evangelisation of others.

In search of God (Mission)

My earliest introduction to the missions came when I was in infant school. It took the form of a mite box. It was stuck under our little noses every Monday morning in the convent school where my education began and rash indeed was the child who dared to barter his 'pennies for the black babies' for a toffee sweet. The salvation of Africa, it appeared then, depended on them. Our proselytism started very early.

It was a time when the 'foreign missions' loomed very large. That expression, I think now, was ill-chosen. The two words make an odd couple. There is a certain arrogance about the notion that one should set out to convert others in far-distant places. Historically, the word 'foreign' appears to have become attached to the word 'mission' in the wake of the overseas discoveries in the fifteenth and sixteenth centuries. Missionaries followed the conquistadors in the newly discovered lands of the Americas. Spanish priests, mostly Franciscans, established 'missions' all over South America and the southern states of North America. Undoubtedly they did a lot of good, protecting the natives from exploitation by the colonisers. But there was a debit side too. They were the spiritual wing of the white man's conquering armies. With the Christian faith they brought European languages and civilisation. Their progress inevitably entailed the loss of the indigenous culture. The gospel might well have enriched these cultures. It is doubtful whether it could ever compensate for their loss. Now at last, the church is aware of its mistake and is belatedly supporting the 'Africanisation' of local churches.

At the turn of this century, a young girl in her early teens entered a Carmelite convent in France. She exchanged the sheltered life of a close-knit family for the convent enclosure. A few years later she died. She kept a diary recording the stages of her own missionary journey. *The Little Way*, as it was called, profoundly influenced our thinking on the missions. After her death, the church took the unlikely step of declaring St Thérèse 'patroness of the missions'. It was a return to an earlier, more authentic Christian tradition when the early Irish saints fled to Europe in search of a hermitage where they could discover their innermost selves and their God. People flocked to them, attracted by their transparent goodness. Their self-conversions converted Europe. Aggressive salesmanship might be good for Coca-Cola; it has no place in evangelisation. We are all missionaries. Our

mission is to journey deep within ourselves in search of God. It
is a life-long undertaking. Others will be converted only by the
grace of God and the quality of our lives. An early Irish monk
summed it up in a verse, warning his fellow missionaries:

Pilgrim, take care your journey's not in vain,
A voyage without profit, without gain.
The God you seek you'll find in Rome, 'tis true,
But only if he travels on the road with you.

Suggested additional Bidding Prayers
We pray
– for ourselves, that we may find God and be converted to live
the gospel.
– for missionaries everywhere, that their conversion may lead
others to Christ.
– for peoples in the Third World, that Christian missionaries will
protect them from exploitation.

Mothers' Day

Readings: for the Sunday.

Introduction
To honour our mothers is one of the commandments. We
cannot honour them while we continue to discriminate against
their sex.

Burning issue (Feminism)
There are certain moments in our lives which we are forced
to confront ourselves and our attitudes on certain important issues. It is not that we change our convictions dramatically: circumstances have simply never obliged us to make a stand. One
such occasion occurred in my life some years ago when my
father died. He was a country schoolmaster and the sole bread-
winner in our family. He had taught school for fifty years and
died shortly after his retirement. My mother, who devoted her
life to being a wife and mother, was now a widow. Worse still, as
I discovered to my consternation, the moment my father died,
his pension was discontinued. Within days more bad news followed. My father had died intestate which meant that my mother

was legally entitled to only one-third of what had up to then been their mutual estate. My father's marriage vow, 'With all my worldly goods I thee endow,' delivered no doubt with all the ardour of a young man in love more than half a century earlier, was now posthumously reduced by two-thirds. At one stroke my mother was widowed, pick-pocketed and dispossessed. Had my mother died first, apart from losing his life's companion, my father would have suffered no other inconvenience. Such were – I speak of twenty years ago – the inequalities between the sexes. Small wonder that the question of women's rights should have changed overnight for the child of that couple, from an interesting topic of conversation to a burning issue of social justice.

Today is Mother's Day. On such a day we tend to become very sentimental about mothers. We send them cards, we give them flowers and we dedicate one whole day out of 365 days to mothers. The irony of that is that mother dedicated 365 out of 365 to us most of her life. This commemorative day itself was born out of the war, when sons languishing in the trenches had nothing more to keep their hopes alive than a mother's letter. 'Say it with flowers', the song has it. All the flowers in the world cannot disguise the inequalities women still suffer. Say it with laws. They express our love much more succinctly.

It is probably from our mothers than we gain our earliest and deepest experience of love. Whatever inkling we have of Christian charity derives from that. Their dedication to their children is unconditional. A mother devotes all her energy, all her time to others. When the rest of the family is stricken with the 'flu, she alone remains the ministering angel. As the expression puts it: 'Mothers have no time to get sick.'

God is love. Mothers – at least for their children – are probably the best human expression of that love.

Suggested additional Bidding Prayers
We pray
– for mothers, that home-making will always have a special place in their lives.
– for working mothers, that society will accord them the rights which are their due.
– for single mothers, that they will find support in their communities.

Thematic Index